Difficult

Difficult

Mothering Challenging Adult Children through Conflict and Change

Judith R. Smith

ROWMAN & LITTLEFIELD
Lanham • Boulder • New York • London

Published by Rowman & Littlefield
An imprint of The Rowman & Littlefield Publishing Group, Inc.
4501 Forbes Boulevard, Suite 200, Lanham, Maryland 20706
www.rowman.com

86-90 Paul Street, London EC2A 4NE, United Kingdom

British Library Cataloguing in Publication Information Available

Library of Congress Cataloging-in-Publication Data

Names: Smith, Judith R. (Clinical social worker), author.
Title: Difficult : mothering challenging adult children through conflict
    and commitment / Judith Smith.
Description: Lanham : Rowman & Littlefield, [2021] | Includes
    bibliographical references and index. | Summary: "Difficult presents
    detailed stories of how women balance their desire to protect their
    challenging adult children alongside feelings of resentment,
    helplessness, isolation, shame, and fear for their children's future and
    their own safety"—Provided by publisher.
Identifiers: LCCN 2021046381 (print) | LCCN 2021046382 (ebook) | ISBN
    9781538138885 (cloth) | ISBN 9781538192733 (paper) |
    ISBN 9781538138892 (epub)
Subjects: LCSH: Parent and adult child. | Mother and child. | Problem
    children.
Classification: LCC HQ755.86 .S5846 2021 (print) | LCC HQ755.86 (ebook) |
    DDC 306.874—dc23
LC record available at https://lccn.loc.gov/2021046381
LC ebook record available at https://lccn.loc.gov/2021046382

To my son, Matthew, and my husband, Neil.
They, along with my parents, Marsha and Alex,
provide the heart of what I know about love and family.

Contents

Acknowledgements

This was my first attempt to move from teaching, research, and being a therapist to writing a book. I was inspired to take this leap because of the wisdom that I gathered from each of the stories shared with me by over 50 mothers. Each woman helped me see a different, and often overlapping, aspect of how "difficult" it was to be the mother of an adult child who was struggling with mental illness or substance use disorder. I am forever grateful to each of you for speaking with me.

Since the publication of the hardcover version, I keep learning from readers with "difficult adult children" who have joined one of the support groups that I facilitate. This is a family situation that touches many people.

My journey to become a writer was nurtured by several close friends. Jessica Lipnack, a friend for over 50 years, an essayist and novelist, provided unwavering support and hands-on advice. She was my first reader and first critic. Pat Brownell, a leader in the field of elder abuse, pushed me to use my knowledge of child development to understand adult children's aggressive behavior towards their own mothers. Barbara Glickstein, a health media professional, interviewed me for her radio program, HealthCetera. This interview was the catalyst for the decision to turn my academic research into a book for a general audience. She continued to be a visionary and hands-on media mentor with me during the launch of the book.

I owe tremendous gratitude to Brenda Copeland for her excellent editing. She allowed me to turn my ideas into this book. Many thanks to Ethan Ellenberg, my agent, who recognized the value of this project from the beginning, and helped me to connect with my editors at Rowman & Littlefield, Suzanne Staszak-Silva, and Christen Karniski.

This project could not have happened without the many social service agencies that helped me during the recruitment stage of the research. These include Central Harlem Senior Citizens Centers; Eileen Dugan Center; Goddard-Riverside Senior Center; JASA/LEAP; National Adult Protective Services Association; NYC Elder Abuse Center at Weill Cornell Medicine; Weinberg Center for Elder Justice; and 1199 SEIU United Health Care Workers.

The section on Getting Help is informed by the experience of leaders in the fields of aging, mental health, social work, and elder abuse, including: David Levy, Esq. Kings County District Attorney; Helle Thorning, New York State Psychiatric Institute; Joanne Sirey & Jean Wynne, Weill Cornell Hospital; Lisa Dixon, New York State Psychiatric Institute; Lisa Furst, Vibrant NY; Miriam Goldberg & Takai Forde, JASA/LEAP; Nancy Needell, Mt. Sinai Hospital; National Center on Elder Abuse; Patricia Degan, CommonGround; Paul Caccamise, Lifespan of Rochester; Richard Velleman, Addictions Research Group; Risa Breckman, NYC Elder Abuse Center at Weill Cornell Medicine; and Teri Brister, National Alliance of Mental Illness.

Finally, I could not have persevered with this project without my husband, Neil Grill. His enduring support and sense of humor were invaluable. Marrying in later life, we had the opportunity to learn together about responding to the accomplishments and struggles of each of our adult children.

Author's Note

The experiences of older mothers and their difficult or challenging adult children have for too long been overlooked by mental health professionals, journalists, and self-help books. This book is the result of eight years of research and interviews. I talked to more than fifty women who shared with me the intimate details of how their adult children's problems were affecting their lives. Many told me that our conversation was the first time anyone showed any interest in their situation; several sighed with relief to have an opportunity to put into words what they had been hiding for years.

Having spent most of my early career studying mothers and their young children, I was excited to turn my attention to the lives of mothers whose children had grown. My work as a clinical psychotherapist, along with my tenure as an associate professor of social work at Fordham University, provided me with the foundation to study these experiences. My research revealed that a mother's internalized mandate to protect her child does not end when her children are grown. But the challenge of protecting adult children who have serious problems can be filled with frustration. Mothers described that although they were trying to help their "kids," they often were met with disrespect, anger, and sometimes physical violence. Many blamed themselves or felt blamed for their adult children's problems. Talking to these women, all over sixty years of age, helped me realize the unique dilemmas of older mothers and their challenging adult children.

I am indebted to each of them. In presenting the accounts of their relationships with their adult children, I have taken the utmost care to represent their situations with respect and honesty. To protect their anonymity, I have changed their names and, sometimes, distinguishing characteristics.

Because my research was only with mothers, I cannot with certainty talk about the experiences of fathers who are navigating the same terrain. However, I hope that this book will also speak to them.

I am interested in hearing from parents who want to share their experiences or comment on this difficult topic. I invite correspondence at judithrsmith@difficultmothering.com, through my website (https://www.motheringinlaterlife.com), or on Facebook (https://www.facebook.com/difficultmothering).

Part I

THROUGH A MOTHER'S EYES

In this section, "Through a Mother's Eyes," you will discover, as I did, what occurs in the lives of mothers whose adult children are facing prolonged obstacles that interfere with independent adulthood. Each of the adult children profiled in their mother's stories had had a period of independence outside of the family home, but they had each returned for emotional, financial, or residential support from their families. It was a return that affected their mothers in profound and difficult ways, often upending the women's lives.

People will choose to read this book in different ways. You might want to jump to the chapters specifically geared to your adult child's issue—such as mental illness or substance abuse—in order to hone in on your family situation. While this approach may be appealing, I'd like to suggest that you start with the first five chapters as they present the themes that are common across difficult mothering:

- Chapter 1: What Is a Difficult Adult Child?
- Chapter 2: Once a Mother, Always a Mother?
- Chapter 3: Give Me Shelter
- Chapter 4: Guilt, Shame, and Mother-Blame
- Chapter 5: Torn in Two

Chapters 6 to 8 are specific to mental illness and substance abuse. Chapters 9 to 11 return to issues that may occur in many homes.

The problems experienced by the children in this book may vary widely, but the accounts of their mothers have a great deal in common. This first section will show just how widespread the *difficult* issue is. It gives a name to what may feel like a unique family problem, but is actually experienced by many. Reading this and knowing that there is a name for what you are feeling may help to break feelings of isolation, bringing relief and empowerment.

Chapter One

What Is a Difficult Adult Child?

When I began this project, I was in some ways similar to the women I was hoping to meet. I was older (in my mid-sixties) and the mother of a son in his mid-twenties, on the cusp of adulthood. I was also a feminist gerontologist interested in family relationships. Having spent most of my early career studying mothers and their young children, I wanted to understand the experience of mothers whose children were adults.

My earlier work explored the needs of young children—first as a psychotherapist, then as a filmmaker, and finally as a PhD researcher. As I aged, perhaps matured, I became interested in the mother and child relationship for older women with adult children. Yet a search for professional literature and self-help books turned up very little on this topic. Nearly all the resources were geared toward parents of young children, with scant information on how mothers managed their lives alongside the lives of their adult children. Surely being a mother doesn't end when your kids are in their twenties? I know from my own experience that this is not the case.

You don't stop being a mother just because your kids are grown.

I wanted to use my clinical and research skills to understand the relationship of mothers and their older children. More to the point, I wanted to use my experience to study how problems in the lives of adult children affect a mother's sense of self as she, herself, was aging. As far as I was aware, no one was yet talking about these two topics together.

A LIFELONG ENTANGLEMENT

As a social work professional and psychotherapist, I was surprised at how eager women of all ethnic backgrounds and income levels were to talk about themselves as mothers, even though their kids were grown. Some told me about their disappointment when their kids dropped out of college, others about their endless attempts to get their younger kids tutors and therapists, and many about the joy they derived from their grandchildren. What shocked me the most was when a mother calmly walked me through the incidents when her son or daughter physically assaulted her. Although I had read about elder abuse and even knew that dependent adult children were the most likely perpetrators of elder abuse, I had never sat with someone who had lived through this experience. Before meeting my interviewees, I had tried to make sense of the possible family dynamics that might be related to this dynamic. Had these adult children always been aggressive toward their mothers, or had something happened later in life to explain this? Why were these women allowing their abusive adult children to remain in their homes when the situation had become clearly dangerous for them?

Witnessing my mother's lifelong entanglement with her sister, who suffered from depression and was phobic, I saw how one person's problems could reverberate through an entire family. As a young child, I was angered and confused by my mother's relentless devotion to her sister, despite my aunt's aggressive and hostile behavior. It was hard to observe the struggle between my mother's lifelong attempt to balance her commitment to her sister and her desire to focus on her family and her own happiness. I wondered if older mothers of adult children with problems were feeling similar conflicts. I began a research project to find out.

I started by reaching out to women whose grown children were struggling as adults. I recruited women from senior centers, YMCAs, drug treatment centers, health clubs, meetings of retired workers, and elder abuse centers. I did not, however, interview any of the adult children. My focus was on discovering the perspective of the mothers, each of whom was over sixty. I spent several hours with each person. I did not use cookie-cutter questionnaires or surveys with "yes or no" questions. I simply asked them to tell me about the highs and lows of their parenting journey with their adult child.

Before they shared their life stories with me, I asked each woman to tell me in just a few sentences how she would describe her adult child's current problems. The women responded with accounts of substance abuse disorder, mental illness, gambling, unemployment, underemployment, lack of citizenship papers, domestic violence, anger management, attention-deficit/hyperactivity disorder (ADHD), and undiagnosed malaise. They talked to me about their sadness and concern, their ambivalence and fears. Most of all, they talked about their priority of keeping their child safe.

Each woman's narrative illustrated how the problems of adult children create tension in the parent-child relationship, how they affect a mother's physical and mental health, and how they influence the options they see for their future. Half of the women I talked to were poor (family incomes under seventeen thousand dollars for a family of two). Half had family incomes of at least thirty-five thousand dollars a year. Some were affluent. Half of the respondents were women of color; half were white. All the women were married when their children were born. Many were widowed or divorced by the time we spoke. Most had more than one child.

THE DIFFICULT ADULT CHILD

Despite the unique circumstances of the women's lives, I discovered many commonalities in their stories. Nearly all had reopened their homes to their adult child when they had nowhere else to go. Many of the adult children had mental health problems or substance abuse disorder— or both. None had expected their own later years to be framed by active worrying and providing support. Yet for all the many similarities, there were also unique circumstances in each child's life. That's what led me to search for a name to describe what I was seeing and to ultimately settle on the term "difficult adult child." I chose this name to acknowledge not just the challenges faced by the grown children, but the hardships passed along to the mothers who cared for them. If "difficult" seems a harsh label—one that blames, not just identifies—consider how the dictionary defines the word: (1) when something is hard to do or carry out; (2) hard to deal with, manage, or overcome; and (3) hard to understand. Mothering adult children is *hard to do*. Tolerating the tensions in a relationship with a struggling adult child is extremely *hard to manage*. *Understanding* the problems that might have caused your child's situation is *hard*, and knowing how to intervene can feel impossible.

The term "difficult adult child" acknowledges not just the challenges faced by grown children, but the hardships passed along to the mothers who care for them.

As I was analyzing my research, friends and colleagues would ask me about my study. When I said I was focusing on mothers with difficult adult children, nearly all mothers to whom I spoke said, "You should talk to me." I was taken aback by this response, as I knew that these women's children were not similar to the adult children in my book. In fact, their children were thriving. But their comments did make me consider that while mothers of difficult adult children are a particular niche of the population, nearly all mothers struggle to find the right balance in their relationships with their adult children. They wonder how much advice to give or how much financial assistance to offer. They get angry when someone hurts their child. They want to do everything that they can to make their child's life better, despite the pushback they may get from their kids, who cherish their independence. These mothers also feel foolish for being too easily hurt when their sons or daughters are too busy to see them, or for being competitive with their in-laws. So while this book is for mothers of difficult adult children, the issues may also be relevant to your friends whose kids seem *fine*. Mothering in later life is hard for many of us.

HOPE AND SAMANTHA

Hope reached out after hearing me interviewed on public radio. We spoke in her apartment on the outskirts of Boston. She was sixty-five when we first met; her daughter was thirty. She divorced when Samantha was seven years old and had returned to school to get a master's in education. Hope had been doing art therapy with middle-school children for over fifteen years. She began painting in college and was looking forward to her upcoming retirement when she could paint full time. The table where we spoke, with the tape recorder between us, was framed by two of her colorful abstract paintings. Hope was soft-spoken yet eager to communicate with me the journey she has been on with her daughter.

The youngest of two girls, Samantha had been a very social child. Other children always wanted to play with her, and she received invitations all the time for birthday parties, sleepover dates, and trips to the mall. Although Samantha had learning problems, she was a smart and funny girl. Yet while her most serious issue, with drugs, did not begin until she was twenty-three, the years leading up to that were not easy. "There was always something. It was the suicide attempt. It was the stealing with the credit card. It was not going to classes when she was enrolled in MassBay Community College. Those were like the big events and then there was the sex with the boy in the attic . . . a lot of events that I felt personally hurt by."

The hurt that Hope felt resulted from having to see her daughter in a new light each time something unpleasant happened. She was not just the smart, social young girl her mother appreciated and enjoyed. She was also troubled and dishonest. Hope found a therapist for her daughter after the suicide attempt, which had actually been a call for help and not a serious attempt. But after six months, the therapist called Hope to let her know that Samantha was not speaking in any of the sessions. She just spent the hour looking at her phone.

Hope learned about her daughter's drug problem by discovering that valuable items were missing from a locked cabinet in the apartment— her father's gold coins and her mother's silver. Upon realizing that it was Samantha who had been the thief, Hope felt a tremendous sense of betrayal. Confronted, Samantha admitted that she had stolen the items, sold them, and used the money to buy crack. Hope was shocked and concerned. She made calls to locate an inpatient drug treatment center but was told by the intake workers that her daughter had to be the one to contact them. Samantha had no interest in going into a treatment center, and her mother couldn't force her to get help.

What Hope could do—and did, to her own amazement—was insist that Samantha move out. She wouldn't be allowed back unless she was clean. Samantha moved into a homeless shelter that also provided drug counseling. She remained there for nine months, during which time her mother brought her books to read and clean clothes when she asked for them. Samantha stopped using drugs while in the shelter. Hope thought that perhaps she had been chastened seeing the terrible effect drugs had had on the older women who were in the residence and whose current status perhaps frightened her.

I met with Hope several times over three years. The first time was about twelve months after Samantha had left the shelter. This was a relatively stable period for Samantha: she was working as a food delivery person for a new online grocery company and was not using. She had a new boyfriend, and they had their own apartment, which they shared with a third person. While there were periods of conflict for Hope, who worried about her daughter's financial situation—Should she help them out? How much?—there were also good times between them. Samantha and her boyfriend would come home for dinners and there would be lively, although not intimate, conversation.

Hope was always aware of Samantha's refusal to discuss more personal topics or to revisit any clashes that she and her mother had. Nevertheless, she accepted these limits and did what she could to maintain the relationship. When I first spoke to Hope, Samantha was not using drugs and was calling her mother often as she delivered groceries, and they both enjoyed their daily chats. Hope would also get a call when the young couple was not able to meet their monthly expenses, when the electricity or cell phone service had been turned off, or they couldn't pay other bills. Hope, worried that her daughter and her boyfriend could become homeless again at any moment, was glad that she could help.

Yet, even during this relatively stable period in Samantha's life, Hope suffered. Worried whether her daughter would ever earn enough money to be fully self-supporting, she knew that she would not have the money to look after her once she retired. Hope would go back and forth, trying to figure out what was okay to buy for her daughter and whether she was being foolish by not saving money for when Samantha would really need it. What was hardest was realizing that she was holding on to unrealistic expectations for their relationship. Hope had begun attending Al-Anon meetings where she attempted to follow the takeaway lesson, "If you don't expect anything, you won't be disappointed." While this generally referred to not expecting that the addict will recover, Hope was applying it to her hopes for a more reciprocal relationship between herself and her daughter.

Unrealistic expectations can cause a great deal of distress and sadness.

To illustrate this, Hope told me about the time when Samantha called to say she would be getting out of work early and could take the train to see her mom and be there by 7:30. Hope was pleased and decided to make dinner, cooking one of Samantha's favorite dishes, eggplant parmigiana. The plan was for Hope to pick up her daughter at the commuter train at 7:30. At 7:15, as she was getting ready to leave the house, she put the finished eggplant dish on the counter and called her daughter's cell to make sure the train was on time. Samantha hadn't left yet. This meant she would not be there for an hour and a half. Instead of suggesting they postpone the get-together, Hope agreed to pick her up at a different train stop, which would make it easier and faster for Samantha to get there. In other words, Hope put herself out even more in order to have time with her daughter.

At the appointed new pick-up time, she waited in a deserted car park. The station was poorly lit, and groups of street people were mingling about. Hope felt vulnerable and conspicuous being this "white-haired lady" hanging out in her car. When the train arrived, Samantha did not get off with the others. Worried, Hope called the boyfriend and then Samantha, and learned that she had taken the wrong train and would be arriving at a different station. Hope was livid, but instead of telling Sam to turn around and go back home, she told her that she would get to her as quickly as she could. Driving there—"like a maniac"—she imagined her daughter alone in a deserted station. Hope was relieved to see Samantha in one piece, but she was also in a rage. She handed her the seventy-five dollars that she now realized was the real reason for the visit. Hope told Samantha to not call again. They didn't speak until several weeks later when Hope called Samantha for her birthday.

"My daughter doesn't know what it's like to have to make it work," Hope lamented. "To not get on the wrong train. To call when you're not able to leave on time. To me, those are just normal things. And to her, I don't know what. I still don't know why she wouldn't call beforehand

and say, 'listen, it's really late. Let's make another plan or something.' It would have definitely taken the edge off for me."

On the one hand, Hope recognized that her daughter had serious problems that led to her being late, etc. At the same time, Hope believed that she, herself was really the problem. She wanted to stop herself from so quickly responding to her daughter's requests or offers to visit, as they almost always ended up being disappointing and frustrating. "I feel trapped in this relationship that I'm not willing to give up. And unlike a divorce, where you really can give the person up, I just really don't feel able to give her up."

> You can divorce a difficult spouse. It's much harder to give up on a difficult child.

Three years later, Hope had retired. Worn out and unable to stay attuned to the rollercoaster that had become her daughter's life, she described herself as feeling her age. Samantha had left her boyfriend and had found a new one; she was using heroin and living on the streets. She had been arrested and had been in jail for six weeks. During Samantha's confinement in jail, mother and daughter were in constant contact. Samantha would ask Hope to bring her clothing or books or to get in touch with the boyfriend and tell him when he could call. Hope realized that she was being used by Samantha; nevertheless, she was still glad to be in touch with her daughter, who seemed relatively upbeat in the protected environment of the county jail. She had also started on methadone.

Immediately after leaving jail, however, Samantha started using heroin and was again living on the streets with a group of new friends who all were also using. She stayed in contact with her mother, but calling only infrequently, which Hope appreciated. "I'm content if she calls me just every once in a while, so I know she's alive. But the craziness is too emotionally draining. I can't do it." Hope's prior dream of painting again during her retirement seemed to have been shelved.

NAMING THE PROBLEM

The term "difficult adult child" accurately describes the situation that Hope and countless others like her are facing. To be able to say, "Hope has a difficult adult child" rather than "Hope's daughter is a 'drug addict'" changes everything. It moves the descriptor away from Samantha alone to a family situation in which the parents, and perhaps siblings, are also affected. While Samantha might not be able to change, perhaps they could. While "difficult" may sound like a pejorative term, from a mother's lens the situation is exactly that—difficult.

Giving a name to a family problem is the first step in being able to take action. It was only when domestic violence, child abuse, and elder abuse were named that attention to these problems occurred in health care, the law, and government social policies. Child abuse was first named in the 1960s,[1] domestic violence in the 1970s,[2] and elder abuse in 1975.[3] On a personal basis, for a woman whose boyfriend or husband was hitting her, having the name of "domestic violence" gave her a tool to link her experience with that of others, and the first step toward seeking help.

Sociologist C. Wright Mills was one of the first to draw a distinction between "personal troubles" and "public issues." He suggested that although individuals may experience many "troubles" or "problems" in their lives, not all of these emerge as "public issues." That is, only situations that command public interest or are seen as requiring a public response. (What can we do about ___?) If only a few people experience a particular form of trouble, then it is likely to remain a private matter. If, however, large numbers of people begin to experience this same trouble—or fear they might—it may become a public issue.[4]

> Giving a name to a family problem is the first step in being able to take action. It can also go a long way to break feelings of isolation, as well as bring relief and empowerment.

There is no way to know how many parents are struggling with difficult adult children. It is not a question on the census form; there's no particular place where mothers with "difficult adult children" gather. Having a name that women can use to openly seek help or readily explain to friends and family about their current situation may go a long way to break feelings of isolation, bringing relief and possible empowerment.

The absence of a public conversation about difficult adult children contrasts dramatically with the myriad of books, magazine articles, mommy blogs, and even television shows about the difficulties faced by

mothers with infants and toddlers. National newspapers devote whole
sections to parenting advice to mothers and fathers of young children.
In this book, I present what I learned from women about the strains
that occur in later life, among mothers who had adult children with
different types of problems. I only interviewed women for this book.
I believe that women process and experience parenting responsibilities differently from men. A separate study is needed on the internal
world of fathers with difficult adult children. Some of the issues may
be similar. Others will be different. The women who spoke to me came
from a wide spectrum of economic situations, and their adult children's
problems were all different. But they were all eager to talk to me about
how the problems in their adult children's lives had impacted their own
well-being. As one mom said to me, "Nobody before ever asked me
about this."

SOMETHING'S HAPPENING HERE: PROLONGED
DEPENDENCE OF YOUNG ADULTS

Difficult adult children who return home because of obstacles in maintaining their self-sufficiency may be seen as part of a larger historical
trend, that is the dramatic increase in the number of intergenerational
households in the United States. Starting with the sharp economic
downturn of the 1980s, more and more young people in their twenties
have returned home or never left. The share of older young adults between the ages of twenty-five to thirty-four who live with their parents
increased from 11.9 percent in 2000 to 22.0 percent in 2017, which
translates to more than 5.6 million additional young adults living under
their parents' roofs.[5] In 2020, over 50 percent of young people aged
eighteen to twenty-nine were living with their parents.

   The pattern is so widespread that new terms have been created to
describe the phenomenon. "Emerging adulthood" is now used by psychologists to describe the expected longer road to adulthood that young
people today will experience.[6] "Boomerang kids" describes young
people who move out, then move back in, only to bounce back out
again after a short time in the parents' home. The same pattern is occurring throughout the European Union and in the United Kingdom. In

Australia, a popular television reality series called *The Nest* comically referred to returning adult children as "Kippers," or "kids in parents' pocket eroding retirement savings." This name reflects a concern (and a reality for some) that older parents' willingness to offer financial support to their adult children can endanger the parents' financial future.[7] What's happening here is more complicated. Although similar to Boomerang kids, each of the adult children portrayed in this book had moved out of the family home for a while, and then moved back in. Very few of the women assumed that their kids would soon "bounce back" into independent living and self-sufficiency. The mothers' perceptions of the possible chronicity of their adult children's problems made the situation particularly difficult for them.

THE GOAL OF THIS BOOK

This book goes beyond describing a social problem in our society that needs attention. It also includes a model of change to help readers consider how and if they might want to gradually alter their current situation. There are different models of change, and the one I am offering is adapted from the transtheoretical model developed by psychologists James Prochaska and Carlo Di Clemente, which has been used worldwide to help people change addictive behaviors. The approach starts with the assumption that it is extremely hard for people to change behaviors that seem unhealthy to others.[8] Motivation to change must come from within the person. Finding the resolve to change can only come from feeling the discomfort of maintaining the status quo.

Whether you are a physician, mental health professional, or friend of someone with a difficult adult child, this book will help you become attuned to the complexity of the challenges faced by mothers whose adult children are struggling. If you have a difficult adult child, you will discover that you are not alone in your feelings of worry, disappointment, conflict, and ambivalence.

Part I illustrates how different women experience mothering in later life and argues that this is a social problem that needs public attention— not just a personal problem. The dilemmas of the thirty-five different mothers with difficult adult children reveals common themes:

- How do I protect my child without hurting myself?
- What did I do wrong that my child treats me with such disrespect?
- How do I handle the disappointment that I feel?
- How do I forgive myself for the mistakes that I made?
- Why can't anyone suggest a solution that can help me and my child?
- What is wrong with our mental health and criminal justice system?
- How can I enjoy my later years and take care of my adult child?

Part II introduces a gradual model for considering changes you might want to make in your current situation. Part III illustrates the actions that mothers can take to get help for themselves and/or for their adult children. These include:

- Getting formal and informal support for yourself—from friends, mental health professionals, and support groups.
- Setting boundaries, which may or may not involve using legal and/ or social services to regain a sense of safety and control within your home.
- Becoming involved in political action to transform the current services for the mentally ill and substance addicted.

The women's stories, as well as knowledge from the fields of psychology and human development, are woven into each of the chapters.

For a mother with a difficult adult child, changing can feel like abandoning her role as mother and endangering her adult child. For many, it is an unsolvable situation, a real-life catch-22. Many feel unable to act and change their situations to ensure their and/or their adult child's safety. I have come to respect how difficult a mother's situation is when there are no clear alternatives for her as a parent to meet her own needs and that of her adult child.

Part III offers resources recommended by experts from social work, psychiatry, criminal justice, elder abuse, and aging services. You'll find examples showing how the mothers highlighted in the book were able to access and use similar services. Finally, I discuss the gaps in our social fabric regarding care for the mentally ill, treatment of substance use disorder, affordable housing, and educational opportunities for struggling adults.

I wrote this book for mothers trying to find the right balance between their own needs as individuals and the needs of their still struggling adult children. This is not a book that will provide suggestions on how to change or motivate your adult child to get a job, take psychiatric medication, stop using drugs, or go back to school. And while it is my hope that physicians, mental health professionals, and legislators will find much to engage them, this book is directed at the mother of the difficult adult child. I hope that by reading about other women's successful and unsuccessful attempts to navigate the late-in-life parenting demands with adult children who are not yet succeeding, you will feel less alone and maybe find a possible new path for yourself.

Chapter Two

Once a Mother, Always a Mother?

Jillian, at age seventy-six, described her situation as being like a mule held back by a harness. The harness was her commitment to providing shelter and safety to her daughter, Celia, who had her first psychiatric break at twenty-two. The next twenty years in Jillian's life were framed by finding and re-finding new apartments for her daughter. She moved Celia twenty-one times in twenty years, setting up each place with new curtains, new dishes, and a hope that *this time* it would work out. And every time, Celia's mental illness reemerged in the form of paranoia, which triggered her anxiety, fights with neighbors, and recklessness. Friends thought that Jillian's doing the same thing over and over again was pointless. Others said she was only being a good mother. Jillian explained to her friends that she had to keep doing what she was doing because Celia "needed to eat . . . she needed a place to live." She believed her efforts were necessary to protect her child.

Most mothers of difficult adult children do not have the resources that Jillian and her husband did. Nevertheless, each woman I spoke to took steps to protect her adult child in crisis, no matter how old her son or daughter. The types of protection and mothering work they provided included sharing food, advocating for a daughter during psychiatric hospitalizations, giving advice (often unwanted), taking care of grandkids, paying for psychotherapy, chauffeuring a son to methadone, and "putting up with her" as one mother succinctly put it.

There's no shortage of opinions on what it means to be a good mother. No shortage of saccharine quotes as to how a woman's fulfillment is based on her child's happiness. "You are only as happy as your least happy child." "Being a mama isn't the easiest job you'll ever have, but it's definitely the best." Consider, too, how one of the oldest images, that of the Madonna, exemplifies the view of the dedicated, selfless, nonsexual, faithful woman devoted only to her son. Every mother measures herself against the particular images, or myths, of motherhood within her culture. "Intensive mothering" has become the norm, and mothers today spend more time in childcare, whether or not they work outside of the home, than their mothers and grandmothers did, often sacrificing time with friends or for hobbies.[1] Hollywood films portray the best moms as ruthlessly protecting their children, like Sarah Connor, the young mother in *Terminator 2* who uses her wiles to save her son and outwit the robots. Another twenty-first-century maternal ideal is the supermom who works outside the home, keeps her body trim, is sexual, and also completely devoted to her young children. Women's magazines highlight celebrity mothers who "have it all." I have yet to see the film that offers a glimpse into the complicated set of feelings of the mature woman who is engaging with her adult children.

MATERNAL WORK

It was the psychologist Sarah Ruddick who named the work that women do in response to the needs of their young children as "maternal work." Most mothers understand this maternal work as the need to protect, hold, foster growth, and train their child. Each woman brings her own strengths and anxieties into her role as a mother. Right from the start, newborns engage their parents in what psychoanalyst Daniel Stern called a "dance." An interaction that provides most mothers with a feeling of competency and satisfaction, the mother-baby dance is a back and forth in which the mother follows the baby's lead. The baby smiles, the mother says "yes," and the baby smiles back. The baby gurgles, and the mother responds, "I know, you're still hungry," and offers the bottle or breast. Our culture celebrates and appreciates this maternal capacity to create the mother-child unity. Yet this beatific exchange, this feeling of oneness, is not static. Mothering also includes giving the child a gentle push, encouragement to explore the outside world and eventually to move away from the nest.

Some fully enjoy the complete dependence of their newborn infants, while others only can relax when their toddlers can communicate their needs with words. Some mothers' traumatic histories in their own families interfere with their ability to tune in to the emotional world of their young child. Yet, due to the enormous plasticity of young children's brains, most can adapt to their own mother, regardless of her strengths or vulnerabilities.

> Our culture celebrates mother-child unity. Yet mothering also means giving the child a gentle push to explore the outside world, eventually supporting the move away from the nest.

Ruddick also included "preservative love" as a critical part of maternal work. Preservative love concerns a mother's ability to contain her mixed emotions about the demands of caring for her young child. A mother's feelings toward her children can vary from hour to hour, year to year. A typical day may encompass joy, fury, infatuation, boredom, and even simple dislike. Just as mothers must keep their infants and young children safe in a world that itself may not be safe, they must also protect or preserve their children from their own mixed feelings and failings.

Looking after the well-being of a young child is not the same as protecting an adult child. Mothers of young children foster the growth of a being whose emotional, cognitive, sexual, and social development changes every day. It can be a fascinating and enriching experience. In contrast, mothers of difficult adult children encounter another person who may be depressed, anxious, mentally ill, or despondent. This relationship offers none of the magic a young child can provide. Instead of witnessing daily changes, parents of a difficult adult child often feel trapped in their child's despair and bad decisions. The interaction may be additionally strained because the adult child resents her new dependency on her parents and may become sullen, uncommunicative, and angry. This is a hard burden for a mother to bear.

Parents of difficult adult children may feel trapped in their adult children's despair and bad decisions.

INTERGENERATIONAL SOLIDARITY

An older mother who willingly interrupts her life when her adult child is in trouble because "that's what a mother does" is demonstrating what sociologists refer to as the "societal norm of intergenerational solidarity."[2] Parents will protect their children in need, even when those children are adults. But side by side with this notion is the belief that it is a parent's job to usher in a child's ability to become an independent adult.[3] These two obligations require opposite behaviors and create ambivalence for all parents.[4] No wonder parents struggle with how much financial and emotional support to give their adult child.

"Am I hindering my child's independence by helping him out?" There's no easy answer to this common question. Recent data shows that 59 percent of parents (not just those with difficult adult children) gave financial support to their adult children between the ages of eighteen and thirty-nine who were no longer in school.[5] The average amount parents spent on children when they are between the ages of eighteen and thirty-four is $65,912 in 2019 dollars. The calculated "average" is skewed by the inclusion of high-income families.[6] One sociologist called parents' ability to help their adult children, particularly when they are in need, as acting as a "Family National Guard."[7]

Parents are expected to protect their children in need, even when those children are adults. They are also expected to support and usher in their children's ability to be independent and autonomous adults.

Family obligations—shared understandings about responsibilities, informal rules that determine how family members should help each other—vary from family to family and within cultures. The majority of families provide important, but typically intermittent, support when there are changes in their children's lives. They may help around the birth of a grandchild, offer assistance when there is a serious illness, and step in with financial help when a security deposit is needed or a job loss has occurred. Yet not all events have a clear ending. If an adult child develops a serious illness that does not allow him to continue working, who will he turn to? If a daughter gets divorced, or her partner dies suddenly leaving her with young children and no place to live, she probably hopes to "return to the nest" of her family home. When a mother is faced with her adult child's long-term need for support, she then faces a different kind of conflict—weighing her own needs over her adult child's.

FAITH

Faith met me at an agency that offers services to older people with legal and other family problems. She wanted information on how to deal with her forty-two-year-old daughter and nineteen-year-old grandson who had been living with her, once again, for over two years. A well-dressed woman who looked much younger than her eighty years, Faith had been a nutritionist at a large urban hospital. She retired at age sixty-two because her grandson Lester was going to be placed in foster care due to her daughter's drug use. Faith has no regrets about having made the decision to raise her grandson and protect him from what she believed might be harm in the foster care system. Like many women in her position, she was glad she could step in.

When Lester was fifteen, his mother, Ebony, was clean of drugs and in a position to set up her own apartment for herself and her son, close to Faith. One year later, her daughter was diagnosed with breast cancer. Weakened by the treatments for her disease, Ebony could not cook or manage other tasks of daily living. It was at this point that Faith let them both move back in with her. "That's my daughter," she had said. The most compelling of all reasons. In addition to Ebony's weakened physical condition, she also had mental health challenges, as did her son. Both had been diagnosed as bipolar.

After two years of living with her daughter and grandson, Faith had come to the agency to find out how to evict them. "I'm still trying to help. But at the same time, I can't keep on leaving myself out. I have to help myself. And I'm at a crossroads here. I don't know what to do now to get over that hurdle, just to make that jump. I have to stand up to them. At the same time, I have to understand that they have real problems. And I have to understand that, no matter what, I want to help them. I don't want to give up on them. If I step back, something could happen to them and I'll be sorry that I didn't continue to try to keep working with them."

> The majority of families provide intermittent support to their children. But not all situations have a clear ending.

Faith could not choose one action over the other. She wanted to help Ebony and Lester, but this entailed "leaving herself out." The doctor was worried about her high blood pressure, which was exacerbated by her living arrangements. "I have to stand up to them," she said, meaning she couldn't continue putting them first. At the same time, she understood that they had real problems and couldn't manage on their own. If she "stepped back," she would be faced with guilt and regret if they got hurt, as if she herself was responsible. Her dilemma was based on the reality of two conflicting situations: her children's vulnerability and her own physical and emotional needs.

When our interview was over, Faith thanked me. She seemed relieved. I felt as if she was thanking me for understanding the bind that she was in, without judging her. I also had quietly communicated that her problem was not unique. Others were also in the same situation. As we parted, I did not think that she would choose to push her daughter and grandson out until she was sure that they could manage independently in part, because, if she put herself first, the regret and self-blame would be too much for her. She told me, "I'll be sorry that I didn't continue to try and keep working with them."

Faith described herself as still "working with" her adult daughter to secure her capacity to live safely on her own. Ebony is forty-two years old; Faith is eighty. According to most textbooks on typical adult development, Faith should be in the post-parental stage or the "empty nest" stage,[8] which is assumed to occur when one's children are all out of the parental home. Obviously to name Faith or Jillian's current stage in life as "post-parental" does not reflect their reality.

A CHANGING VIEW OF ADULTHOOD

Parents' legal responsibilities end when a child reaches the "age of majority"—either eighteen or twenty-one, depending on the state. In the eyes of the law, once this milestone has been reached, a person is given the right to vote, join the military, and sign a contract. This same law also limits a parent's right to see her now adult child's medical records, grades, and bank statements, unless willingly shared. But beyond legal definitions of adulthood are the more subtle discussions of how adult children and their parents measure a young person's capacity for independence and autonomy.

Ideally, adult children attain a healthy sense of their own autonomy beginning in adolescence. Parents play an important role in supporting their child's efforts to become less dependent and make decisions for themselves, to live as autonomous, self-directed people. Working, moving out on their own, and becoming a parent are all possible motors of autonomous actions for young people. Clearly, having to move back into the parent's home can be seen and felt as a giving up of independence—not something desired by either the parent or the child.

DIFFICULT MOTHERING:
THE CONTINUED COMMITMENT

The relationship a mother has with her adult child is the longest phase in the parenting career, lasting fifty or even seventy years. Yet no one has come up with a model to describe how this relationship changes over time. Most parenting books end with adolescence, perhaps with a little attention to the "launching stage" when children are in their early twenties and assumed to be on their way to living independently. The work of parent educator Ellen Galinsky is an exception. She describes the final stage of parenting, which she names "Departure,"[9] as being a process in which the parent loosens control over the adult child's choices. The parent-child relationship shifts in the Departure Stage during which mothers and fathers search for new ways to stay connected to their adult children.

As of yet, there is no agreed-upon name for the stage in life in which an older mother has to resume worrying about and trying to protect her adult child. During COVID-19 a *New York Times* reporter called mothers' new role as becoming the "shock absorbers" for society. When schools were closed and learning moved to the home, more women than men dropped out of the work force—four times as many.[10] Being a shock absorber for society is also the position that older mothers of difficult adult children often assume. Most of the women whose stories are shared in this book responded to a crisis in an adult child's life: a break-up of a marriage or romantic relationship, the birth of a new baby, or a mental health, physical health, or substance use issue. High rents, lack of paid maternity leave, and limited facilities for mental health and substance abuse treatment are all structural problems that have created a widening gap in the safety net, a gap into which mothers often step.

One sociologist used the term "linked lives" to describe how changes in the lives of adult children impact their parents and vice versa.[11] I suggest the name for this maternal work as "difficult mothering." When adult children get into a situation where they can no longer support themselves and/or have no place to live, "difficult mothering" begins. It is "difficult" because it is not what most mothers hoped for or expected for their adult children. Nor was being responsible for another what the older mothers imagined for themselves in later life. As both mother and adult child adapt to a new and unexpected dependency of the adult child, both live with the uncertainty as to when this will come to an end.

> When adult children can no longer support themselves or have no place to live, "difficult mothering" begins.

JILLIAN

Jillian has been providing financial and other direct support for her daughter, Celia, for twenty-five years—twenty-five years beyond the legal "age of majority." In listening to her talk about what she has done for her daughter over the years, it became clear to me that her attitude toward her protective maternal work did change over time. There were four phases, each having a different sense of urgency, each requiring energy directed in different ways to address her daughter's and her own needs.

The first was the realization of a problem: "Something's wrong: I have to help." All of Jillian's kids were out of the house. Celia, her youngest, had graduated college six months prior and was living near the school. Jillian got a phone call from someone who lived in her daughter's building, saying that Celia was "acting weird." Jillian got on the first plane to discover that Celia clearly looked distressed (she was not washed, she looked like she hadn't slept, and she was flimsily dressed) and was hearing voices. Jillian was not comfortable seeking medical advice in Baltimore, where she knew no one, and decided to take her daughter back to Michigan to their family doctor, whom she trusted. After seeing Celia, the doctor sent them to the emergency room, where she was admitted for the first of many psychiatric hospitalizations.

Celia was kept in the hospital just for a few days, discharged with medication and a plan to return to see a therapist. Jillian could not remember if her daughter had followed through with the therapist that first time, but she told me that a pattern emerged in which Celia would pull herself together once in the hospital and on medications, and would be discharged within a few days with a follow-up plan to continue the medications and engage in talk therapy. Celia never did either of these plans. "She did not think that she had a problem. And she was smart enough to comply while in the hospital so that she would be let out within a few days."

After her daughter's discharge from the hospital, Jillian became busy with trying to find a place for Celia to live, close to her but not with her and her husband. Jillian met with realtors and located a nice, safe building where Celia could live. She bought her new furniture and made the space welcoming. She also flew back down to Baltimore to close Celia's apartment and arrange for all the furniture to either be shipped out west or sold.

The next twenty years in Jillian's life could be called "this will be a new start." Jillian's feeling of being the mule on the harness included dreading each time the phone would ring and she would have to respond to either Celia, a landlord, or a police officer reporting another disaster. The most labor-intensive work for Jillian was having to move Celia each time she was evicted or was driven out by her own paranoia. Celia would tell her parents how she couldn't stay in a particular apartment because her neighbor was out to get her, or the neighbors were making too much noise. When Jillian would show up to help Celia move, she would discover that, as in the apartment in Baltimore, Celia was living in a "total mess." Rather than get into a screaming match with her daughter, she would quietly clean up the mess, find a new realtor, and move her, again and again.

> It was horrible. It was horrible because I thought, oh, another place; either she has to leave or she's—like the time we bought her a condo, she kept complaining and complaining to the management company. And she'd complain about neighbors and things like that. I was just getting call after call, and it was just awful. Each time I'd think, "Well, I have to find her another place to live." And, of course, every time I had to co-sign the lease because she didn't have any money or capital. . . . And it was just . . . I would foolishly make an effort to make it nice, and that didn't make any difference at all because she would just trash it. And I even had my cleaning lady go over once a month or something and clean and thinking "that would solve the problem."

As the years progressed, Celia's symptoms and behavior got worse. But beyond the financial outlays and the exhaustion from the endless moves, something changed when Jillian turned seventy-five. Celia crossed a line by breaking into the family cabin on Lake Michigan, where she was forbidden to go, and she trashed their belongings and the cabin itself. Even though Celia had already broken into their suburban home several times, her breaking and entry into the family cottage pushed Jillian into a new level of fury and shock. She entertained (then rejected) the idea of cutting off Celia's money or calling the police. "It's like lead in your stomach." I named this new period in Jillian's view of her parenting role "crossing the line." Although Celia continued to be in and out of psychiatric hospitals, Jillian stopped investing in setting her daughter up in new apartments. Instead, she supported her in a rooming house, where she could stay and go without consequences for the family.

The final (or next-to-last) period in Jillian's career as a mom, I call "running out of gas." Jillian was tired and worn out.

> So, I just want to go into a hole and a cave and have nobody bother me. . . . I think that I finally began to detach (a little). Of course, at this age [seventy-six] that's when you naturally start detaching. I think I realized that friends or people I know are dying and that I want to have quality time for the rest of my time with my husband, and that my main responsibility is

with that relationship. I have to start taking care of me because I think all
of this has really done a number on my health. I have bad irritable bowel
syndrome. I've had ulcers, and I think that—I would say that I've run out
of gas. I just don't have the emotional reserves to tap in to. I just don't.

You can become an ex-wife by divorcing or an ex-schoolteacher by
retiring, but you can never become an ex-mother.

Jillian started to set new limits to protect herself and her time. While
Celia had always been included in Sunday family dinners, this open
invitation was stopped. Instead, the only way she could join them was
if she was taking her medications. "I mean, it's kind of an injustice to
the rest of the family—because you just don't have that much psychic
energy to disperse in equal amounts to everyone. . . . I just feel that we
have dispersed as much physic energy as I want to give. And I've got to
save some for myself and the rest of my family." She tried unsuccess-
fully to hire a lawyer to apply for state guardianship for Celia with the
hope that this could include mandated medication to treat her psychosis.
When this failed, she found a cousin who was willing to move in with
Celia. She paid the cousin a stipend for living there. The cousin also had
health problems and had to take daily medications. It became the cousin's job to also give Celia her antipsychotic medications each morning.
    While the new arrangement was bringing greater stability to Celia's
life, Jillian turned her energy to planning for the future—how would
Celia manage when they were gone? Jillian and her husband had located a fiduciary agent who would be responsible for administering
monthly allowances. This search for "after I'm gone" is the last stage in
some mothers' and fathers' worrying and planning for their challenging
adult children.[12]

AFTER I'M GONE

The late Alice Rossi, a University of Massachusetts' sociologist, wrote
that there is "little cultural prescription about when the authority and
obligations of a parent end."[13] As a role, being a mother is unique from
other roles because you can't quit, retire, or be fired. You can become

an ex-wife by divorcing or an ex-schoolteacher by retiring, but you can never become an ex-mother.

Looking at difficult mothering as an arc that extends into old age offers new insights. Rather than thinking about the mother-child relationship as spanning a limited twenty-something years, I have shown that mothering work may last fifty or sixty years. "How are the kids?" is a very familiar question that accompanies so many mature women's greeting of one another. Yet this question is often asked with the unspoken assumption that the answer will include just a positive breezy report. An acknowledgment of the potential complexities of mothering in later life, this question might shift to "How are you?" Whether we have difficult adult kids or highly achieving kids, or children who are no longer talking to us, mothers' well-being needs to be considered as both affected by, and also, separate from the ups and downs in the next generations' lives.

Chapter Three

Give Me Shelter

"He's a good kid, why not?" That was what Loretta said to herself when her son, Jason, asked if he could move back home with his girlfriend, Zahra, and their new baby. The young family had been living with Zahra's mother since the child's birth, but after a year, Zahra's mom had had enough and wanted them to leave. That's when Jason asked his mother if they could move in with her for a while. Loretta knew that her son had had problems getting along with others, particularly in work situations. But she still saw him as a lovable kid. She wanted to help.

Retired and living on a fixed income, Loretta had a small house in Brooklyn that she and her late husband had purchased years ago. Now that Jason had no place to live, she didn't want to put him in a situation where he would be at risk. Besides, there was a child involved, her granddaughter. That changed everything. Loretta said yes to a temporary stay. But short-term has a way of becoming long-term when a difficult adult child is involved. In Loretta's case, Jason was unemployed and he and his family stayed for twelve years.

The women I spoke with came from diverse backgrounds with varied resources at their disposal. Nevertheless, the one resource common to all the mothers I spoke to was a home, no matter how small. Whether they rented or owned, the mothers could provide shelter. In fact, all of the women I interviewed had opened their homes to their adult children when their "kids" were in the midst of a crisis with no place to live. Most had assumed that their adult child (and often family) would stay only for a short time. Many stayed for years. In the vast majority of situations, it was the mother, with or without the help of the legal system, who made the leave-taking happen. These were not "boomerang" kids who eventually bounced back into independent living.

SHARED LIVING

Many people assume that when adult children live with their older parents, it is the older parents who benefit. This belief is based on an antiquated notion in which a widow or widower with few resources is invited to live with their offspring. The assumption from years back is that older parents are physically and economically vulnerable, socially isolated, and in need of protection. Today, however, older people are on average healthier, live longer, have greater financial security, and value their privacy more than their predecessors. It is the adult child who is the likely beneficiary of an intergenerational household.[1]

The most obvious gain for an adult child returning to the family nest is a reprieve from having to pay rent or maintain a mortgage. With the current high costs of housing, this is a tremendous saving, particularly for a young person who may be going back to school or is finding it hard to secure full-time employment. Being back home can also include the companionship of parents and siblings, not to mention the comfort of home-cooked meals, cable, and laundry.

There can be benefits for all if an adult child returns home for what they see as positive reasons. With today's high housing costs, many young people move back in with their parents to be able to afford an advanced education. Not having to pay rent allows them to afford graduate school. If they also work, they may be able to contribute to the household financially. In such instances, co-residence is viewed as positive by both the adult child and their parents. Living together in such a situation allows both generations to experience a new adult-to-adult relationship in which the adult child has more autonomy and the parents have less responsibility. Parents can take satisfaction from facilitating their child's efforts toward independence. The new roommate can provide companionship and emotional support, and help with household chores. The younger person can be relied on to troubleshoot computer problems or run out at night to do last-minute errands. During COVID-19, a mother whose fifty-year-old daughter moved in with her temporarily felt warmed by her daughter's concern for her when she would volunteer to do the dishes, noticing when her mom was more tired than usual. Feeling seen in this way may not occur in more typical short family visits.

A short-term stay has a way of becoming long term when a difficult adult child is involved.

Shared living situations vary tremendously. The size of your apartment or house will have a large effect on how much you and your adult child have to negotiate in order to accommodate each other. In addition, your flexibility, your adult child's ability to be respectful and even help out, and your other commitments will make this new situation more or less stressful. What's more, the way the adult child views their return home—as a personal failure or as a stepping stone to future goals—will influence their attitude toward their parents, which itself will affect their willingness to contribute to the shared living environment.

Yet among adult children returning home, a number of parents report feeling resentful at having to give up their newfound freedom as "empty nesters." For those parents who had gotten used to living without any children in the house, they may feel resentful. When the adult child returns, parents have to re-shift the lifestyle they had created when living alone. Some find this change unwelcome.[2]

SOCIAL CLOCKS

We measure ourselves through social clocks and timetables. That is, there are accepted societal timeframes during which major life roles are expected to be accomplished. At what age should people marry? Live on their own? Be self-supporting? These schedules change over time and place. In the 1950s, for example, a woman who wasn't married by her early twenties might be regarded as an "old maid." That's certainly not the case now. It is now also accepted that young adults will remain dependent on their parents much longer than in previous generations.

The markers of independence, of whether a child achieves autonomy "early," "late," or "on time," are not as rigid as they once were. They also differ across cultures. Look at the different trends in the south of Europe (Italy, Malta, and Greece) and the north (Finland, Denmark, and Sweden). Almost 50 percent of Italians aged twenty-five to thirty-four still live at home, compared to 3 to 6 percent in Denmark or Sweden. This is due not just to poorer labor markets in Italy, but to the cultural and political contexts. In Finland, Denmark, and Sweden, parents place much greater value on autonomy. These northern countries also have government support systems to facilitate the independence of younger and older generations. In contrast, in southern European countries, including Italy, government policy and family cultural values support the reliance of adult children on their parents. Italian young men living at home are called "mamoni," or men who are tied to their mothers' apron strings, without many negative associations attached to this trend.

> The markers of independence, of whether a child achieves autonomy "early," "late," or "on time," are not as rigid as they once were. They also differ across cultures.

U.S. economists explain higher rates of intergenerational living as a by-product of changing employment opportunities and the declining financial situation of young people. Lower wages for entry-level workers and longer paths to career development, coupled with higher housing costs, have made it difficult for young adults to secure independent housing.[3] Scholars have shown how living with parents is a critical safety net and a way of pooling resources, especially for low-income families. More non-immigrant Black and immigrant Hispanic and Asian youth live with their parents during young adulthood than white youth. Parents in low-income groups, who cannot offer their adult children the same financial resources as white middle-class and affluent parents, can provide indirect economic support through co-residence.[4]

AUTONOMY AND THE DIFFICULT ADULT CHILD

There are a myriad of issues that can interfere with an adult child's independence, but the event that usually triggers a move into a parents' home is financial. For the difficult adult child, a financial crisis may be compounded by personal factors such as mental illness, substance abuse disorder, unhealthy alcohol use, and depression. Parents who open their homes to their difficult adult children have to cope with more than the end to their "empty nest." They have to deal with the realization that their adult child may have serious problems. Living with adult children who are dealing with mental health problems, emotional distress, financial issues, or legal issues is stressful for parents.[5]

Some parents feel ashamed that their adult children are not self-supporting and still need parental support. One mother feared that others would judge her poorly and assume that she did not instill the right values into her son's life. She quoted scripture to me to illustrate her church community's teaching on the value of promoting self-sufficiency. "The Bible talked about treating the children in a way they should grow and when they grow older, they should not be part of you." A parent's sense of worth can be affected not just by their adult children's accomplishments, but also their failures.[6]

THE DAY-TO-DAY EXPERIENCE

What I discovered from talking to the women in my study of difficult mothering is that while each of them wanted to help their adult child who needed a place to stay, the actual day-to-day experience of living together again was difficult in many unexpected ways. Mothers felt that they were not respected or appreciated by their adult children. They had to cope with their children's (and grandchildren's) lack of cleanliness as their houses moved from organized to chaotic. Many felt powerless, as if they were losing ground and being pushed to the side by their adult children in their own homes.

Lack of Respect

Most of the mothers talked about the strain when sharing a small space. "It just became too much. I'm claustrophobic and she has all these clothes, all these—I tried my hardest—I even went on antidepressants to try to calm myself down, to keep myself, you know, level. I felt we were right back to when she was younger, like there's no escape."

Rebecca gave many examples of how she felt disrespected and intruded on when Brandon lived with her again. She felt he treated her home as if it was no different than living on the street. He would bring unknown men and women into the house at night, and when she would get up to use the bathroom, she would run into "strange people." Rebecca felt that she had to protect her valuables not just from the outsiders he would invite in, but from Brandon himself. "Living with him was like living with ten babies . . . you've got to hide things, put things away so they don't get broken or stolen."

Cleanliness and Chaos

Fights over cleaning the kitchen and bathroom, sharing of chores, and noise at night were constant occurrences in some of the newly reshared homes. Many women mentioned being upset that their new "roommates" could not adhere to their need for cleanliness and order. What the mothers took for granted, their adult children did not.

Esther couldn't tolerate coming home from work and seeing Reggie's clothes strewn all over the living room. When she finally told him that unless he started to clean up after himself, she would take away his keys, he did what was needed. Not all adult children are as responsive as Reggie.

Durene had a long list of Caleb's habits that still got under her skin, even though he had been living with her for more than ten years. She resented being woken up by the sounds of his doing the dishes at two in the morning when he had promised to do it earlier. She was offended by his not cleaning the shared toilet, even though she had shown him innumerable times how it should be done. They also had constant tussles about his helping out with the shopping and sharing expenses. Durene knew that Caleb was getting money each month from Social Security Insurance and that his budget was based on both their food needs for the month, but he used his allotment only for himself. She saw his behaviour as selfish, especially when he would take the food that she had prepared for herself without leaving something in its place. She did add that there were times when he would surprise her with an ice cream late at night. Those were nice moments between mother and son, but there were few of them, and they didn't make up for his general disregard for her welfare.

Overstepping Boundaries

Making room for new people in your home theoretically requires setting up firm boundaries and clear communication. In an ideal world, parents and their adult kids will negotiate with each other regarding their expectations and needs in the now-shared space. Loretta never expected to feel unsafe and pushed out of her own home, but that's what happened when she allowed her son to move in with her. Her small house had a garage that had been converted into a downstairs living space. She had agreed to let Jason, Zahra, and their one-year-old daughter stay in this small room that also had a half bathroom, a hot plate, and a small refrigerator. She allowed them the use of her own full bathroom for showers and baths. Despite these cramped living quarters, Jason and Zahra kept having more children. Loretta would reassure herself. "Well, they'll leave, once this next baby is born." But they stayed until she had to have them escorted out by the police. At that point, their family included six children. Remember, Loretta had invited her son and his baby and girlfriend to live with her temporarily. Twelve years later, there were eight of them, still in that same small downstairs space.

Eighty-two years old when she told me her story, Loretta sometimes had difficulty recalling the details. It was hard for me to make sense of the timeline, especially since I couldn't understand how she and the family could have lived with such discomfort for all of those years. The most evocative image that she shared with me was her description of the dangers she faced in using her own bathroom. One day Loretta needed to get into the bathroom, which was occupied. Her knocks on the door and verbal pleas to "let me in" were ignored. Zahra had locked the door and acted as if she didn't hear her mother-in-law calling.

> It was a constant thing about the bathroom.
> I was going somewhere so I said to the kid, "Oh, please." I begged her.
> "Can you just let me go into the bathroom?"
> The mother came up, slammed the door, and pushed the kid in, while I was standing out there waiting. There she is, with her computer and just— I mean . . . it was just too much. Too, too much.
> The bathroom would be all wet and I could slip.
> They didn't even care. It was a house of confusion, just a house of confusion.

Boundaries Broken on Both Sides

As much as it is hard for parents, adult children also struggle to find comfortable boundaries when they have to once again share a home with their parents. Sylvia's daughter became furious when she learned that her mother had gone into her room when she wasn't there. The reason didn't matter. Sylvia, for her part, couldn't understand why Jasmine was upset. She felt that her daughter should trust her mother and assume that if she was looking through her daughter's stuff, it was for a good reason. Sylvia did not want to be treated like a stranger—or a roommate—and felt hurt by what many would consider the healthy request of one adult to another.

> As much as it is hard for parents, adult children also struggle to find comfortable boundaries when they have to once again share a home with their parents.

Faith had to continually walk on eggshells as she shared her studio apartment with her fifty-two-year-old daughter and her eighteen-year-old grandson, both of whom had mental health issues. She worried if she pushed too strongly to remind them to keep the place neat, as she wanted it, they could interpret it as a put-down and then tempers would rise. She, however, was able to see the situation from their side, as well. Her daughter and grandson didn't want to be monitored all the time. They wanted to be treated as adults. Yet she wanted things run in a certain way. "I have to ask and if they don't do it, I sometimes have to demand." And the demand, she realized, made them feel like they were kids again being monitored by their "mommy." "They don't want me to be overprotective. They don't want me to look at the mistakes they make every day." Faith's ability to see the situation from her daughter's perspective helped when conflicts ensued.

GOOD ADVICE, HARD TO FOLLOW

"Come up with an exit plan right away." That's popular advice for parents whose adult children have moved back home. "Ask about goals, job aspirations, life direction. Revisit it every six months. Be realistic: Consider what is truly achievable in that time frame."[7]

A great many assumptions underlie this advice. For one thing, it assumes that parents have a partnership with their adult child that can include friendly discussions. For another, it would suggest that the adult child can take an active role not only in making plans, but can carry them out. None of the mothers I interviewed had this sort of relationship with her child. Esther's son had moved back in after he and his girlfriend broke up. He was also unemployed. Instead of being goal-directed to find a new job, he seemed depressed and was making poor decisions for himself. Esther was dismayed by his going out at night with friends and coming home at two in the morning, obviously having been drinking and smoking. The few times she tried to give advice about the importance of choosing one's friends and not being at the beck and call of "bad apples," all she got in return was silence or if she was lucky, "You already told me that, Ma." The only words they shared were "Good evening" or "Good morning."

The ethicist column of the *New York Times* provided similarly unrealistic advice in a column titled: "My adult child son moved back in. It's a nightmare. Can I kick him back out?" A mother wrote to the advice columnist describing her dilemma when her thirty-something adult son moved back in with her after being fired. "When he first asked if he could move in and how long he could stay, she replied: 'It depends on how good a roommate you can be.'" Turned out he was a terrible roommate. He called his mother ugly and stupid and accused her of lying when she could not remember something. When asked to move, he refused.

The son wasn't working or paying any rent. His mother, worried about his mental state, offered to pay for his therapy if only he would go. "Given his mental state," she asked, "is it unethical to evict him? I feel like I'm in an abusive relationship and desperately want him out. I realize that if we evict him, it may be the end of our relationship with him, but much of the time that feels preferable (and saner) to me than what I am living with."

The reply she got from the male ethicist presented the view that there was no question that she should kick him out. "You do not owe it to anyone including your own adult children, to let them make a habit of abusing you, whether physically or verbally. Allowing such abuse out

of a sense of obligation is a moral mistake. And it may be a mistake in
other respects too: Once someone feels he has you under his thumb, he
has no incentive to change his behavior."[8] What the *New York Times*
ethicist Mr. Apiah recommended was based on the assumption that
evicting her son would be an easy action for this woman based on what
is right or wrong. What his advice does not contain is an understanding of the complexity of a mother's commitment to protect her child.
Carol Gilligan, a feminist ethicist, might also critique the position
recommended by the *New York Times* ethicist for being based purely
on fairness and equality—what Gilligan calls the "justice perspective."
She suggested an alternative framework: "the care perspective." The
care perspective is used more by women and is based on an evaluation
of how a particular action will impact those involved. The reasoning
the women used to explain why they could not "kick out" their adult
children from their home was because of the negative effect it would
have on them. Many realized that there were no other affordable housing options for their adult children and, as mothers, they could not bear
forcing their child to become homeless.

What Is a Mother to Do?

Sylvia and her husband had opened their home to their two daughters
and their two children several years back. The apartment was tiny. The
grandchildren were sullen and messy. The adult daughters were seemingly unconcerned with their mothers' health and well-being. Three
years back, Sylvia had finally given in to her son's pleading that she
evict her daughters. He believed that the stress of living with them was
destroying her and his father's mental and physical health. Three days
after they were gone, Sylvia got a phone call from a friend who told
her that Jasmine was on the 6 o'clock news talking to reporters. It was
a story about the plight of the homeless. Sylvia was mortified and told
her husband that they had to let them come back home. She felt humili-
ated that others would see her as a "bad" mother. The families returned.
They are still living, and fighting, with Sylvia and her husband.

Tracy expressed tremendous anguish that she could not find a safe
living arrangement for her daughter. Jeannie had been discharged from
her last psychiatric hospitalization to a homeless shelter for persons
with mental illness, not back to live with Tracy because the staff be-

lieved that Jeannie might harm her mother if they lived together again. Jeannie had set a fire in her mother's house during her last psychotic episode. The discharge plan was for Jeannie to live in a nearby shelter that had special support for persons with mental illness. Jeannie, however, was not comfortable in the shelter. Instead, she was sleeping in the park near her mother's house. Tracy knew that she couldn't take Jeannie back into the house, but she also felt that she couldn't live with the worry knowing her daughter was sleeping in the streets.

Giving shelter or providing refuge from the storm is what any parent wants to offer her adult child when in need. Yet the stories that the mothers of difficult adult children shared reveal how difficult this can be. These mothers felt alone and without viable options. When the only alternative to being painfully pressed within your own home is having your child become homeless, what is a mother, or mother and father, supposed to do?

Chapter Four

Guilt, Shame, and Mother-Blame

You know, you want to feel proud of your children.
You want to see progress in their life.
You want to see them do something that will lift up or portray
the kind of life you instil in them, the values you instil in them.
And people tend to point fingers at their parents every time a child
turns bad.
They will point a finger at the parents, like in a way, the parent
didn't do good,
the parent didn't train the children, you know.
And yet, you do your part, and nobody asks if you did it?
Automatically, they already know you didn't.

—Esther

There are many distinctions between the mothers whose stories are reported here. Some were widowed. Some were married. Some were rich, and others were poor. They came from different races and ethnic backgrounds. The type and severity of the children's problems varied greatly, too. Yet, among these distinctions, they shared a view of mothering that led them to become their child's safety net. Although none had anticipated spending their later years living with or worrying about their troubled adult child, each explained their current caregiving situation with this simple sentence: "I'm her (his) mother."

Feminist psychologists have noticed how women develop a moral commitment to care, how being responsible for their children is about "being moral as a person."[1] This notion of *being moral* for women is about relationships and the centrality of caring for others. Guilt is typically about how your actions affect others. Several mothers explained how they would not be able to bear the consequences of evicting their adult child. "I couldn't live with that." Guilt is self-reproach for a specific bad deed. It's tied to an event and is an evaluation of a particular behavior. Shame, on the other hand, focuses on a woman's entire self[2] and is the emotion that results from feeling that she did not live up to her ideals. In the case of the women profiled here, the shame of not being a good mother. As for blame—that comes into play when we hold someone responsible for a bad result, either another person or group of people. And then there's self-blame, which is similar to guilt but includes an assumption of greater responsibility for what happened—or didn't happen. Beyond the particular nuances of the differences between guilt, shame, and blame is the important idea that women suffer when they compare themselves with the internalized ideal of what a good mother is.

A woman may berate herself for having lost her temper at her son's teacher. She may feel shame for the way she spoke harshly to a teacher, and then guilt that her comments might have caused insult. In another example, a mother described her self-blame which also feels like shame, when she discovered that her older daughter was twenty-six weeks pregnant. "I blame myself for all that. . . . I felt so guilty, so terrible that my daughter had managed to go through all this, and none of us had noticed. I felt like a total failure as a mother. I felt that my neglect had ruined her life."[3] Even though her "neglect" could be explained by her having had to attend to a younger child's serious health situation, she still blamed herself for not being able to attend to both.

In all cultures, mothers are expected to be altruistic and, when necessary, give up their own needs in order to feed and clothe their children. In the twenty-first-century world of parenting, a mother's altruism is supposed to extend to her providing deep, exclusive, and full attention to her children. The assumption is that children need an adult who will be at their disposal to listen, hear, and play. Mothers who are not "one with their children" or have conflicts about being a mother, even momentarily, can be made to feel as if they are failures. They label their behavior as "appalling" if they feel angry at their children. They believe that "good mothers" don't have any negative feelings about their children.[4]

In all cultures, mothers are expected to be altruistic and to give up their own needs in order to tend to their children.

In a study carried out by two Finnish researchers, mothers were asked to keep a journal of their forbidden feelings while caring for their young children. The most-reported feeling was guilt. Guilt for not being more present. Guilt for aggressive feelings. Guilt for wanting a break. Guilt for favoring one child over another. Guilt for not living up to the idealized image of a good mother. We know much more about mothers' feelings of responsibility for their young children than we know about how they feel about their obligations to their older children. Nevertheless, research has shown that women are more prone to feeling guilty than men,[5] creating what has been named the "guilt gap" between husbands and wives.[6]

Evolutionary psychologists remind us that guilt may have had an evolutionary purpose in ancestral times. Psychologists Anna Rotrich and Katrina Janhunken suggest that human evolution may explain gender differences in experiencing guilt. They define *guilt* as an emotion that stops people from causing harm to others. A woman's heightened ability to feel guilt within relationships serves an evolutionary purpose—it protects the young. Guilt inhibits aggression.[7] When this mother wrote in her journal, "My own feelings scare me the most. The rage that possesses me is scary. I have often cried when I think that I am a bad mother or even the only mother in the world who treats her child like this," she may have been berating herself, but the evolutionary psychologist would recognize her guilt as a protective force to inhibit her aggression.

Vivian's global self-reproach of her parenting is an illustration of both shame and guilt. "I mean, I used to think about that constantly. Like how could I do that? What did I do? What did I create? If I had been a stronger person. If I had had more patience. If I handled things differently, maybe it would've had a different result."

"If only I had insisted . . ."

"Why didn't I realize . . ."

"What was I thinking . . ."

THE GOOD MOTHER

When it comes to young children, there are many qualities that are associated with being a good mother. Being loving, a good listener, in control, patient, fair, and responsible[8] are just a few. When it comes to mothers of adult children, the list of commonly accepted qualities is much smaller. Some recommend "bite your tongue," meaning don't give unwanted advice or try to control your adult children. Others recommend "*don't* bite your tongue," encouraging mothers to engage in more open and genuine dialogue.[9]

Parents of adult children feel better about themselves and rate themselves more positively based on how their children are doing.

What do we do know is that parents of adult children feel better about themselves and rate themselves more positively based on how their children are doing.[10] Psychologist Stella Chase considers it remarkable that mothers are ever able to relax because of the sense of responsibility they carry: "There are very few jobs in which one individual will be blamed for anything that goes wrong, and fewer still in which what can go wrong, and the feeling of being blamed, is so devasting."[11]

Feminist authors have suggested several different names to describe the ideology about ideal motherhood that affects all women, "whether they are buying it or not."[12] This has been called "total motherhood" or the "motherhood myth." Still, others refer to it as "intensive mothering."[13] The idealized image of mothering depicts women as selfless beings able to make their needs synonymous with their young children. Starting when they become pregnant, mothers are told that if they do all the right things, they will have fully healthy and perfect children. The responsibilities that women are expected to take on for their children are not confined within the family. They bear the burden for an entire society that depends on the maternal work of ensuring the well-being of the future generation.[14]

SELF-BLAME IN MOTHERS OF YOUNG CHILDREN

Mothers across economic and racial groups blame themselves for nearly each glitch in their child's development. And feelings of failure can begin right at birth. Joan Wolf describes total motherhood as "a moral code in which mothers are exhorted to optimize every dimension of children's lives, beginning with the womb."[15] The pregnant woman who hopes to give her new baby the best birth possible, which in today's culture is a "natural" vaginal birth, can feel devastated if instead a Cesarean section becomes necessary. Similarly, women who cannot breastfeed feel ashamed that they are failing their babies and not living up to their own ideals of a good mother. For example, this was posted by a mother on a site for new mothers:

> I've tried exhaustively—and unsuccessfully—to breastfeed my baby. It was always a struggle, even after I got professional help. During my pregnancy I was so excited about the idea of breastfeeding. *Now I feel like a failure*, especially because of all the information out there about breast milk being best. What should I do?[16]

Maternal guilt and shame are also felt by mothers because of their poverty status, work situation that conflicts with time at home, and being a single parent.[17]

Parenting books have promoted the idea that infants and toddlers need to receive exclusive attention from a caregiver, usually the mother, who is expected to experience only joy and happiness from childcare. Consider this example from the popular book *Your Baby and Child*: "[T]aking a baby's point of view does not mean neglecting your own, the parent's view. Your interests and his are identical. You are all on the same side—the side that wants to be happy and have fun. If you make happiness for him, he will make happiness for you."[18] This advice completely ignores the reality that mothers and young children are, in fact, separate beings who have very disparate needs. Yes, being able to enjoy moments of oneness with your child is an essential part of attuned mothering, but they are not possible all the time. Women get tired, they have other relationships, other children, even, and need or want to work outside of the home. Each of these needs as separate people can bring feelings of guilt and shame for not doing what is assumed to be "best."

While most theories of child development credit mothers as having enormous power as the holders of their children's emotional and psychological health, no one can protect a child from every danger. If a toddler who is learning to climb suddenly finds himself up on a high table, and in his excitement slips off and hits his head, his mother will likely berate herself for not having gotten there two seconds sooner. She can also expect to be blamed by others. Similarly, when walking down a city street, a joyous interaction between a mother and her child can suddenly change into the mother screaming at the five-year-old who has stepped into the gutter without waiting for his mother. The panicked mother is fearful that her child will be hurt and that she will have failed to protect him.

SELF-BLAME BY MOTHERS OF ADULT CHILDREN

A mother's self-blame and her internal mandate to protect her children do not dissipate as her children age. Many studies have documented how mothers negatively react to problems in their adult children's lives. They experience distress and feelings of failure that can undermine their maternal identity.[19] Karen Gueta and Einid Peled documented the distress that Israeli mothers experienced when they learned that their daughters had experienced domestic violence. "I used to be an ordinary mom . . . it's really a disaster that happened in our family [daughter's experience of domestic violence]. . . . This is not the daughter we have dreamed to have. We wanted her to be happy, to have a normal husband."[20] Another mother said, "Of course I am ashamed. Because no matter what, as a mother you always think that if you take responsibility, somehow, always, [things will be fine]. It is possible, that maybe, somehow, I made a mistake. You cannot shake off that responsibility, it's impossible."

> A mother's self-blame and her internal mandate to protect her children do not disappear as her children age.

The women I interviewed all accused themselves of having done things that could explain their grown children's current problems.

"I spoiled him."

"Their father was not around when they were older."

"She followed in my footsteps and married the wrong person."

Many wondered if they had "been stronger," "paid more attention," or "been around more and not at work" if the outcome would have been different. Perhaps their child would have been more self-sufficient, less prone to anger or substance abuse issues. *Perhaps* and *if* are the words women use to wound themselves.

AM I A BAD MOTHER?

Lucy described her life as an emotional rollercoaster. One minute she felt guilty for the person her son had become, the next she rejected that blame as unrealistic. "I feel angry with myself because I'm the one who made him the way he is; but then again . . ." I felt her sadness.

> Sometimes I say to myself, "No, Lucy, no matter what you would have done, that's the way he was going to be." So, in one part of my mind I think "you don't make people be the way they are." But in the back of my mind, I tell myself over and over again I *could'a should'a would'a.* I yoyo myself. And I'm saying what the hell am I yoyoing myself for? I keep on saying to myself I did the best I could to the best of my ability, so don't feel any guilt. But no matter what, you're going to feel it (the guilt). So that's why, you know, it bothers me. It bothers me. But, yet, what's done is done.

Sylvia had stage IV cancer. Her two daughters and each of their two children had been living with her and her husband for almost ten years, rent free. The daughters each had trouble keeping a job and the grandchildren had multiple behavioral problems in school. While both daughters were self-absorbed, Jasmine was the difficult adult child who Sylvia wanted to talk to me about.

Sylvia was torn. On the one hand she felt like a generous mother who had invited her daughter and grandchildren to live with her. On the other hand, Jasmine's neglect made her feel like a failure. Sylvia wanted to believe she had been a good mother. She had been involved in the Parent-Teacher Association, had always dressed her children well, and earned enough money to be able to take them to special events in the city. She was shocked that now that she was ill, Jasmine and her sister were not reciprocating by showing love and concern when she was undergoing treatment for her cancer. When she would remind Jasmine to buy fruits and vegetables when she went out to shop, Jasmine would often "forget" or say that she didn't have enough money. Sometimes she'd come home with potato chips, something her mother could not eat. Her daughter's inattention to Sylvia's need for healthy food was more than annoying, more than disrespectful. It was neglect—a form of abuse in which the family member of caregiver fails to care for someone she is responsible for. Sylvia did not name her daughter's behavior as neglect. Instead, she wondered what she might be doing wrong.

> Am I expecting too much of them? You know, you get to a point where you don't know what's right. When they see me lying in the bed, I would like for them to come in the room and say "Ma, did you eat? Is there anything I can fix for you to eat? How are you feeling? Are you in pain? Do you need some—do you need your medicine?"

Sylvia felt embarrassed that none of her children accompanied her to her monthly chemotherapy appointments. Her choice of the word "embarrassment," rather than "angry," underlines the self-blame she carried. Rather than holding her adult children responsible for their choice to not accompany her to the doctor, she is blaming herself for having raised children who now ignored her when she needed them. She does not want other people in the waiting room to see the evidence of her adult children's neglect—she does not want to be seen as a bad mother.

BLAMED BY YOUR ADULT CHILD

Several mothers reported that their adult children accused them of willfully hurting them. Loretta's son believed that he, rather than his eighty-year-old mother, should have ownership of the family home. Jason's father had died when he was ten years old. Even though there had been no will, Jason assumed that the family home was meant for him. Now forty-two—unemployed with five children—he still believed that his mother was withholding property that was rightfully his. Loretta had to spend four years in court fighting her son's relentless attempts to turn his wishes into reality and take away her house.

Tracy's daughter, Jeannie, blamed her mother "for everything," especially when she was in a psychotic episode. She blamed her mother for the times she had to call 911 to have Jeannie taken to the hospital. Like Loretta's son, she also blamed her for mother for not giving her the proceeds from the house when it was sold. Although Tracy realized that it was her daughter's mental illness talking, it still hurt her to hear Jeannie say that she hated her and believed that she had actually stolen from her own daughter.

When Sylvia's unmarried daughter had her first baby, she blamed her mother for never talking to her about birth control. "I couldn't believe her," Sylvia told me. She was twenty-five.

> Mother-blaming holds mothers responsible for the behavior of their (even adult) children.

BLAMED BY PROFESSIONALS

"Mother-blaming" has been defined as holding mothers "responsible for the actions, behavior, health, and well-being of their (even adult) children," writes nurse researchers Jackson and Mannix, who interviewed mothers who had sought help when their teenagers were in trouble and starting to abuse drugs. The mothers reported that rather than having their child's situation addressed with helpful resources, the women felt blamed.[21] This assumption—that mothers play the lion's share in determining the person their child becomes—was most dangerously promoted by in the 1950s by psychiatrists who stated that autism was caused by "refrigerator mothers." Of course, we know now that autism is a genetic and neurological deficit, but consider that seventy years ago many people thought that autism was the result of a cold, distant, and rejecting mother who did not awaken the child's emotional capacities. It led to the simplistic and harmful misconception that autism is caused by inadequate parenting, which in turn resulted in many parents blaming themselves for their child's difficulties.

Although later research documented the inaccuracy of this, the theory that mothers are the explanation for their children's problems continues today. Psychologists Paula Caplan and Ian Haii-McCorquodal found that "mothers were blamed for seventy-two different kinds of problems in their off-spring ranging from bed-wetting to schizophrenia from inability to deal with color blindness to aggressive behavior, from learning problems to 'homicidal transsexualism.'"[22]

> Women are being held accountable for social problems beyond their control.

Mothers therefore are being shamed by social norms based on gender. The assumption that mothers should be held accountable for their children's behaviors and traits has also been extended to being blamed for their male partner's aggressive behavior. "Failure to protect" is the accusation made against mothers in the child welfare system whose children have witnessed domestic violence or been abused.[23] Blaming a mother for not protecting her child from her partner's violence omits the man's accountability for his actions. Mothers are not the only forces responsible for positive child development. Fathers (whether absent or present), schools, pollution, gun violence, and neighborhood resources all affect the person we become.[24] To only point a finger of blame at mothers for all of our social problems is unhelpful, sexist, and unwise. Nevertheless, mother-blaming is built into the child welfare system, the educational system, the health care system, and the legal system. Women are being held accountable for social problems beyond their control.

Current parenting research provides strong evidence that the person a young child becomes is explained by the interrelated effects of heredity (genes), parenting influences, nonfamily influences such as peers and schools, and the broader environment such as growing up in poverty or affluence. Families are seen as important influences on children, but the effect is understood only in light of the simultaneous influence of heredity (child's temperament) and the larger environment.[25]

Alana hated it when she was called in to see her daughters' teachers or therapists. She worried that they would only see the problem through her daughter's eyes and blame Alana for the terrible fights at home. Deborah had attention-deficit/hyperactivity disorder and behavioral problems starting in middle school. Alana acknowledged to me that she, too, had suffered from depression and could become argumentative with her daughter when she tried to help. But when she met with these professionals, she felt like they only saw her as the problem. She wanted to ask for help, but she felt attacked instead.

When Loretta called the Department of Aging to ask for protection from her son and his five young children, the call was routed, instead, to the Department of Child Welfare. Social workers arrived with measuring tapes and insisted that Loretta create more space for her son's growing family. This was the opposite of what Loretta needed. She had made the phone call to report feeling pushed out and abused by her son and his many children. The person who responded to Loretta's call for help had assumed that the children's needs ought to have priority, even though Loretta was the one at risk.

MOTHER-SHAMING BY OTHER MOTHERS AND STRANGERS

Mother-shaming—letting a woman know that her behavior with her child is unacceptable—can occur in supermarkets, on the subway, or online. Anywhere, really. The journalist Ayelat Waldman, mother of two children and author of the book *Bad Mother*, admitted that prior to becoming a mother, she had also engaged in mother-shaming. She wrote that "one of the darkest, deepest shames so many of us mothers feel nowadays is our fear that we are Bad Mothers, that we are failing our children and falling far short of our own ideals."[26]

Waldman described how, before becoming a parent, she "busted my first Bad Mother in the spring of 1994, on a Muni train in San Francisco." She was watching a mother on the bus trying to comb her daughter's ponytail and yelling at the girl to "stand still." Waldman came to the rescue of the girl, or so she thought at the time, and yelled at the woman, "Lady, we're all watching you." Waldman described how when she watched the mother struggle with her daughter, she, who had no children, felt confident that when it was her turn to brush her own daughter's hair, she would never be like that. In some ways, her book is an apology to her prematernal days when she thought she knew so much—but actually was so ignorant of the real lives of mothers with children.

The COVID pandemic brought mother-shaming to a new level. With actual dangers at stake and no clear answers available, mothers attacked each other for taking one choice over another. A *New York Times* reporter shared the tension and personal attacks that arose when she and a mommy-friend took opposing routes for coping with the shutdown. "No one has said so aloud, but our choices express what we would never say: Each thinks the other is wrong. Maybe reckless, selfish, and privileged too."[27] The pandemic was a time with no obvious right answers, and yet mother-shaming increased. When the reporter took her children out of daycare, her friend immediately scooped up the same daycare slot. She included her parents in her "pod," while her friend thought that other families with kids were a better choice for exposure and seemed to look down on her friend's choice.

Terri Peters, a journalist for *Today*,[28] reported on one mother's attempt to speak back to someone who had tried to put her down as she was grocery shopping.

To the man at Costco today who glanced over at me on my phone while my babies were fussing and felt the need to say, "You see these babies? They fuss like that because they want your attention. Maybe you should get off of your phone and give them your attention."

First of all, I had no idea the toddler saying, "Mama, pizza, mama, pizza" over and over and making pre-cry warnings to alert me that if we don't move soon, he's going to lose it—wanted my attention. Thank you for that brilliant analysis of the situation.

Secondly, I had been in the Membership line for 15 minutes already. I pulled out books, snacks, patty cake and even took to creepily pointing out items in buggies as customers left the store to entertain them.

Thirdly, you had been in the Refunds line next to me for a total of two minutes or else you would have seen the smiles and laughs and interaction.

Lastly, after 15 minutes, these babies got a bit fussy. And on the meltdown scale, they were barely even at a 1. Sensing the meltdown brewing, I took out my phone, downloaded the Costco app, and texted my husband to ask what our log-in is, an attempt to just get my membership card on my phone. Because I ran out of tricks and my kids ran out of patience, and now my goal was to just get us out of this line as quickly as possible before they released their screaming. But thank you for your parenting advice. Thank you for taking the time out of your day to shame a young mother with two tiny children. Thank you for seeing a stressful moment and deciding, "I think I'll make this worse for her."[29]

THE DANGER OF SHAME

Shame can make people with problems turn inwards and want to hide, rather than looking outwards, speaking up, and asking for help beyond themselves. A "veil of secrecy" can turn lethal when mothers of abusive adolescent or adult children refuse to seek help because they fear being labeled a "bad" parent. Mothers of aggressive adolescents who have called the police to help protect themselves and their families from their children's aggressive outbursts have, instead of getting help from the police, been given a referral to a parenting group as if the issue is the mother's fault.[30] Similarly, among older parents with an aggressive adult child, there is a reluctance to reach out and make the problem public. Most incidents of elder abuse are not reported. Older parents fear that a call to the police will only lead to harm for the adult child, who will likely be treated as a criminal, or shame for themselves that their older children are problematic.[31]

> Shame can make people with problems turn inwards and want to hide, rather than looking outwards, speaking up, and asking for help beyond themselves.

A feminist philosopher, Jill Locke, writes that "One of shame's most poisonous consequences is the way in which it overwhelms the subject so that she is unable to think beyond herself. Rather than focus on changing the world in ways that might lessen her shame, the shamed subject focuses on changing herself so that she might accommodate the demands of her milieu." Working mothers in the 1950s were blamed for their children's juvenile delinquency; in the twenty-first century, the media and public opinion continue to blame mothers for children's overuse of video games, the epidemic of childhood obesity, childhood poverty, and domestic violence in the home.[32] What do you blame yourself for in your adult children's lives? Self-forgiveness does not come easily for women. We have internalized society's dependence on us as the caring ones, without demanding the resources we need. I hope the women's stories shared here may allow you to have empathy not only for them, but for yourself as well.

Chapter Five

Torn in Two

I'm grateful my husband is not alive to see this mess! I'm a 73-year-old senior citizen taking care of two middle-aged men!!! I'm sick of it!!!

–Priscilla, "Difficult Mothering" blog on Facebook

Parents are supposed to be the emotional and practical support system for their children when they're in trouble.[1] This is the norm of family solidarity, and it's the rationale behind the choice of a woman to interrupt her focus on herself in later life and become a support system for her adult child. So why, then, do mothers report mixed feelings about the new situation in which they find themselves.

Ambivalence, that state of simultaneously holding positive and negative feelings about a person or situation, is something we all share. When we feel ambivalence within a powerful and intimate relationship, such as exists between a mother and her child, it can shake us to the core. Ambivalence can also occur on a structural level, involving dilemmas created by the expectations of society. The message that mothers should always be available to their young children conflicts with the other reality that women must work outside of the home in order to help support their families. Where adult children are concerned, there is a tension between the expectation that parents are responsible for ensuring that their adult children become independent, self-supporting human beings, while at the same time acting as a safety net. We are expected to be there for our adult children when they need us, but we also must not infantilize them.

INTERGENERATIONAL AMBIVALENCE

The term "intergenerational ambivalence" was suggested by psychologists Karl Pillemer and Karl Luscher to describe the opposing mandates that all parents of adult children juggle: be there when your children are in need while facilitating a child's independence.[2] The concept of intergenerational ambivalence promotes the understanding that family relationships should not be characterized using a dichotomous, black-or-white lens. There isn't one group of families that experiences conflict and another group that comfortably supports each other. Mixed feelings are part of all relationships and all families.

Pillemer and Luscher suggest that every parent experiences this state of ambivalence, but parents whose adult children are struggling and have not reached the typical milestones of adult success feel this contradiction more acutely. Their research shows that mothers and fathers experience heightened ambivalence when their adult children are not married, have not completed their education, and have mental health or substance abuse problems. These parents experience more negative feelings about themselves and their children.[3] Intergenerational ambivalence is especially strong for those who see no escape from providing support, which is the situation of parents of many difficult adult children.[4]

> Conflict is built into all intergenerational relationships. The younger generation's job is to separate and form their own lives, whereas the older generation is trying to preserve the connections and build a positive family legacy.

Parents universally have been found to have stronger and more positive feelings about their children than adult children have for their parents. This phenomenon is called the "developmental stake," referring to the fact that parents invest more in their children than children invest in their parents. This situation often prompts parents to emphasize their positive feelings as a way to make sense of this unequal investment.[5] In most families, intergenerational tensions are highest during transitions in the family, specifically when new members come in or out, such as marriages, new babies, and older parents' need for care.[6]

Beyond these predictable tensions between the generations, parents' disappointment and ambivalent feelings increase when their adult children do not achieve the adult roles that are indicative of independence.[7] Difficult mothering often includes coping with the effects of an adult child's lag in achieving an autonomous life. The adult child's lack of success impacts the mother's feelings about her adult child and herself. The adult child's problems create conflict for her about her maternal role and her need to also take care of herself. What is an older woman/mother supposed to do? Ambivalence is a useful term to describe her dilemma.

THE MOTHERHOOD IDEAL: SECRECY AND MATERNAL AMBIVALENCE

Mothers of young infants become unsettled when they discover that, side by side with their loving feelings toward their baby, they also harbor feelings of resentment, anger, and sometimes dislike. Negative feelings—what has been called "the darker side" of mothering[8]—conflict with the myth of motherhood as presented in the Hallmark card version of what mothering is supposed to look like. Thanks to changing views on a woman's place in larger society as well as in the home, the idealized image of a selfless woman who derives only pleasure from the demands and isolation of motherhood is slowly fading away.[9] Women with young children are now more able to acknowledge mixed feelings and are aware of the importance of being connected to other mothers in support groups or by openly acknowledging the strains of mothering with family and friends. When sharing not only information, but the pressures and joys of beginning motherhood, women can learn to accept the feelings of uncertainty and contradiction inherent in their new role. We can thank the women's movement for that. Following on the heels of the consciousness groups of the 1970s, mothers' support groups were subsequently developed to offer the same camaraderie to women caring for young children. Not only do these groups provide a safe space for mothers to openly discuss their fears, joys, and questions about raising their children, they mimic their earlier counterparts by creating an opportunity for women to talk about feelings that go against the cultural stereotypes of what a good wife or mother should do or feel.[10]

Yet it wasn't that long ago when a mother with, for example, a colicky baby would keep secret her reactions to her crying infant. She feared that acknowledging any feelings of helplessness in her maternal role could lead to disparagement of her as a good mother. To talk publicly about her difficulties in soothing her baby, she would be admitting that her feelings toward her baby also included anger and powerlessness. The impulse to keep feelings secret was likely based on embarrassment about her own reactions, as well as lack of information about colic, which can make even the most confident woman feel like a failure. Acknowledging negative feelings about being a mother or one's child have been called the "darker side of mothering"[11] and women go to great lengths to deny these emotions.

> Negative feelings—what has been called "the darker side" of mothering—conflict with the myth of motherhood as presented in the Hallmark card version of what mothering is supposed to look like.

Mothers of young children can reassure themselves that, in time, their children will sleep through the night, be toilet trained, and eventually move away, go to college, or get married. But older mothers of difficult adult children cannot necessarily anticipate a time when conflicts or issues will abate. Many older women with difficult adult children try, at least initially, to also keep their feelings and situation secret. Patricia, quoted in the epigraph, added to her post that she could never reach out for help. "The embarrassment is so real. I present myself as a strong individual . . . I could NEVER OPEN UP TO ANYONE!" I heard the wish to conceal the "darker side of mothering" of adult children from many of the women who I interviewed. Wendy, who was helping her daughter who had her first psychiatric break at age forty-one, was at a loss when she tried to write her annual Christmas letter. "How can I put this into words?" she asked. Leslie, a physical therapist, stopped chatting about her family to clients, as she was wont to do, once her son became ill with mental health problems. It's understandable that a family may want to keep family problems private; nevertheless, the question remains about the price women pay by shutting down and not sharing their complicated situations with others.[12]

The women I interviewed were still actively committed to supporting and protecting their adult children, despite their mixed feelings about resuming a responsibility they thought was behind them. For the woman who had hoped for a happy and active retirement in which she could at last indulge her own interests, having to become a caregiver again can be depressing and frustrating. Women with adult children with serious mental illness or substance use disorder have to learn about community and psychiatric services to help their adult children. And grandmothers raising their grandchildren have to learn to negotiate the school system and the health care system, and, for some, locate income support.[13] Many feel a desperation surrounding the impossible choice: me or them? While there have been a great many changes in family life, and women's views about their options as mothers, women are still expected to sustain motherhood as a beacon of order in changing and disordered times.

> While there have been a great many changes in family life, and women's views about their options as mothers, women are still expected to sustain motherhood as a beacon or order in changing and disordered times.

Painfully conflicted about the right thing to do, several women presented scenarios that they believed had no positive resolution—either their son or daughter would be hurt, they might hurt someone else, or the mothers, themselves, would suffer. I heard strong negative feelings of hopelessness and anger toward their adult children who they, at moments, perceived as trapping them and hurting them. Many had no one to turn to. They did not want to make public their adult children's problems and their own sadness and vulnerability.

"I'm at a crossroads. I cannot keep leaving myself out. But do you just throw them away?" Faith asked me. Alana said, "It's her or me. I have to move away. But she won't survive without me. I'm trapped in this relationship; I don't feel able to give her up."

And the shock of Rebecca's statement, "I love him too much, I don't have the strength to put him out, even though he will kill me there."

Mothers of both young children and adult children struggle with ambivalence, that is, accepting their mixed feelings toward their children.

It was Rozsika Parker, a British psychologist, who named the experience of maternal ambivalence as being "torn in two."[14]

Mother and child face the task of negotiating a sequence of separations from the moment of birth onward. While it is socially acceptable to view young children as increasingly gaining a sense of themselves as separate from their mothers, women, too, evolve from one maternal identity to another. It is essential that she be able to accept her mixed feelings about herself as a mother.

When mothers are encouraged to acknowledge their ambivalence, they find new ways to handle uncertainty and become stronger in their roles.

Women can benefit tremendously by examining their own mixed feelings. Consider the lessons gained in therapeutic groups with disengaged mothers struggling in the care of their young children. When given a safe space to examine their ambivalence about their offspring and about themselves, these mothers were better able to make parenting decisions that they were comfortable with, decisions that benefited both the mother and her child.[15] So many mothers of young and adult children feel undermined by their own feelings of ambivalence. This, in turn, creates guilt and anxiety, the sense that they are failing in their role, a role that we may feel is the most important one we'll ever have.

Things change when mothers are encouraged to acknowledge their ambivalence and hold in their minds both positive and negative feelings toward their child. They find new ways to handle uncertainty and become stronger in their role. The alternative is to escape this complexity and only ruminate by running to one or the other end of the two opposite poles of feelings or alternative actions. Thinking about ambivalence allows a woman to reclaim herself, rather than feeling helplessly divided.

MIXED FEELINGS AND DIFFICULT MOTHERING

Ellen, a successful business manager, told me: "I just expected and assumed that she would have an interesting career that was fulfilling. She would be independent, emotionally as well as physically . . . but she's not living in the world like a grown-up." Esther, too, had always assumed that children who are raised well by their families would ultimately become independent and live on their own. Now that Reggie, age thirty-two, was again living with her, she felt embarrassed. "I'm angry because he's not supposed to be depending on me. He's supposed to be on his own, by now. He should have a family of his own." As Paulette shared, "Parents want to feel like their kid is like a feather in their hat." Corrine described the sadness at seeing how her daughter's substance abuse was destroying her future as an attorney. "I think she's brighter than I am—and I am a bright woman. That is part of my depression, seeing someone with her promise, and it's all going to waste." Each mother I spoke to tried to find a way to support her adult child while managing her own feelings of disappointment. Of course, their strategies for handling their mixed feelings varied. Some used encouragement and continued to intervene in the hope that growth and change were still possible. Others stopped trying to help out, but still wanted to believe that their son or daughter who was using drugs, for example, might someday "wake up." Others, based on their assessment that change was not possible, altered their expectations for their child, the relationship, and the future.

Handling ambivalent feelings about the right way to respond to your difficult adult child is obviously different than it is for mothers of young children. Here, we are dealing with an adult-to-adult relationship. Adult children cannot be given a time out or "made" to do one behavior over another. Yes, boundaries can be made. Expectations can be set. But mothers with difficult adult children struggle to find a comfortable way to continue the relationship with their adult children.

MIXED FEELINGS ABOUT WHAT TO DO

If ambivalence is an expected aspect of family life, how do mothers with difficult adult children experience and manage their conflicting feelings? Nearly all the women I interviewed felt the discomfort of ambivalence. Those older mothers who did feel torn in two described that underneath this conflict were two central quandaries, which in turn could be summed up as the tug between the allure of freedom and the weight of responsibility:

1. Whose needs should take precedence: mine or my grown child's?
2. Can I bear the consequences of not protecting my child? (And the flip side of this: Can I bear the consequences of continuing to protect my child?)

Wanting Him Out, but He Will Get Hurt

Georgia was tired of having Desmond live in her home. She saw no positives in the situation for her. He didn't pay rent. He didn't clean up after himself. He was rude. She asked him on several occasions to please find his own place, but he wouldn't. The only option she saw for herself was getting a court order for his eviction—an option she couldn't bring herself to do.

> Well, I feel—he doesn't have a job. If I go to the legal system and put him out on the street and something should happen, how would I live with it? It's a difficult decision to make, very difficult. I want him to leave on his own. But for me to force him out without his having a job and just throw him out on the street—and God forbid something happen. Then, I would have to live with that for the rest of my life. I'm afraid of things like that. So, that's my problem right now. I just don't know what to do.

Similarly, Durene described how her neighbors and family members have begged her to remove her son from her home. They worry about her health and safety. She is seventy-three and has Parkinson's disease. They worry about the stress she experiences living with her son who has mental illness and has already threatened her on several occasions with physical violence. She, however, has come to a resolution and has decided that her son's safety should take precedence over her own.

> I know he needs to be out of here. He's thirty-six years old this year. I'll be seventy-three. He needs—*we need*—to be separated. I don't need all these on me at this age in my life. But I don't want to see him, you know, become homeless because he won't survive. He won't survive. He will not survive. So that's what I feel. You know, fears that there's harm would come for him. I mean that could come to me, too, but I just fear harm coming to him.

Aware of the danger this choice could bring to her, she reached out to a social service agency to arrange unannounced police surveillance. Durene has resolved her ambivalence by finding a way for her to feel safe and not endanger her son.

Wanting Her Out—This Is Dangerous for Me

Many of the mothers reported that their health was suffering as a result of the stress of caring for their adult child. Many were depressed. Jillian reported having irritable bowel syndrome. Faith was worried about her high blood pressure, Tracy was having anxiety attacks. While each knew that these health issues were related to their choices, none of them were willing, at least when I spoke to them, to make a change. As Jillian summed it up, "I can't walk away. I am like a mule on a harness, keeping my daughter afloat."

A recent widower, Natalie, was using whatever financial resources she had to ensure that her son, Chip, got the medical attention he needed to address the multiple serious health complications he was experiencing as a result of his alcoholism. Her resolve to do all she could to help her son was costing her a lot of time and money. It was also creating distance with and resentment from her other three sons. They didn't like how their mother was using up all her resources to help Chip, who they did not feel deserved saving. They started to cut back on attending family holiday dinners and refused to even visit their brother in the hospital during his two-year ordeal. On top of managing her sons' resentment and Chip's care, she was feeling the rebuke she imagined her husband would have made: She had allowed the family to come apart. And, like Durene, she had made a decision: she would not give up on her son.

If Not Me, Who?

Many of the women who sought help from the courts or police reported that there were no resources that would help them in the manner they wanted with their adult children. Instead, the options were about punishing them, as if they were criminals. Lucy went to family court to see if the judge would help her by ordering her son to start paying her child support for his daughter, her granddaughter, whom she had been raising for over thirteen years. Now that Carlos was succeeding financially in a new store he had opened, she was enraged and disappointed that he did not offer to help support his daughter. Lucy filed a complaint and waited to see the judge. In the courtroom, she saw a neighbor who was a clerk and had read her complaint. He told her that if she continued with her case, Carlos could be sent to jail for six months. Apparently, he had lied on his child support application for his other children. He had said that he was already paying Lucy support, which had therefore lowered the amount he had to pay to his former wife. This lie was an act of perjury, she learned. Lucy thanked the clerk and left the court. She did not want to be the one responsible for sending her son to jail, which would have led to Carlos's small business having to close. This was not the remedy she was after. She wanted her son to stop being selfish and help her out.

When Mirabel's daughter, Lena, cut up all the family photos with a pair of scissors and threatened her mother with a hammer, she called the police. When they arrived, Lena quieted down. When the officers asked Mirabel if she wanted her daughter arrested, Mirabel said "No, that's my daughter." The police informed Mirabel that arresting her was all that they could do. But this is not what Mirabel wanted. She wanted someone to help her understand her daughter's anger and behavior.

Many women who seek help from the courts or police find the responses punitive rather than supportive. They don't know where to turn.

From a mother's point of view, when a child is in a psychotic rage and becoming violent, calling 911 is often the only option. But later on, many adult children resent the mother's actions that brought in outside help in the form of the police. Calling the police can also escalate the situation, creating even more danger. This was particularly true for those mothers who were African American. Durene's son, Caleb, is Black and six foot three. When she had to call for help because he was threatening her with a knife, she realized as soon as she opened the door that she would have to take control of the situation. She could see that the officers were frightened of Caleb and were reaching for their mace and billy clubs. Durene was able to instruct the officers and bring calm to the situation, and no one was hurt.

Tragically, this is not always the outcome. In 2020, an unarmed, forty-one-year-old Black man with mental health problems was one of many who were killed by police who pinned his naked body to the ground and pressed his chest into the pavement. A video of the event went viral, sparking protests across the nation and renewed calls for officers to use less aggressive tactics during encounters with people who are mentally ill.[16] Too many other examples are still occurring.

THE TUG BETWEEN FREEDOM AND RESPONSIBILITY

Alana, age sixty-seven, had been battling with her daughter for over fifty years. She desperately wanted to have a few years before she died where she could live without the constant fighting. She, like other older parents, felt the pressure of the limited time left. Her plan was to move away from her daughter, to a small town in the West where she could afford living in a senior community. Alana's plan sounded well thought out. She would even let her daughter, Deborah, stay in their rent-controlled apartment. But while going over the details and enthusing over all the "positives" she would derive from this new start, Alana then told me, with the same forcefulness, that she could never move and leave her daughter. "She will not survive without me."

A closer look at Alana's situation illustrates how a woman's inability to openly explore her mixed feelings or work through her ambivalences can lead to paralysis. Alana has not been able to let herself weigh her two divergent plans. She presented her opposite goals, to move and to stay, without the acknowledgment of the impossibility of following both. In order for Alana to come to terms with her opposing wishes, she would have to tolerate the discomfort of having disparate wishes. If she could let herself weigh both proposals, she could do the psychological work of problem solving, which is a rational process of identifying the pros and cons of a particular action.

Ideally, Alana would carefully question her emotional assumption that her daughter "won't survive without me." She would gather and weigh the evidence to determine whether her negative assumptions about her daughter's capacities were accurate. If she determined that her daughter really could not live on her own, then Alana could look at other options for Deborah's living situation, beyond the two of them continuing to share an apartment. She might also want to assess what it would mean to her if her daughter did actually become homeless. Could Alana live with this outcome? In this way, she could use her ambivalence to engage in a more realistic evaluation of her daughter's situation and her actual goals.

Tracy, on the other hand, is more able to express and explore her ambivalent feelings. As a young woman with three children, Tracy had felt pleasure and a sense of competency. But she also looked forward to the time when her kids would be launched, and she could travel and write. Tracy recounted having had an earlier experience in which she successfully found a way to live with her ambivalent wishes. She told me that she remembers when her husband asked her to marry him, wanting to marry but also wondering if she could accept a domestic life. But she pushed through these doubts—"at the time, it was what everyone was doing"—and enjoyed her life as wife and mother.

She managed her ambivalence about accepting a domestic life by sharing her love of adventure with her children, each of whom then traveled and studied overseas. She felt she was a good mother, but she was always looking forward to when the time would come for them to "leave the nest." When she and I met, that time had been temporarily postponed. As she was getting ready to put her house on the market and use the money to travel, her middle daughter, Jeannie, was hospitalized for what became a series of ten subsequent hospitalizations within a period of fifteen months. After each hospitalization, Jeannie refused to take the prescribed psychiatric medications and never returned to see a therapist. The times in between each hospitalization became shorter and shorter due to her noncompliance with the follow-up plan and the resulting reoccurrences of her psychotic behaviors.

Tracy put off selling the house, but she still was torn. "This whole year I've been exhausted from it all. There's a little knot inside of me, saying, 'you're being selfish if you want to keep moving on with your own life. You must stay and be there for Jeannie.' But then I say to myself, 'that's exactly what you shouldn't do.' I tell myself, 'How are you going to be good for anyone else if you don't take care of yourself?'" She also wants to be a role model for her other children that women should be able to self-actualize.

Tracy is willing to verbalize and experience both sides of her internal battle. She is able to use words to describe her contradictory feelings. She articulates the conflict she experiences. "But it's a very, very difficult line to walk. I try very hard to take my emotions out of it, but, you know, you're a mom. How do you do that? I've been told by the medical staff that I cannot allow her back in the house with me because it is too dangerous; but to go to bed at night and say, 'my daughter is on the streets, sleeping in a park, okay; and god knows what could happen to her,' it takes a lot tougher person than I am to do that."

On the one hand, she knows the downside of allowing her daughter to move back in with her: she could get hurt. (Jeannie set fire in the house the last time she lived there.) But she also knows how hard it is for her to know that her daughter is sleeping on the streets. She also expresses what is named "structural ambivalence." She is aware that there are not adequate resources to protect her daughter, beyond her own home. Her mixed feelings are partially based on structural realities—the absence of societal supports for persons with serious mental illness are creating conflict for her. "So, that's why now I'm nervous, what's going to be the solution? Because there's no halfway housing places. And reading about our mental health system—and I'm sure you know that—they closed all the horrible institutions. And I'm in agreement with that, but nobody put anything else in place."

Mothers and fathers with adult children with serious mental illness, substance use disorder, and chronic unemployment experience internal conflicts that are created by far broader structural forces. Tracy is having to deal with a problem that can only be solved by an institutional change regarding the care of those with mental illness.

> Mothers with adult children with serious mental illness, substance use disorder, and chronic unemployment experience internal conflicts that are created by far broader structural forces.

She is trying to sort through her multileveled feelings of ambivalence. It's not just about her mixed feelings toward her daughter for being ill. It is not just about whether to let her daughter back into her home or feelings of being let down by society's treatment of the mentally ill. She's also struggling with whether she has the right to follow her own dreams when her daughter is so ill. But Tracy's capacity to be able to give words to both sides of her conflict will allow her to eventually come to terms with a choice. She will decide how much discomfort she can live with from each of the alternatives. She is also doing research to inform her decision. She has learned that people with Jeannie's diagnoses may never recover. This information reminds her that her staying or going will not alter the outcome of her daughter's disorder. She was also aware of how vulnerable she is to other people's judgments about whether she is a "good mother" in their eyes. When we spoke, she had not yet made a decision about whether she would go or stay. She did not yet feel "strong enough" to leave and have to live with her family's and society's scorn, as well as her own guilt.

There are parents who become estranged from their adult children and adult children who become estranged from their parents. I did meet two women who did eventually cut off all ties with their adult child, and two moms whose sons cut off from them. Their experiences are interspersed in the book. But most of the women who were part of my study, despite feeling conflicted about their mothering role in later life, remained committed to what they saw was their new maternal role, regardless of the conflicts they were experiencing. Their stories illustrate how they each tried to cope with a situation that felt like it had no exit. Difficult mothering is a situation with no easy answers.

Chapter Six

Mental Illness in the Family

On pins and needles.[1] Walking on eggshells.[2] Peace at any price.[3] Those are the evocative terms that have been used to describe what it feels like to be a family member caring for a loved one with serious mental illness (SMI). It's a large demographic. Eight and half million older adults in the United States are taking care of family members with mental illness, most of whom are adult children financially dependent on their parents, many of whom also live with them.[4] Surprisingly, the women who spoke with me whose adult children had an SMI did not refer to themselves as caregivers, even though they described their lives as framed by their children's illness and the obligation to care for them. Perhaps because they were talking to me about the stressors on them as mothers, adding the term "caregiver" was superfluous.

Family caregivers provide unpaid care for frail or dependent adults. (In this case, "family" also includes friends and other nonfamily supports.) Caregiving includes the emotional work of helping a dependent family member or friend manage their feelings and maintain relationships, as well as the more concrete tasks of helping with specific responsibilities such as negotiating with doctors, organizing medications, and preparing meals. Without the unpaid work of family caregivers for people with an SMI, the number of people requiring publicly supported long-term care in psychiatric hospitals would increase astronomically, as would homelessness.

I agree with the feminist authors who remind us that the gender-neutral term "family caregiving" disguises what remains primarily a female role.⁵ Certainly, the term reflects the societal expectation and ideology that family caregiving belongs in the home, which is generally seen as the women's domain and caring a natural female characteristic. There can be no doubt that women's identities, and later life financial security, are shaped by family caregiving demands, so the inclusive term "family caregiving" does seem to misrepresent the realities of the burdens that unfailingly fall to women.

Adult children with SMI experience challenges that interfere with their ability to maintain employment or live independently—both of which can restrict their independence and their ability to separate from their families. While SMI has a tremendous impact on the person with the illness, it also changes the fabric of the family forever, affecting not only mothers, but fathers and siblings too. Caring for a family member with SMI has been equated to experiencing an earthquake whose long-lasting aftershocks affect the emotional, financial, and physical health⁶ of the entire family.

TRACY

Tracy's life, for example, was upended when her youngest daughter, Jeannie, was in her freshman year in college and had her first psychiatric hospitalization. Jeannie had been away with friends on spring recess when she became anxious and paranoid. She started accusing her girlfriends of stealing things from her and thought they were talking behind her back. Her friends, unable to reassure her, telephoned Tracy. She told them to put her on a plane back home, and Tracy would meet her at the airport. After a few days in the hospital, Jeannie was diagnosed with post-traumatic stress disorder. The doctors believed that because she had been near the Twin Towers on 9/11, she had been traumatized. This diagnosis led the family to believe that Jeannie would be able to bounce back and recover from post-traumatic stress disorder, which is a stress-induced disorder. But over time, and after many difficulties and additional hospitalizations over the next five years, the doctors changed her diagnosis to schizophrenia. When I met Tracy, Jeannie was thirty-four years old. Tracy was feeling the anguish of not knowing what her or Jeannie's future would be. Tracy's plans to travel and enjoy her "empty nest" had been put on hold. Yet, even with her own plans shelved, she didn't see a way to protect her daughter. She could not allow her back into her home because of her previous violent behavior: Jeannie had attacked Tracy and set a fire in her home when she had last been living with her. She felt helpless and constantly worried knowing that her daughter was living on the streets.

Just as women take on family caregiving in disproportionate numbers, so do mothers report higher levels of emotional pain than fathers when caring for an adult child with SMI. Jillian in her interview with me described herself as "always bleeding inside," but told me that she did not think that her husband was paying the same price. His insides were not turned upside down when responding to the weekly crises with their daughter, Celia. He could be calm and would sometimes even use humor to deflect the situation. Jillian could not. David Karp, a writer, sociologist, social psychologist, and professor of sociology at Boston College, reported gender differences in his study on how families cope with mental illness. Many women complained how their husbands "put things in compartments" and did not experience their child's situation in the same way as they did. Karp relates how one woman described the way her ill son dominated her thoughts. "I honestly don't think there is a minute of the day that I am not thinking about . . . my son. I wake up thinking about him. I go to bed thinking about him. If I wake up in the middle of the night . . . I think about him. . . . It's my existence. He's my child."

WHAT IS A SERIOUS MENTAL ILLNESS?

One out of five Americans—forty-six million people[7]—have a mental health problem. That large number is 20 percent of our population and includes people with any type of psychological issue or illness with mild to severe symptoms, including neurotic and psychotic conditions. In contrast, severe disorders (SMI) only affect one in twenty-five in the United States.[8] People who have an SMI experience symptoms that can cause substantial disruption in their everyday life, including the need for being hospitalized. Bipolar disorder, schizophrenia, schizoaffective disorder, and major depression with psychotic symptoms are the most prevalent of these severe disorders. The most common challenge for persons with SMI is psychosis, a state of mind characterized by loss of contact with reality. Persons with psychosis perceive things in a way that is strikingly different from those around them. They may experience delusions, hallucinations, disorganized thinking, and unusual behaviors, all considered "positive symptoms" because they become additions—new ways that the people present themselves in the world and with others.

• Delusions are false beliefs that are not subject to reason or contradictory evidence. You cannot argue someone out of their delusions, which may range from the bizarre ("That bird told me that I have to kill you") to the non-bizarre ("I am being robbed of my inheritance by my siblings").
• Hallucinations take the form of false perceptions (hearing, seeing, or feeling something that is not there), the most common of which are auditory, involving one or more talking voices.
• Disorganized thinking is symptomatic of schizophrenia. It is a chaotic thought process that shows itself in the person's speech, including unrelated or weakly linked topics strung together to form full or partial sentences.
• Unusual behaviors of a person who is in a psychotic episode can include dressing oddly, sexually inappropriate behavior, or unpredictable swearing or yelling.

While the explanations for the cause of these illnesses have changed over time, the current prevailing wisdom in American psychiatry is that these are diseases of the brain. That certainly was the understanding of the women I interviewed, each of whom believed that there was a biological basis for their family member's mental illness.

Describing her family's relationship with Jeannie as a Jekyll and Hyde situation, Tracy told me of an incident when she was with Jeannie and her other two daughters, just chatting together in the kitchen. Suddenly Jeannie turned on them. "We weren't agreeing with something she said. She responds by saying that she was going to kill her sister because her sister stole her boyfriend. All of this was delusional. None of this happened. And then she tells us that Grandma and Grandpa are talking to her, even though they are dead. And then, because I guess we still weren't agreeing with her, she starts to fling glasses across the room. That's when I called 911."

LACKING INSIGHT

The experience of caring for someone with SMI is different from caring for a person who has a physical illness, like cancer, for the simple reason that a person with the physical illness usually wants to engage in treatment to get better. A physical illness may have a course of treatment that leads to the alleviation of symptoms and their underlying causes. In contrast, as of now, there is no "cure" for schizophrenia or other SMIs. Medications may regulate a number of the symptoms, but control is not the same as a cure.

Another factor that separates the person with SMI from the person with a physical illness is that many with an SMI do not see themselves as ill. Consider that fewer than one-third of patients discharged from short-term psychiatric hospitalizations return for follow-up appointments,[9] and many do not stay on their medication. One reason given for the common rejection of follow-up appointments for talk therapy or to take the antipsychotic medication is that people with an SMI do not see themselves as ill or benefiting from medical care. This absence of awareness of a psychiatric illness, often called "lacking insight," has recently been compared to a neuro-psychological deficit called "anosognosia." *Anosognosia* is derived from words that roughly mean "disease of knowledge," which is also found in patients with brain injury who are also unable to perceive the realities of their conditions. It is very frustrating for a mother whose son or daughter does not see their illness in the same manner as the parent. This difference in perception creates tremendous tension and frustration for both parties.

ASSESSING THE FAMILY BURDEN

In order to help plan out interventions to support family caregivers, social scientists examine what particular aspects of caring for a family member with SMI are most stressful. Because family caregiving affects the caregiver's physical and psychological health, objective and subjective aspects of the caregiver role are studied separately. Objective criteria include the adult child's actual symptoms, as well as the related behavior within the family environment. For example, if the adult child hears hostile voices that command them to hurt other people, this would be an objective burden measured by the number of fights that erupt in the home. Or if the son or daughter keeps showing up at the parent's worksite, or calling them all during the day, these behaviors will directly impact the parents, leading to actions such as having to change jobs or work schedules.

A different term, subjective burden, focuses on the family's feelings about providing care and the emotions they experience about their adult child's SMI. Feelings of stigma, loss, fear, grief, and worry are all too real for the family caregiver, and they can create stress. Subjective burdens related to feeling stigma and worry are a big part of the negative impacts on a parent's health. While none of the mothers in my study reported positive feelings of purpose from caring for their adult child with mental illness, other researchers have documented that many people do find satisfaction in the role of caregiver for their mentally ill adult child.[10]

It has been found that those parents who report less family burden in caring for their adult children with SMI are those who had found a way for the adult child to contribute to the family. Older parents who had adult children with SMI who did errands in the house, took their older parents to the doctor's or to go shopping, experienced greater satisfaction and less burden. But the cyclical nature of SMI means that these simple things, also, cannot be taken for granted.

LOSS AND GRIEF

Parents who have an adult child with SMI deal with loss, grief, and chronic sorrow over the adult who will never be. Jillian's daughter would not go on to become a classical musician, and Iris' daughter would miss seeing her sons grow into young men. Instead, each of these families would be adapting to their child's SMIs that would last a lifetime and would involve cycles of stability and instability, periods of clear thinking, and then a return of the psychosis.

When a child is diagnosed with serious mental illness, they do not die—but they are changed. Not only is the person you are grieving still alive, but a parent's grief in response to their child's psychiatric illness is not recognized and shared with friends and neighbors.

There are no rituals to support the family as they mourn what could have been—for their adult child and for themselves. The feelings of loss that parents report is both similar to, and different from, traditional grief, which refers to the process of letting go of a loved one who has died. When a child is diagnosed with SMI, they do not die—but they are changed. Not only is the person you are grieving still alive, but a parent's grief in response to their child's psychiatric illness is not recognized and shared with friends and neighbors.

One author has suggested the term "disenfranchised grief" to describe "the grief that persons experience when they incur this loss that cannot be openly acknowledged, publicly mourned, or socially supported."[11] This type of loss has also been equated to families coping with Alzheimer's disease, traumatic brain injury, or a family member missing in action during war. It is an ambiguous loss.[12]

The "Wonderful Before" is how Leslie references their family's happy life before her son's mental illness. He was a star baseball player and an excellent student, and he had a lot of friends. Then one day she got a call from Leon saying he felt sick and was going to leave school early. Hearing something in his voice that worried her, Leslie left work to meet him at home. Leon wasn't spread out on the couch watching television, the usual place for a sixteen-year-old who was feeling under the weather. He was upstairs in his bedroom and on his desk was a large carving knife. She asked him what he was doing with the knife. When he said he was going to make himself a sandwich, she told him that we don't make sandwiches with that kind of knife. That's when he spoke about his plan to end his life. She and her husband sought care for him and he was admitted the next day for the first time to a psychiatric unit. That was when the "Terrible After" all began.

Leslie's life has been framed by Leon's twenty-one hospitalizations over the past twelve years. He was also in four residential care facilities, three substance use treatment programs, and four different group homes. Having dedicated her life to learning about the illness—and to being her son's advocate in each treatment facility—she makes sure that each care team knows his medication history, especially what has worked and what has not. Because his voices command him to commit violence when he is in psychosis, including violence directed toward his mother, the family, similar to Tracy's situation, can no longer allow Leon to live with them.

Leslie has come to accept that her son will never be able to pick up where he left off in the "Wonderful Before" time. Her most optimistic hope for him is that he is able to live in a supportive housing situation where he could also find meaningful employment or purpose via volunteer work. Leslie has turned her own grief about her son's incurable illness into a fierce commitment to being an advocate for changing the mental health system for others. She lives in Iowa and has developed with her husband an advocacy group that educates politicians about needed mental health policy reforms.

The most common age of onset for SMI is during the late teens to the early twenties, ironically, what we may consider to be a time of great promise for a young person and their family. Leon became ill at sixteen. Even though the women in my study, all over sixty, had been coping with their adult children's illness for more than forty years, the day they first became aware of their child's illness is forever marked in their memory. When telling me about their sons and daughters, each shared what their child's pre-illness passions and talents had been. Jillian's daughter, Celia, was a talented musician in college. Durene, in her seventies when we met, described to me with pleasure her memory of Caleb before he became ill. He had a beautiful voice and loved singing in the Harlem Boys' Choir. Tracy's daughter, Jeannie, was getting all As in her college courses in business when she suddenly had to be hospitalized. Each mother mourned her child's foreshortened future and her own anticipated pleasure in watching her child blossom. None of these mothers had ever considered that their son's or daughter's career would be as a person with mental illness.

Life events in the family that remind the parent of "what might have been" can suddenly reawaken a mother's feelings of loss regarding her child's potential. Mothers described different ways that their lives included actual loss. Several had to ratchet down their career ambitions when their child became ill. Others talked about missing the companionship they once had and the child they had once known. A final loss for some mothers with adult children with SMI is that, rather than being able to lean on their adult children for caregiving later in life, they worry about who will be able to take their place as their child's protector once they are gone.[13]

FEAR

The fear that a child with mental illness will harm himself or others, or be harmed themselves, can be a major source of distress. Women can be burdened by both managing their fears, as well as having to come up with a safety plan in the event that their adult child may strike out at them.[14] Although most persons with SMI are not violent, the violence that does occur is most frequently targeted at family members, and most often takes place at home.[15] Persons with SMI are also at greater risk of being victims of violence themselves.[16] Among adults with SMI, younger adults are more likely than those who are older to commit violence toward family members.[17] Other risk factors include drug and alcohol use, the number of psychiatric hospitalizations, and the patient's refusal to take medication and attend mental health treatment.[18] An adult child's financial dependence on the family has also been shown to be a risk factor, with a demand for money often identified as the impetus for violence and aggression.[19] Finally, some studies have shown that limit setting—such as insisting that a mentally ill family member take their medications—are strongly associated with family violence.[20]

Very little has been written about the fear that family caregivers experience and the actual risk that exists for family violence among patients with SMI. This is despite the fact that studies have found that one-third of mentally ill persons have threatened or committed a violent act within the past eighteen months, and that more than half of these violent acts were against relatives, particularly mothers who lived with the adult child.[21] Another study reported that 40 percent of people with psychiatric disabilities who lived at home had subjected families to threatening, intimidating, and violent behavior.[22] One reason given for the limited amount research given to family violence by persons with psychiatric problems is the reluctance, even among mental health researchers, to further stigmatize persons with mental illness.[23] Yet the dearth of reliable information means that caregivers often do not get the assistance they require, and public health policies that could help both persons with mental illness and their families are stalled.[24]

Being physically attacked by your son or daughter hurts on too many levels. Not only is there the actual fear that occurs if anyone were to throw things at you or try to choke you, but there is the additional shock, and feelings of shame, when the person trying to hurt you is your own child. Mothers wonder if this means that their daughter or son never loved them. They fear that their child's irrational behavior is a sign of the family's pathology. Such feelings of shame can get in the way of the mothers getting outside help and reporting the violence. Not to mention that parents are reluctant to report their adult child's violence to the police because they fear that criminal prosecution will hurt, rather than help, their child.

MOTHERS' WELL-BEING

A mother's devotion to overseeing her adult child's situation can affect her well-being in a number of ways. Some mothers abandon their own careers in order to monitor their adult children's mental health problems; others borrow money from relatives or banks in order to pay for needed treatments that are not covered by insurance. One mom told me "I'm part of the two hundred billion dollars of ancillary costs for mental illness due to lost productivity in the workforce."

Another objective measure of how the stress of caring for an adult child with mental illness affects the family is the impact on the parent's physical health. In a national report on family caregiving, twice as many mental health caregivers reported that their role had made their own health worse, compared to caregivers of physically ill family members. Emotional stress and not having enough time for oneself are factors too. Just one in three mental health caregivers describe their health as excellent or very good, while 27 percent say it is fair or poor.[25] Leslie lost a lot of sleep and had difficulty focusing. Greta had to take antidepression medication for years. Faith worried about her high-blood pressure being exasperated by continuing to live with her daughter and grandson. Jillian was "exhausted, worn out, from years and years of this. It's like when your cortisol levels are firing all the time. . . . You're always on edge." Iris decided to move: "I can't help her, and I don't really want to live in the same town watching her do the things she is doing." When Leslie realized she couldn't change the downward trajectory of her son's mental illness, she left her job and became an advocate to improve mental health legislation to help others like her son.

COMMON MENTAL DISORDERS—
SERIOUS MENTAL ILLNESS

Mothers are much more likely to be able to name what they think is "wrong" with their adult child if he or she has a substance abuse problem and/or serious mental health problem that has observable behavior (intoxication or being stoned) or obvious symptoms from psychotic thinking. Yet there is an even bigger group of young adults who suffer from the more common mental disorders that do not have obvious observable symptoms. These include anxiety, depression, alcohol use, and phobias. These psychological problems can also affect a person's motivation and ability to function well in the world, and most of these problems go untreated.[26] Common mental disorders can grow into larger more serious issues such as suicidal behaviors, social withdrawal, or unexplained physical symptoms, or may recede as the young adult moves into their thirties or forties. Several mothers described to me that their sons or daughters seemed depressed, based on their being uncommunicative, more introverted, and generally having a low mood. But the women's observations did not lead them to have a clear explanation for their adult children's difficulty in looking for work, lack of motivation to return to school, moodiness, or getting along better with them or maintaining friends. While some mothers hoped that their children would seek counseling, because their sons and daughters were adults, the decision was theirs to make.

THE STIGMA OF MENTAL ILLNESS

Mothers whose adult children display symptoms of SMI often report feeling embarrassed when this bizarre behavior becomes public. The women also talk of feeling ashamed of themselves for being embarrassed about their family member who is ill. It's a catch-22, but mothers do worry about how others will perceive their adult children and themselves.[27]

While most people no longer view mental illness as a sin or a moral failure, societal stigma toward mental illness continues. The notion of a stigma dates back to Old English and refers to a scar left by a hot iron—that is, a brand. That's not far off the mark of shame that people who care for someone with a mental illness feel. When discussing the stigma associated with mental illness, the scar is figurative and refers to the unfair beliefs that a group of people have about persons with mental illness. People with mental illness often report feeling unworthy and incapable. They speak of feeling that others only see their personhood as their illness or diagnosis. The threat of stigma, and the effort to avoid the label, are so great that more than half of the people with mental illness who would probably benefit from treatment never obtain or seek an initial interview with a professional. People of color are even less likely to use psychiatric services.[28]

Family members may also experience rejection and blame for a family member's illness. There is even a name for this common occurrence: associative stigma,[29] or guilt by association. Uneducated neighbors or friends may fear people with mental illness and assume that the family home is a threatening place. They may also blame the parents, assuming that they might be the cause of an adult child's illness. Leslie's father-in-law kept reminding her that it was her side of the family that had the genetic history of mental illness.

When parents experience this associative stigma, they can become withdrawn, depressed, and feel even more guilty for the causes and courses of their child's mental illness. Some families choose to cut off from relatives and neighbors rather than share the reality of their situation, even though maintaining a curtain of secrecy can lead to a dangerous condition of social isolation. Parents may be reluctant to invite friends and neighbors to their homes to minimize the possibility that their adult child will experience stigma. Yet by limiting their contact with others, they are also constricting their sources of available social support. One family who had been actively involved in their church reported being shunned by their former friends when their son was discharged from the psychiatric hospital. They responded by living a double life in which they hid their needs and emotional pain from others. When asked by neighbors and casual friends how everything was going, they'd respond with "Oh, fine. Everything's fine." Nothing was further from the truth.

Chapter Seven

Who Cares for the Mentally Ill?

"The most persistent critics of psychiatry have always been former mental hospital patients."[1] That's why psychiatric care is gradually being transformed by reforms ushered in not just by advocates, but by former psychiatric patients themselves. These people have dedicated years to changing laws, treatments, services, and public policies that serve people with mental illness. And now we are seeing a paradigm shift, one based on the belief that people with mental illness can recover and lead meaningful lives.

The new Recovery Model understands that to become symptom-free should not be how wellness is measured. Instead, this framework focuses on helping people with mental illness harness their individual strengths—with or without symptoms. A breakthrough in the field of mental health care, the Recovery Model is built on the belief that people with mental illness should not be confined by their diagnosis. They can contribute to society. Their lives can be rich and satisfying. Federal mental health policy is now based on the recovery framework: to identify and build individual strength, personal agency, and competence to encourage meaningful participation in the greater community.[2]

Pat Deegan is a PhD psychologist and a leading advocate in the recovery movement. A star athlete who was looking forward to college, her life came to a complete standstill when, at age seventeen, she was diagnosed with a serious mental illness (SMI). Doctors told her she had schizophrenia. At discharge, she was told to go home and avoid all stress. Furthermore, she was told that she would never recover, that she should accept herself as a "mental patient." Over time, with the hopeful encouragement of her grandmother, Pat had a revelation: "I am going to become a psychologist and change the field of mental illness." And she did,[3] creating the CommonGround Program, an approach to supporting the recovery of people diagnosed with mental illness.

The goals of the Recovery Model are to identify and build individual strength, personal agency, and competence to encourage meaningful participation in the greater community.

The Recovery Model was a response to the norm that existed fifty years ago when treatment for SMI was based on containment. Back then, men, women, and even children could be institutionalized or placed in long-term psychiatric hospitals without concern for their rights. Rarely given treatment plans, patients were confined to sanatoriums located in desolate areas, miles from their family and friends. Haunting photographs exist from this time, showing patients in restraints, chained to their beds in dirty clothing.

Advocates worked hard to change these asylum-like conditions. In the 1960s, after years of challenges in the courts, large psychiatric hospitals were closed, and thousands of persons were discharged in a process called deinstitutionalization.[4] The promise of deinstitutionalization was that patients would be returned to the community where they could access locally available services, including counseling, vocational training, and housing. Family and other personal networks would offer support *when needed*. But funding never materialized for these necessary community resources. As a result, most people with SMI were not provided with the services and support necessary to live independent lives. Without the creation of subsidized housing, for example, many former psychiatric patients became homeless.[5]

Deinstitutionalization included an unstated assumption that relatives of a person with an SMI were under an obligation to care for their family member. It didn't seem to matter if this was a responsibility carried out willingly or one that was thrust upon them. Because this was an unstated assumption, rather than a clear policy mandate, it led to the exclusion of family members in the decision-making process.

If patient and caregiver well-being was the priority, an agreement would have been made between the institution and those who would be affected, including family caregivers, patients, and professionals.[6] But there was no such agreement, and policy makers and health professionals took the support of family members for granted.

Interviews with family and friends who became these default caregivers show how they felt excluded by the treatment team. With no support or education for their new role, they were adrift, unsure of what to do and what their rights and responsibilities were.[7]

Today, many family members are in the position of caring for their loved ones without the support that would make such a situation manageable. This is undoubtedly true of many of the mothers whose stories are presented here. Perhaps policy makers and professionals assumed that mothers, who are the primary family caregivers, have "natural" abilities to provide care for their adult children. Stereotypes about women's roles and obligations to their children, despite their age, have blinded professionals to the need for a binding covenant with family caregivers. Like so many people let down by the system, these women are left to come up with their own coping mechanisms and to find their own ways of reframing the experience of caring for an adult child with SMI.

Each mother's story is different, depending on the severity of her child's illness, the quality of treatment the child received, and the stage of life that she herself was in when her child became ill. Not to mention her support system. Yet, despite significant differences in the gravity and course of their sons' and daughters' illnesses, there were commonalities. Each of the women's lives had to change course to some degree. Each of them had to discover ways to interact with their child, who was also an adult and had rights and wishes independent of their mothers. Each had to decide for herself what and how much she could do and how to balance these decisions with her child's safety, autonomy, and her own needs for self-care.

FROM BEWILDERMENT TO ACCEPTANCE: ADAPTING TO AN ADULT CHILD'S MENTAL ILLNESS

Many are familiar with Dr. Elizabeth Kubler-Ross's five-stage model of the ways in which people process their grief. People move, she said, from denial, to anger, to bargaining for more time, to depression, and then acceptance. These stages aren't linear or fixed; nevertheless, they have helped a great many people (and their caregivers) navigate the complex terrain of grief. Similarly, Dr. David Karp, a professor of sociology at Boston College, created a model to describe the stages that family members experience when a family member has an SMI.[8] These include:

- Bewilderment and confusion
- Getting a diagnosis
- Cycles of stability and instability
- Acceptance of permanence of the disease

Bewilderment and Confusion

In the first phase, parents try to make sense of witnessing the uncharacteristic and bizarre behavior in their adult child. Wendy and her husband, Ralph, were confused about their daughter Mindy's behavior. She was acting differently than she ever had. She started to make changes in her life that were surprising, including getting a divorce and leaving her high-paying prestigious job to become a yoga teacher. But Wendy and Ralph told themselves that they had always trusted Mindy and her judgment had always been sound, so beyond asking many questions about the new choices, they chose to live with their confusion. But this all changed on one visit when Wendy had a "light bulb moment" which confirmed for her that their daughter was in trouble. "We got in the car, and I rode in the front seat with her. She took a right turn out of the driveway. I just casually said, 'Oh we usually go the other way.' My saying that caused her to go into an 'episode,' only I didn't know at the time that it was an 'episode.' But there was this frozen look on her face. I tried to keep her calm by saying each wrong turn she took was still 'ok.' After many wrong turns, Mindy stopped the car, took a breath, and looked at me and said, 'Wow, that wasn't real back there! Sometimes it's hard for me to tell real from unreal.'" Wendy and Robert then knew for sure that their suspicions were correct. Something was amiss with their daughter's mental health.

Getting a Diagnosis

Most families learn that their son or daughter has schizophrenia or bipolar disease when their behavior necessitates them having to be hospitalized.

Cycles of Stability and Instability

Living with a family member with SMI is cyclical. The person can recover after a course of medication within the hospital and have a period of stability, until a stressful event again triggers the illness, and the person becomes actively psychotic again. For many, there is a brief hospitalization and the use of antipsychotic medications. The patient is discharged after a few days with a plan to continue the medications and seek talk therapy. Unfortunately, most patients with SMI do not continue taking their medication upon discharge.

Most people with SMI struggle with the illness throughout their lifetime—as do their families. At age seventy-five, Jillian has seen her daughter through almost fifty years of stability and instability. When she spoke with me, Jillian couldn't remember all the details of when, and if, Celia had seen which therapist, or what diagnosis her doctors had given or when. What she did tell me about was the objective ways she had to be involved to keep Celia safe. She had moved her daughter in and out of twenty-one different apartments over a twenty-year period.

Jade, at eighty-two, was tired and worn out. She, too, had only vague memories of the course of her daughter's illness. What she spoke most clearly about was an incident a few years ago when her daughter attacked her. That's when, with the help of the police and social worker, Jade obtained an order of protection forbidding her daughter from moving back in.

Acceptance

When patients and their families get a diagnosis of SMI, they are, in effect, being told what they already know—something is wrong. Learning the name for that *something* can be met with a mixture of relief, fear, and despair. Ultimately, this can lead to acceptance.

The last stage in a family's adaptation to their loved one's illness, acceptance recognizes that parents cannot control their family member's mental illness. The 4C mantra of Al-Anon—"I did not cause it; I cannot control it; I cannot cure it; all I can do is cope with it"—applies not only to a loved with a substance abuse problem, but also to living with a grown child with mental illness.

To be able to accept that you cannot control your adult child's illness is to radically change the parent/adult child relationship from one of moral obligation to care for a dependent, to one of separateness and respect for the other's control of their destiny.[9] A mother's acceptance of her lack of power and ultimate inability to manage is not easy. Women grow up believing that as mothers we have an enormous opportunity and responsibility to shape the next generation. Each person who comes to the acceptance stage does so at her or his own time and to a different degree.

Most of the mothers whose stories are shared here had at least an intellectual understanding that their efforts to control their child's illnesses were fruitless. Yet the heart does not always agree with the head. This realization did not end their felt connection. As Faith told me, "Am I just supposed to throw my daughter and grandson away?" Even Iris, who moved rather than witness her daughter's "destructive" behaviors, found a way to check in on her daughter. She used Facebook to see if her daughter was posting. If several days went by without a post from Fern, Iris would call the local shelter and food pantry to see if the workers there had seen Fern. The staff were glad to help. Knowing that others had put eyes on Fern, that she was okay, helped Iris manage being at a distance.

WENDY

Wendy's daughter did not fit the typical age of first onset of SMI, which is late teens or early twenties. Mindy, forty-five, was happily married and had a successful career as an executive-level scientific researcher. At sixty-five, Wendy was glad of her empty nest, which meant that she could travel and enjoy time alone with her husband. She had always assumed that once she had raised her children through their teens, they would go off and live their own lives. Family vacations and weekly phone calls were how they would stay in touch.

This all changed when Mindy told her parents that she was planning on selling her apartment, buying a camper, driving toward the North Pole, and starving to death when she ran out of food. This came months after she had announced that she was divorcing her husband and quitting her job. While Wendy and her husband had been dismayed by the divorce and job change, they had confidence in their daughter to make her own decisions. It was when she started talking about suicidal plans that their bewilderment changed to alarm. Wendy and her husband, Ralph, who had never had any knowledge about mental illness, realized that they better get educated very quickly. After googling "mental illness," they met with doctors in their community, spoke to lawyers, and started checking in on and visiting Mindy much more often.

Now more informed about mental illness and different routes to getting their daughter treatment, Mindy's parents were prepared when she told them she was thinking of shooting people from her rooftop. Putting their already researched plans into action, Ralph flew from Boise to Pittsburgh, where Mindy lived. In the cab from the airport, he prayed that she would let him into the building. She did, and she showed him the gun. Ralph knew that she could hurt other people, maybe even him. He got her to put the gun down and hand it to him. They went inside and had a cup of tea. He told her he needed to take care of some things and would be back soon. With the help of Mindy's friends, who lived nearby, Ralph took the gun to the police station, where it would be used, along with the suicide note that she had emailed to her brother, as evidence in the involuntary commitment process. The police returned with Ralph to Mindy's apartment, and she was taken (against her will) for emergency psychiatric care.

Because of the extensive insurance Mindy still had from her job, she was able to afford an excellent, long-term stay in the hospital. Wendy and Ralph were back and forth to the hospital over the entire year that she was hospitalized. While Wendy originally kept Mindy's situation private, with time she decided to go public and tell her brothers and sisters. Rather than being judgmental, they provided information, resources, and created a prayer team. Every day at 3 pm, they each would join Wendy in prayer.

Upon discharge, Mindy's doctors believed that based on their current hypothesis about her illness, she had experienced a single episode of psychosis and would most likely not have a recurrence, along with depression. Mindy emerged emotionally strong enough to return to her demanding job. She was fortunate that her employer took her back, yet she also lives with the fear that her illness might recur. She made up a list of behaviors that might indicate that her disease was resurfacing and asked her parents and siblings to remain alert. These included the following: *Am I acting as if the world revolves around me? Am I seeing things or hearing things that are not there? Do I notice random words and make meaning of them?* Wendy told her and me that this list would not be sufficient. What would matter was that they all stayed in touch and talked openly if they became worried.

Wendy hopes to write a book to help other parents learn about the mental health system and the many barriers they, and their adult children, will confront as they attempt to get the care that they need. Wendy said her life will never be the same. While she remembers believing when her kids were little that mothering would end when they left the house, she now knows that watching out for Mindy's possible relapse will be with her forever. This realization, however difficult, has helped Wendy. She no longer harbors false hopes and does what she can to help her daughter to live the best life possible.

COPING WITH NEGATIVE EMOTIONS

A number of the mothers I spoke with acknowledged having powerful negative feelings about their son or daughter—including hate. Sharon, who feared foreclosing on her house because of having to support her daughter, shared that she almost wished she had never had a second child. Wendy had a hard time facing her anger toward Mindy for having become ill and requiring so much assistance from her parents. When talking about her son, Eric, during his drugging days, Brenda said she had wished that he had been someone else's child—not hers. Revealing these taboo emotions were usually offered with a disclaimer—that what disturbed them was not the person, but the person's behavior or illness.

Tracy had reframed Jeannie's physical attacks on her. She told herself that it was the mental illness, not her daughter, who was hitting her in an angry rage. Tracy's attempt to see her daughter as someone who has a mental illness, but is not defined by it, allowed her to hold on to the positive parts of their relationship. She knows that when Jeannie is between episodes, she can feel close to her. Jeannie will call, they will go for walks together, or they will share a meal.

Not all mothers are able to separate the person from the illness,[10] particularly when they are attacked or told by their own child, "I hate you." Iris invited her daughter back into her home after she became very ill and could no longer live on her own. "I wanted to be there for her because she was my daughter and if she's sick, she needs help. You know, that's what you do or at least that's what I actually did." But after a year, when Fern screamed at Iris and said that she was a terrible mother and that she hated her, Iris's emotions took over. She became enraged and grabbed her daughter and slapped her. Fern, who was stronger than her mother, held onto her mother's wrists and looked her straight in the eye. "I could kill you," she said. In telling me about this episode, Iris wanted me to know that Fern had said "I *could* kill you," rather than "I *will* kill you." That Fern had been restrained in her choice of words was important to Iris. This was her way of protecting her tie to her daughter.

FAMILY INTERVENTIONS

Although not geared to the needs of parents, per se, family psychoeducational groups are effective in helping family members manage their adult child's illness. The groups are led by mental health professionals and include content about the specific mental illness, medication and treatment management, assistance in improving family communication, and ways to engage in structured problem solving and crisis management. For the intervention to be most effective, a family should begin the group soon after the patient's initial discharge from the hospital. Despite research that has shown the positive value of these groups for the patients and the family, there has not been sufficient government funding to make this treatment accessible in most communities.[11]

PEER SUPPORT GROUPS

Peer-led groups provide parents of adult children with SMIs with information about their adult children's illness, as well as much-needed support. The National Alliance of Mental Illness (NAMI) offers support groups in most cities. The organization was started in the 1960s by Joyce Burland, a mother who felt dismissed by her son's psychiatric treatment team. She realized that families had an unmet need to be educated and informed about mental illness. As most people with SMI live with or are supported by their families, "Family to Family," a nine-session group learning experience, provides a forum for parents to both be supported by others in a similar situation and learn about resources and strategies for communication with an adult child with SMI.

When Leslie's son was first diagnosed, she and her husband wanted to understand his condition. They looked for and devoured as many books on the subject of mental illness that they could find. Although they had heard of the peer-led organization NAMI, they did not get involved for more than seven years after Leon's first hospitalization.

> We waited too long. But getting there was transformative. We had re-sisted it, because we were both working full time jobs, and we were try-ing to keep our daughter's life normal. We didn't want to give up more time out of the house. And we thought this was all about his illness and how broken the system was, we didn't really recognize that we needed something. . . . But getting involved with NAMI for me was huge. It helped me process my grief over losing our son to this illness. It helped me to learn to let go of feeling like we had the sole responsibility for his ultimate outcome.

BARRIERS TO FAMILY INVOLVEMENT

The open sharing of information is essential to a good relationship between patients, their families, and health care professionals. Yet ob-stacles to cooperation between professionals and parents exist. Profes-sionals rely on a medical model that focuses on the patient/professional relationship, often ignoring the needs of family caregivers. Some may even resent family members for "intruding" on the treatment plan, mak-ing family caregivers feel as if they are being too aggressive or "pushy." Family members report that their knowledge—gained from being with the patient twenty-four/seven—is often ignored and devalued. Even worse, professionals who are influenced by outdated psychological models that blame families for a child's mental illness may trigger feelings of guilt in parents who themselves may have internalized these mother-blaming models.

Privacy rules, such as the Health Insurance Portability and Accountability Act (HIPAA), can be used as an excuse by professionals to avoid meeting and sharing information with family members. HIPAA was intended to protect the security of sensitive health information of patients. It was never meant to prevent health care providers from listening to the concerns of family members or to provide much-needed information about the patient's care. Family members need to push professionals to share information, without jeopardizing the privacy of the patient.

> The open sharing of information is essential to a good relationship between patients, their families, and health care professionals.

Some women are too easily dissuaded from getting information that will be vital for their future caregiving. Iris hadn't seen her daughter for several years when her grandson called to say that his mother had been hospitalized in North Carolina. Iris flew down and was shocked to see how her daughter's life had been totally transformed by her illness. She was no longer living with her children. They were with their dad. She was living in a large house without any furniture and had posted religious sayings all over her walls. When I asked what the doctors had told her at the hospital about Fern's condition, she reported that they couldn't give her any information because of privacy rules. If she wanted information, she would have to go to court and become her conservator.

There is no way to know how accurately Iris remembered what the doctors said. When she arrived at the hospital, Iris was under enormous stress and shock. She had not seen her daughter for three years. Overnight, she had to absorb that Fern had lost touch with reality. Her daughter could not care for herself or her own children. Iris must have been struggling with her grief and ambivalence about taking Fern back home with her (which she did). Iris needed staff to partner with her and educate her about her daughter's needs and situation. Instead, her situation was ignored by the physicians using HIPAA as the excuse.

Deinstitutionalization brought important changes to the way we care for those with mental illness. But the institutional approach to care has not yet been replaced with an adequate community-based system that integrates the needs of the persons with mental illness and their families. Persons with psychosis need safe, affordable, and appropriate housing; help with reintegrating into school or work; and health insurance to pay for medication and services. Without these services, family caregivers are left with an unfair burden. Because most persons who experience psychosis are often young and living with their family when the illness emerges, families assume the role of informal caregivers. They become involved in all aspects of treatment from initiating help-seeking, accessing services, attending appointments, managing medications, and continuing to monitor their child's well-being and/or illness. Family members report feeling frustrated that there are not sufficient opportunities for them to contribute meaningfully to their loved one's treatment plans. Misinterpretation of confidentiality laws and mental health practices continue to exclude families and their concerns.[12]

Most of the women who shared their stories with me had been coping with their son or daughter's illness for more than twenty years. Many were feeling alone and without support. Family caregivers' views of their own and their ill loved one's responsibilities do evolve over time as their understanding of the illness changes.[13] Although many clinical studies extol family support and involvement in treatment and recovery, too many barriers still exist.[14]

ADVOCACY

A transformative moment occurred for Leslie during a family-to-family class offered by NAMI. Pete Earley, the Washington, DC, journalist and mental advocate, was speaking about the many structural problems that interfere with the availability of quality services and treatment for mental illness. "I was sitting there in tears, and anger and went home and made the decision that I would have to give up our privacy to be able to work on changing things. . . . I started to move from hiding and crying, to speaking out." One of her first actions was to write an opinion piece in the *Des Moines Register* after a mass shooting to rail against the typical conflation of this public safety concern with the need for improvements in the mental health treatment system.

Leslie's phone blew up with responses. As a result, she and her husband got connected to the Treatment Advocacy Center and then to their State Senator. Together they drafted a new bill that he presented to the legislature. With time, she retired from her job as a physical therapist and became a full-time lobbyist and advocate for improved mental health procedures nationally and in Iowa. She was able to turn her personal grief into action. She has made many new friends and colleagues who have become her new extended family.

Chapter Eight

Substance Abuse in the Family

Corrine was in her seventies when we met. Her daughter, Alyssa, was in her early forties. Alyssa began drinking as a teenager, but Corrine was not aware of it until later, although problems with alcohol were not new to her. Corrine's father drank. So did her grandfather. Corrine also married a man (Alyssa's father) who was an alcoholic. Thus Alyssa had a family history of alcoholism and addiction from both sides of her family. The odds seem to have been stacked against her.

Although alcohol has biological roots, it's often a crisis that triggers a person to turn to a substance to soothe their discomfort and regain equilibrium. Alyssa was a teenager when she was attacked at a club. A young man slashed her face because he was insulted when she refused to dance with him. She was taken to the emergency room. She spent the next few years having plastic surgery on her scars. Despite this trauma, she recovered well enough to succeed in high school and college. She went on to become a lawyer. Corrine, who was also a lawyer, described her daughter as being much smarter than she was. But Alyssa had a doubly hard task. Not only was she competing with other high-powered lawyers, she also had a drinking problem that she could not control. As time went on, her ability to perform at work diminished. Fired more than once, she was caught in a revolving door of working, drinking, losing her job, getting treatment, and starting again.

The five years before Corinne and I met had been chaotic for both mother and daughter. Corrine herself had been ill and had to be hospitalized. Meanwhile, Alyssa was back and forth alternating between rehab programs and living with her mother. Their shared living arrangement did not go well. On one occasion, during an alcoholic rage, Alyssa grabbed her mother and punched her in the chest, causing her to fall backward down the stairs. Corrine was taken to the hospital with the help of a neighbor, and the police were called. Then, with the help of a social worker, Corrine got an order of exclusion forbidding Alyssa from entering her mother's home. Corrine's respite lasted less than a year. When Alyssa became ill and lost another job, her mother let her move back in.

THE BLAMING FRAMEWORK

Some might call Corrine's decision to take Alyssa back "enabling" or "co-dependent." But to do so would be to judge her, to assume that she is doing something wrong. It's part of a blaming framework that holds family or close friends accountable for the problems of their loved ones, in this case being blamed for not enforcing "tough love." Much of the professional and academic literature on substance abuse comes from within this blaming framework.

It has even been suggested that the nonalcoholic family member is satisfying their own neurotic need by living with someone who drinks or uses drugs excessively. In 1953, Thelma Whalen was one of the first researchers to blame wives for playing a role in their husband's alcoholism. Whalen wrote:

> The woman who marries an alcoholic . . . is usually viewed by the community as a helpless victim of circumstance. She sees herself and other people see her as someone who, through no fault of her own and in spite of consistent effort on her part, is defeated over and over again by her husband's irresponsible behavior. This is certainly not true. . . . Her personality was just as responsible for the making of this marriage as her husband's was; and in the sordid sequence of marital misery which follows, she is not an innocent bystander. She is an active participant in the creation of the problems which ensue.[1]

Much like the wife-blaming of spouses in Whalen's worldview, mothers of adolescents with drug problems report feeling blamed and unsupported when they try to get help for their children and themselves. Although there are excellent family interventions for parents and their substance-abusing teens,[2] many families do not have access to these evidence-based treatments. Debra Jackson and Judie Mannix interviewed mothers of teens whose children had developed serious problems with cannabis. They learned that the mothers were under both the strain from worrying about and trying to protect their children, as well as feeling blamed by others for their teens' drug use and associated violent behaviors. When the mothers sought outside help for their teens and themselves, instead of getting support, they felt an undercurrent of being blamed—as the mother.[3]

> New treatment options understand that family members cannot stop a person with the addiction from using or drinking. Their goal is to find more effective ways for family members to cope.

Jim Orford and his colleagues from the United Kingdom have challenged the family-blaming ideologies that are prevalent in the treatment of substance use disorders. They propose a new model that is based on helping family members of addicts learn to better cope with what is acknowledged to be a very stressful situation: living with someone who has a substance use disorder.[4] The Orford stress-strain-coping-support model assumes that there are many ways to respond to a loved one who has a drinking or drug use problem. Rather than blame family members, this approach helps them cope with their stressful situation.[5] The treatment is not aimed at helping the family stop the person with the addiction from using or drinking. Instead, the goal is to find more effective ways for family members to manage. Rather than blame mothers like Corrine, or the many other mothers, wives, and sisters who are trying to help their family members, researchers in the United Kingdom have recommended that government policy and services shift to directly include the needs of family caregivers.[6]

Brenda and her husband, Anthony, would have benefited enormously by discussing the strain they were under as family caregivers, but they never met with the staff at their son's methadone clinic. The parents had been under the impression that methadone would be a temporary solution to help Eric wean off heroin. Each morning they drove their twenty-six-year-old son for treatment. They did this for two years, taking three hours out of their workday to drive Eric to the nearest methadone clinic. Each morning they got up early to get him there at 6:30 am. Their lives (and marriage) were completely turned upside down by the schedule. Brenda later learned that Eric had chosen the morning appointment so that he could be stoned all day. After two years, exhausted and broke, having paid for the methadone clinic out of their own pocket, and seeing no positive changes, they decided that another plan had to be found, whether or not their son would cooperate. He agreed to stop the methadone. As a family they searched online for how to help him detox. They spent a grueling month, on their own, supporting him while he accomplished this.

GRIEF AND STIGMA

The needs and experiences of mothers of adult children with substance use disorders are not a focus of most clinical and public discussions of addiction. Yet addiction impacts more than just the life of the addict. If adult children have a drinking or drug problem, their parents, their siblings, and their own children will be affected. Very few programs for substance abusers include services for the family member whose life is also being impacted; instead they only focus on the person with the drug or alcohol problem. Over one hundred million family members worldwide are estimated to be affected by their loved one's alcohol or drug problems.[7]

Enormous stress is felt by all those living with someone who has a drinking or drug problem, especially a parent. Of course, there is the actual worry for the safety and health of the addict. There may also be the need to respond to the addicted person's aggressive, dishonest, or threatening behavior in the home. And then there is the heartache that a parent feels when witnessing their adult child's life deteriorating. In my conversations with mothers whose son or daughter was drinking, gambling, or taking drugs, I learned about their years of worrying, trying to find them help, of disengaging and reengaging, and, for some, eventually stepping in to support their grandchildren.

In addition to the worry, parents with children who have a substance use disorder experience stigma, which some believe is greater than that experienced by parents whose child is struggling with mental illness or other issues. There is more public stigma or negative attitude toward a condition if it is felt that the sufferer is somehow personally responsible for their situation. Addiction is often assumed by the public to be the result of an addict's "choice." While most people view individuals with mental illness as having little control over the onset or course of their disease, this is not the case for those who misuse alcohol or drugs. By contrast, those with substance use disorders are generally viewed as being personally responsible for the onset of the problem through their own choices, as well as being ultimately accountable for and able to choose to end their addiction. Similar to the associative stigma of mental illness that parents experience if their adult child has a psychiatric problem, parents of drug-using adult children also experience, perhaps even greater, stigma.

> Most people view individuals with mental illness as having little control over the onset or course of their disease. This is not the case for those who misuse alcohol or drugs.

Surveys done in the United States and in Europe show that there is a lot of anger and blame aimed at drug users, especially those who use heroin. One study in Scotland found that 45 percent of the respondents agreed with the statement "most people who end up addicted to heroin have only themselves to blame."[8] Heroin users have been found to experience more discrimination than those who use other substances. This might be explained by the fact that there is wider public knowledge of the physical signs of heroin use (track marks, droopy eyes, drowsiness), or because of the needles and other paraphernalia that are required for heroin injections.[9]

DIRECT HARM

Parents living with an adolescent or adult child who is abusing drugs and is still dependent on them for housing and/or other income support are at risk of becoming the victim of theft and even violence. The parents may have resources, and the adult child is likely unemployed and short of cash but in need of money to fund the substance use problem.

In addition, alcohol or drugs can inhibit the child's judgment and their ability to maintain self-control, making them volatile and difficult to live with. There is very little data on the frequency of violence committed by adult children with substance use disorders toward their parents, but research on elder abuse shows that parents who house an adult child with a substance use disorder and/or mental illness are at high risk for abuse and neglect.[10]

Parents living with an adult child who is abusing drugs and is still dependent on them for housing and/or other income support are at risk of becoming the victim of theft and even violence.

There is more research on the experience of parents with substance-using teens than on parents with substance-using adult children. Researchers who study child-to-parent violence with adolescents found that often the child who verbally, physically, and emotionally attacks their parents (primarily single mothers) often also has a drug problem. Mothers who experience violence or theft at the hands of their child are often shocked and confused. If a teen attacks their mother, she has to protect both herself and her young children. One mother who was interviewed for a study on child-to-parent violence reported that instead of seeking help, she withdrew because of fear of judgment. "It's just that judgment that we get for him and for me, we both get judged in a certain way by people that don't really have any right to judge us. So yeah, I feel embarrassed."[11] The feeling of shame may keep a mother from seeking outside help. In addition, many parents have reported that when they did call the police, instead of feeling supported, they felt blamed by authorities who acted as if somehow the mothers should have been able to have prevent their teens from engaging in wrongdoing.[12]

UNDERSTANDING ADDICTION

Both alcohol and drug addiction are now understood to be biological diseases of the brain rather than voluntary behaviors caused by failures of self-control or poor morality. These medical and legal definitions of addiction are significant, yet they haven't done much to change the negative public opinion about people who use substances. Many still believe that addiction is a failure of personal and moral responsibility, the result of poor choices.

In 1995, the head of the National Institute on Alcohol Abuse and Alcoholism stated that the disease concept of alcoholism "has helped remove the stigma from a chronic disorder that is no more inherently immoral than diabetes or heart disease."[13] The disease concept definition led to research in the field of neuroscience which has since provided data to show that addiction is a chronic and relapsing brain disease. The National Institute on Drug Abuse and the American Medical Association have both since affirmed the biological basis of alcoholism and that addiction is a disease of the brain. This change in definition helped bring about the passage of the Paul Wellstone and Pete Domenici Mental Health Parity and Addiction Equity Act of 2008. The act states that health insurance coverage for substance use disorders and mental health disorders should be reimbursed by health plans and health insurance companies in the same way as any other medical/surgical health coverage claims.

Despite high profile support for the brain disease model of addiction and universal acceptance of this nonstigmatized definition in medical and legal circles, there does not seem to be increased public support or understanding for individuals suffering from addiction. The general public does not seem to agree with the idea of addiction as a medical condition that requires medical treatment. Public opinion does not yet support the idea that harsh punishment or imprisonment for offenses committed while under the influence may not be the best way to solve the problem. Even the few studies that have examined family members' views on addiction found that, without some sort of explanation of the brain disease model during the study, family members continued to believe that addiction should be described as a symptom of other problems (71 percent) or as a dependency (64 percent), rather than as a disease of the brain.[14]

Despite this lack of understanding of the root cause of their child's addiction, parents of children with substance use issues continue to find ways to maintain a positive image of their child in order to maintain their family commitment and attachment. Mothers of adult children with addiction will sometimes go to extreme lengths to protect their child from stigma and, as we shall see, from the legal consequences of violent or neglectful behavior.

PROTECTIVE STRATEGIES

Parents who live with their adult children with substance use problems are likely to be victims of theft as well as possible verbal or physical abuse. Even though these may be criminal behaviors, the likelihood of them being reported to the police is very low as most parents do not see criminal prosecution as the solution to their adult child's problem. At most, parents may take action to protect themselves by obtaining orders of protection or orders of exclusion to have their adult child removed from the home.

Yet despite anything their child may have done in the past, most parents still want to maintain a good relationship with their child and to continue to think well of them. One strategy is to imagine the adult child as two different people: the real child and the unreal or fake child. The fake child is the person who does bad things, like attacking their own mother while they are on drugs or alcohol.[15] Mothers who have been assaulted by their adult children when they are intoxicated or on drugs protect themselves from feeling devastated by rationalizing that it was the drugs or alcohol that explained the abuses. This is the same coping mechanism that mothers with children with serious mental illness use—making a distinction between the child and their illness. By distinguishing between the genuine person and the fake person on drugs, parents are able to diminish in their own mind the child's responsibility for this bad behavior. They can then believe that their child is really a good person who turns into somebody else through the noxious influence of drugs.

Natalie, a recent widower, balanced anger and estrangement from her two healthy adult sons with her commitment to support her third and youngest son. Chip was living at home and had multiple health issues related to his drinking, including chronic pancreatitis. Natalie's older children resented her willingness to support their brother, who they saw as a "loser" who wouldn't do anything to help himself.

In contrast to her sons' disdain of Chip because of his drinking, Natalie defined Chip's situation as understandable in the light of the many disappointments and challenges that he had to weather, due to his speech defect which started when he was six years old. She described feeling powerless as she waved goodbye to her son as he went off to elementary school each day. Just as she empathized with how difficult it must have been for him to have a speech impediment, she knew she could not protect him. Natalie, too, felt very vulnerable. "How do you think it was to send a child down to school each day—a kid who couldn't talk—and you couldn't be with him. He couldn't possibly keep up with the other kids. And to have to say to him, 'Have a great day, talk to your peers, try to talk to your teachers.'"

Witnessing her son's vulnerability had made Natalie feel vulnerable. Glad that she could do all she could to get Chip treatment now for his medical problems, she had no second thoughts about her decision to commit whatever resources were necessary to aid in her son's recovery. She may have been saddened by her other children's resentment; nevertheless, she had few doubts about her commitment to her adult son. He needed her protection and was going to get it.

> Mothers who have been abused by their adult children who are intoxicated or on drugs protect themselves from feeling devastated by rationalizing that it was the drugs or alcohol that explained the abuses.

PARENTS HIDING THEIR ADULT CHILDREN'S CRIMINAL BEHAVIOR

During the opioid crisis, some older women whose adult children were stealing their mothers' pain medication chose to hide this fact from authorities, rather than have their son or daughter arrested. Researchers who examined the Adult and Protective Services (APS) files of older and frail clients in Appalachia found mothers who had left themselves without their needed medications to protect their adult children who were stealing from them.[16] The APS workers found evidence of substance-abusing adult children stealing their mothers' pain medication. The adult children were using the drugs themselves and neglecting their mothers' needs for pain management—thereby committing neglect and exploitation by stealing the medications. Several of the mothers seemed to be aware of the problem but refused to confront their sons or daughters. The situation, documented by the researchers, illustrates the dilemma that some older frail parents face when dependent on an adult child who has a substance use disorder.

Fran was an older woman whose son, Tim, had a documented criminal history of drug abuse. Tim was also his mother's informal caregiver. APS had found that Fran's health was declining and suspected she was not receiving her pain medications. When APS returned a year later, Fran was receiving hospice services. As part of their routine, the nurses in hospice care count their patient's pain medication pills. They found enough evidence to substantiate exploitation by Fran's son (stolen pain medications). Fran, despite her frail state, realized that Tim would be in danger if anyone found out he was stealing her medications. She told the APS worker that it was her who had taken the missing medications—she said she had flushed her medication down the toilet. Fran did not want any authority to know what she knew. Even as she lay dying, her priority was to protect her son. As a result, no formal charges were made against him for exploitation and neglect.[17]

In another incident, Noreen (age sixty-four) needed help with the basic activities of daily living. Her son Nevin lived with her, helping out with household chores and administering her medications. But APS workers discovered that Nevin was not administering her pain medication when she needed it. Noreen was experiencing pain, and her needs were being neglected. Upon further investigation, APS discovered that although Noreen's doctors would do drug screenings to be sure that she, and not others, was taking her prescribed controlled substances, Noreen and Nevin would frequently switch doctors to hide the abuse.[18] Again, this illustrates an older mother's willingness to hide her dependent son or daughter's neglect and abuse, prioritizing the protection and support of her children over her own health and safety.

DUAL DIAGNOSIS

Many parents whose adult children have both a mental illness and a substance use problem are unable to distinguish whether their child's behaviors are a result of substance use disorder or mental illness. Yet in terms of getting help, knowing the difference can be very important. Some of the more traditional support programs for family members with addiction, such as Al-Anon, assume that there is little a family member can do to help someone with an addiction. The addiction is defined as a disease and the family member cannot cure the disease. Instead, the program can recommend that the addicted person may have to find their way until they "hit bottom." This program may work for those with only a substance use disorder but allowing a person who is suffering from a serious mental illness to "hit bottom" could be catastrophic.

Parents of adult children who have both a serious mental illness and a substance use disorder experience frustration at a system that does address the dual health needs of their children.[19] Health care delivery systems are segregated according to individual categories of disorders with unique admissions criteria, different types of treatment programs, and different philosophies of treatment. This siloed system is both confusing and a hindrance to integrated care.

Treatment facilities that are designed to break down a patient's denial or resistance to their addictive disorder may not admit a person who is using any kind of medication, to avoid their taking any illicit substance. This automatically excludes people who take prescribed medication for their symptoms of mental illness. By contrast, treatments for serious mental illness tend to be more supportive and less threatening. These programs often have criteria for admission that excludes persons with substance use problems. There are some, but not many, programs for people with both disorders.

Many parents whose adult children have both a mental illness and a substance use problem are unable to distinguish whether their child's behaviors are a result of substance use disorder or mental illness. Yet in terms of getting help, knowing the difference can be very important.

Opioid and cannabis use disorders are also more prevalent among people with serious mental illness than in the general population. So is tobacco use. Tobacco use is five times higher among persons with schizophrenia. This in part explains the earlier death rates of persons with serious mental illness. The global efforts to reduce tobacco use in the general population have not yet been mirrored among people with serious mental health problems.[20] This is a preventable cause of death, and programs to help persons with mental illness to stop smoking are being included in many hospitals and outpatient programs.[21]

FACING THE PROBLEM: BRENDA'S STORY

"He's a heroin addict and hasn't been able to hold down a job because of it for years. It's probably five years since he's had any job for more than a month or two, and two years without question that he hasn't been able to work at all." This was how Brenda began her conversation with me about her son Eric.

She described him as very bright but after a year in college, he lost interest and dropped out. He then began working in restaurants. At age twenty-three, he met a young woman and a year later they had a child together. Eric became the primary stay-at-home parent, as he was then unemployed. Within eighteen months, his partner, Sylvie, insisted that Eric and their son, Golden, move out. They went to live with Eric's parents, Brenda and Anthony. Although surprised that Eric and Sylvie were separating, Brenda welcomed her son and grandson into their home. Rather than questioning Eric, she enjoyed watching him be the attentive father that he had become.

All of that changed after six months of living with them.

> In April, I walked into the bathroom and discovered drug paraphernalia— needles and spoons. I had been feeling like something was wrong, I had been kind of snooping around looking, I was looking for papers, rolling papers. I've seen a couple of times on television . . . pictures of cans that people poke holes in and use to smoke meth. I knew what those were. And so that was the kind of thing I'd been looking for. I had not been looking for needles, so to see needles and the spoon and lighter and whatever else I saw, I was pretty shocked. I took a picture. All of these things were on my pretty pink counter. We always did joke that the boys' bathroom had a pink counter but that sweet image was destroyed for me, seeing the needles on it. Just the shock of it, just the rawness of it.

When I asked why she took the picture, she said that she wanted to be sure that Eric knew that she had taken the picture—that she was not going to pretend that it hadn't happened. She and her husband, Anthony, confronted Eric and told him that he could only continue living with them if he entered a treatment program. They consulted with their family doctor who said that Eric should be in a methadone program. "You know when a doctor tells you, 'Oh, this is what your son should go into. He should go into this program. This will help him get off heroin.' I didn't question it. I took the thing that I thought we had to do; and we made it work."

The family spent two years framed by Brenda and Anthony waking up at 4 am to take Eric to the program. Because he was so drugged out from the methadone, Brenda and Anthony took over the care of their grandson during the day. After two years, and thousands of dollars spent, they realized that the methadone was not working. Now he was addicted to the methadone and not functioning. They helped him to go "cold turkey" and detox over a month's time. But a few weeks later, they discovered puncture marks on his arms. He was using heroin once again. Eric's parents gave their son an eviction letter.

Within a month of being out of the house, Eric was arrested. Brenda and Anthony did not pay the bail. This was the first of many decisions not to "bail him out." Brenda and Anthony agreed that they could no longer help Eric. It was up to him. Once out of jail (a friend put up the bail), unable to live with his parents, Eric began living on the streets, in the back alleys of the small suburban downtown where he had grown up. Neighbors and friends in the town had all known Eric for his entire life. Now they could see him, homeless and selling drugs. There was no more hiding. By evicting him, Brenda had opened herself up to painful social embarrassment. She found she could tolerate it.

During the two years that Eric was living on the streets (and in and out of jail), Brenda kept an open door for him. She would invite him for dinner. She was glad that he never asked to stay the night, as it would have been hard for her to have to say no. She would set up times for him to see Golden, who had moved back in with his mother. Brenda and Anthony learned to monitor their possessions. If they discovered that he had stolen money on any of these visits, they would take their son to court. Brenda kept telling herself that this was the only way her son might change. "If change came," she said, "it would have to come from him." Brenda believed that her son was smart and would someday "wake up." When asked what advice she would give to other mothers, she said, "[T]ough love does not feel like love. Instead, it feels like hate. You only do it if you are completely exasperated."

I spoke to Brenda almost three years later. Eric had spent the next two and half years in and out of jail. During his last time in jail, the family

did not send him a penny. He learned to use the barter system among the other men. He would help others write letters and they would give him things he needed. He had to write with a pencil and a little pre-stamped envelope. We totally cut him off. And, oh my goodness, it was wonderful! Every time he (Eric) would be in jail, we would feel like "We can breathe, he is safe! And he is not using." That was how we felt. It would be a huge sense of relief.

About a year and a half ago, Eric met somebody who Brenda described as "a darling girl," but she, too, was involved in the same drug scene as he was. They both ended up in jail at about the same time. She got out last spring, and he got out in mid-summer. "Somehow the two of them kind of, must have, had a come to Jesus moment, they decided— well, Eric said—'you know, I'm too old for this. In a few years, I'll be forty. I'm not going back to jail again for these shenanigans,' and they sobered up. They got married in the summer and they have a new child, a new baby."

Brenda explained that while she had altered her behavior by not giving her son any financial support, the real change had come from Eric himself.

It was within him. It wasn't anything mandated thing by me. Because if he wanted to be using, he could still be using. That's my feeling. He is the one who changed his behavior. I think he was really in love with this young lady. I think he saw all that he had missed in life. She has a couple of very young children in addition to their new baby. The young children that she has are in her mother's custody in a different state, but they are working toward being reunited with them, as a family. Her little children might have had part of the awakening within him because he has gotten a chance to be a dad for them. He really missed it with Golden, who is now twelve. Golden makes his own decisions. He has his own friends. They're happy to see each other, but it's never going to be the same relationship as a kid and his father.

I was surprised to learn of such a happy ending. When I asked Brenda if she believed that her tough love had born this positive fruit she said, "I think I have the sense that it did. But I also knew that even if he hadn't changed—I now realize that setting the limits was the thing to do for us."

Chapter Nine

Chronic Sorrow

"Chronic sorrow" may sound like a very sad song, but it's actually a psychological concept that will resonate with parents who live with unacknowledged feelings of disappointment for "what might have been." All parents hope that their children will grow up to lead healthy lives, that they will be able to work, have a family of their own, experience independence, joy, and love. It can be hard for parents to admit that their adult son or daughter has not achieved their hoped-for scenario. Harder still is letting go of the dreams they harbored for their child.

Sometimes a single encounter will bring up an intense reaction. Paulette recalled,

> The other day, I was emotional because when I opened the door, and I saw him, he was shaven, clean cut. You know, when a man just comes out of the barber's chair, it makes them—even if they're not that good looking— it makes them look good looking. And I'm like, "Oh my God." After he left, I started to cry. This is the kid that I would like him to always be. This is the kid that I would appreciate having for my son. But at other times he is like the big bad wolf, ready to want to devour me.

Just the sight of her son with a shave and a haircut filled Paulette with regret.

For some mothers, even the pleasure of holding her first grandchild in the delivery room can be interrupted by memories of earlier disappointments. One mother described to me that instead of this moment being one of pure joy, as she had anticipated, she felt a sense of loss when she recalled giving birth to her firstborn, who later became mentally ill. Her excitement about the first grandchild was laden with memories of all the suffering her daughter had endured.

The term "chronic sorrow" was coined in 1962 to describe lingering feelings or thoughts of sadness for the lost hopes, dreams, and expectations parents of children with a disability may experience. Simon Olshansky, a social worker who worked with these parents, noticed that they experienced grief. He believed that these parental feelings might come and go throughout their child's life. Throughout the parents' life, too. Olshansky encourages professionals to acknowledge parents' grieving and not expect them to arrive at a premature or permanent "acceptance" of what has been lost.[1]

> The term "chronic sorrow" describes lingering feelings or thoughts of sadness for what might have been.

Living with chronic sorrow is different than mourning a loved one who has died. When a death occurs, society has rituals for mourning. Over time, we expect that the grieving person will accept their loss and move on. But mourning your child's lost potential—while your child is still alive—can be a much more complicated process. Pauline Boss used the term "ambiguous loss" to describe the loss that is incomplete and uncertain,[2] as it is when a child is unable to thrive or meet their full potential—for whatever reason. Boss wrote that ambiguous loss is the most stressful kind of loss because it defies resolutions and creates confusion. Ambiguous loss occurs when a family member is physically present but psychologically absent.

Parents/mothers of difficult adult children may end up experiencing two types of ambiguous loss. For many families, the difficult adult child may, at times, be physically present but unable to function due to their particular dysfunction (mental illness, addiction, etc.). At other times, the difficult adult child may not be physically present but still psychologically present. An adult child who has been removed from the home may be living on the street, in jail, or become estranged from their families, but they are still psychologically alive for the parents, despite their physical absence.

Rosanne lost contact with her son, Dylan, and remains bewildered regarding the reasons for the estrangement. She recounted the ways she tried to cope, which also sound like mourning: "I think my problem is that he has not wanted to have any contact with me for almost seven years. I reach out to him in various ways. I never hear back. And I think it's strange to me not to really understand what the reason is. I wake up with my heart pounding. I found an email I had written to Dylan expressing my concern and regret and sadness and apology. But he had changed his email address." She also decided to take a photo of her son and put it near her night table. Each evening, before going to sleep, she touches the image. Her description of this ritual sounded parallel to when religious Jews touch a mezuzah when they enter or leave a room. "If I touch the photo, I will have made . . . I will have prayed for him somehow."

> Living with chronic sorrow is different than mourning a loved one who has died. Mourning a child's lost potential is an open-ended and complicated process.

Family therapists and group leaders in the National Alliance on Mental Illness's family-to-family program report that parents benefit from having their grief acknowledged and accepted. These counselors and family educators help parents accept their suffering and understand how it may suddenly re-emerge, triggered by a wedding, the birth of a grandchild, or even just watching a movie. Ellen admitted that she found herself unsettled when a neighbor or the parent of one her daughter's friends from high school would casually ask about her daughter. "Even now, running into people, her peers are all getting married, and having all these successful careers, I never know how to answer, because when I answer vaguely, then people ask a lot of questions. But people don't really want to hear; and I don't need to be talking about it."

Every mother's parenting career revolves around not just protecting her child, but also fostering her child's independence. When these achievements are blocked by a child's illness or substance use disorder, a mother can lose confidence in herself and develop low self-esteem.[3] Mothers still grieve for that which is lost, perhaps even without knowing the depth of their own sorrow. Knowing that your experience of still feeling this sadness has a name and is "normal" may help these mothers. It is not pathological to feel the twinges of this past pain in the present. If you find yourself immobilized by grief and loss, however, you may find it helpful to talk to a trained clinician who is knowledgeable about these issues.

Chapter Ten

Violence in the Family

Margie called 311. She told the woman who answered the call that she felt frightened by her son's behavior. Her twenty-eight-year-old son had lost his job because of COVID and had moved back home into her small one-bedroom apartment. Margie described his threats, how he said that he was going to hurt himself and her. He had broken the bathroom door and a table, and she worried there was more was to come.

Not knowing who to call, she started with 311, New York City's referral line providing access to government services and information. Margie called the numbers the agent gave her and a few days later received a return call from a social worker in an elder abuse services agency. She was surprised that the referral was from an elder-abuse agency, as she was only sixty-three years old and still working. Margie didn't think of herself as an "elder," and she certainly didn't think of herself as an abuse victim. Yet, after several conversations with the social worker, Margie realized that she was, in fact, in danger. She was experiencing abuse and needed to heed the social worker's advice.

Knowing about elder mistreatment and community services can save lives.

Most people are aware of the risks of developing diabetes or high blood pressure in later life, but how many know about elder abuse? How many know that approximately one in ten adults over sixty experience elder abuse or that adult children are the most likely perpetrators? Half of the women in my study were recruited at agencies that offered services for older people who had experienced abuse, yet none referred to themselves as victims of elder abuse. In fact, no one used the word "abuse" when describing aggressive incidents between themselves and their adult child. It may be that "elder abuse" was not a term that resonated with their experiences. They, like Margie, may not have considered themselves to be an "elder," or perhaps "abuse" was not a term they could relate to when thinking of their own child's behavior.

Until relatively recently, all types of family violence, including elder abuse, intimate partner abuse, and child abuse, were considered rare and private matters to be managed by and within the individual family. But elder abuse, along with other forms of family violence, are now seen as public health issues. Just in time, too, as the life expectancy of women increases, so does the risk of such abuse. Legal, mental health, and support services are being instituted for victims and perpetrators alike. Of course, the availability of these services varies by geographical area, and many people are not aware of where or how to locate help. Still others lack knowledge as to the definition of abuse and do not connect the aggressive behavior of their adult child with this social problem that has sources for help within the community. Knowing about elder mistreatment and community services can save lives.

VIVIAN AND TONY

Vivian named her son's physical, verbal, and sexual attacks on her as "bothering." Describing how her son took money from her, followed her to work, stole her phone, or broke down the door to her bedroom, she said, "[H]e would always bother me."

> I had a two-bedroom apartment, and when you walked in, there was a dining room, and then the living room and his room was all the way in the back. Then you had to walk down a long, long hallway. To the left was the bathroom and my room was straight ahead. So, I knew when I heard him coming down the hall that he was either going to the bathroom or he was coming into my room to bother me. So just the sound of his footsteps used to put me into a nervous state, because I never knew what he was going to do or what he was going to say.

It was only after getting help and living safely on her own that she was able to admit to herself how frightened she had been for more than twenty years. "I lived in fear of him. I didn't want to admit it to myself then, but now, I know what it was. I was afraid. I was afraid to go to sleep. I was afraid to go to work. I was afraid to do anything. I was afraid to go in the bathroom because the door was like a half a door because he had broken it."

I asked Vivian how many times she had come close to calling the police.

"Never," she said.

"Never?" I asked in disbelief.

"Never," she replied. "I didn't want them to put him away. I kept thinking that I would try something else, and that would finally help."

Vivian's son, Tony, was a troubled youngster diagnosed as hyperactive at a very young age. On the first day of kindergarten, he opened the door on a moving school bus and another kid fell out. Luckily, the vehicle was moving very slowly, and no one was hurt. But this act was a harbinger of things to come. Tony was the smallest child in his class and often teased. He had few friends. People didn't like being around him "because of the way he was," Vivian explained. He was always getting into trouble.

> He became very, very needy. Very needy for friendship, for everything. Shopping with him, like going grocery shopping, was just hell on wheels. And I'm talking about even when he was really young, small enough to sit in those things in those carriages. He would take big cans of tomatoes and just throw them at me if I told him that he couldn't have something.

Tony went from being a hyperactive youngster to a troubled demanding teenager, to an aggressive and isolated young adult. In his twenties, he was using hard drugs and smoking pot. He couldn't hold a job. "I was constantly giving him money, or he was constantly taking money. I would hide it wherever I could, but he would always find it and take it, or take my ATM and threaten me if I didn't give him the code. He would become destructive when I told him I couldn't give him any more money. He would put holes in the wall and constantly broke down my bedroom door." He was shy, and girls didn't like him. "And anything that hurt him he took out on me. I was somehow the cause of all of it."

When Tony was in his thirties, Vivian's father died, and she moved into her mother's nearby apartment. The supposed reason for the move was to care for her aging mother, but living separately gave Vivian a welcome refuge from her son's attacks. She couldn't afford the upkeep of two apartments though; when her mother died, Vivian had to move back in with her son. The problems only got worse.

Although Vivian had not told anyone what had been happening with her son, she did finally reach out to a friend who, upon seeing Vivian's fragile state, insisted she get help. Not knowing who to contact, they opened the Baltimore phone book and looked under "psychiatry." The doctor became her lifeline, giving her antidepressants and listening empathically to her situation. On several occasions, the psychiatrist had her hospitalized for seventy-two hours' rest and observation.

Tony had a tremendous fear of abandonment. Each time Vivian left the apartment for her appointment with her psychiatrist, he was afraid that she would not return. "You're going to come home, right?" he asked. "You're not going to leave me here alone?"

Tony asked her this same question the last time that she ever saw him. On that visit, the doctor assessed Vivian's diminished physical and psychological state and told her that there was no way he could send her back home. He called an ambulance. After a brief period in the hospital, Vivian was transferred to an elder abuse shelter, where she will live the rest of her life.

Elder abuse shelters are similar to and different from shelters for domestic violence. Both provide a residence for women who can no longer live safely at home. The elder abuse shelter model is usually housed within another long-term care setting, like a nursing home, and also provides counseling and legal services. For Vivian, living in the shelter gave her the boundaries she had not been able to establish herself. "I now have a place where I am safe. I can put my head on the pillow and know that I am going to be able to sleep and not be awakened and not be abused. . . . I was just thankful, let's put it that way, very thankful for the roof over my head and the calmness. I have a space that I can call my own. I am no longer a prisoner."

Elder abuse shelters are similar to shelters for domestic violence. Both provide a residence for women who can no longer live safely at home.

She does, however, still worry about her son, who does not know where she is. She wishes that she had been stronger, less reactive, and could have helped him. Last year, she finally located him on Facebook. Even though he is homeless, they communicate weekly, mostly just a few words or the sharing of a joke. She told me that except for doing the interview with me, she does not dwell on the hard times she suffered. When she thinks of Tony, she remembers him as a young boy. She wanted me to see a photo she had of him and a Mother's Day card he had sent years ago. The photo was a black and white photo of Tony when he was seven years old. The last thing she told me as I was leaving was, "You might think I'm crazy, but my only worry now is for my son." This was her way of letting me know that being a mother had not been knocked out of her.

ELDER ABUSE: A BETRAYAL OF TRUST

The World Health Organization defines elder abuse as a single or repeated act, or lack of appropriate action, occurring within any relationship **where there is an expectation of trust**, which causes harm or distress to an older person.[1] Physical harm is only one type of abuse and not the most prevalent. Psychological or emotional abuse, material exploitation (taking the elder's money or property, for example), sexual abuse, and neglect are all elder abuse.

> Adult children who are financially dependent on their parents, living at home with them, and experiencing serious mental illness and/or substance abuse are the most likely group to commit elder abuse.

Health professionals first explained elder abuse as being caused by strained family or other caregivers who were overwhelmed at having to minister to the constant needs of a frail elderly person.[2] This has changed. The dynamics of elder abuse are now understood to be created by people with problems such as mental illness and/or substance abuse disorder and/or a criminal history. Most of the abusers are family members—either adult children or spouses. Adult children who are financially dependent on their parents, living at home with them, and experiencing serious mental illness and/or substance abuse are the most likely group to commit elder abuse.[3] Also, a large percentage of older people who are abused are not frail. In fact, they live independently and have opened up their homes to their adult children. Some of these older adults have allowed their adult children to live with them in order for them to help out with shopping, meal preparation, or medications.

It's difficult to arrive at an accurate measure of the extent of elder abuse. Most elder abuse does not get reported. A U.S. national study in 2010 found that 10 percent of people over sixty have experienced some form of elder abuse, but only a small fraction of these events were reported to the police.[4] When family members are the perpetrator, verbal mistreatment is the most frequently reported (9 percent), followed by financial mistreatment (3.5 percent), and lastly physical mistreatment (less than 1 percent).[5] About 2 percent of those who report abuse experience more than one type of abuse.[6] Sexual abuse has the lowest prevalence. Vivian, who experienced four different types of abuse (emotional/psychological, physical, financial, and sexual), is not a typical portrait. The majority of people who report abuse report only one type.

JADE

Jade, at age eighty-one, did call the police when her daughter tried to strangle her. "When she struck me, I called the cops. Maybe I should have let it go, but I fell to the ground. I said, 'Lacey!' I mean, I was shocked. She went like this [hands around neck] and then I fell down. . . . And then she started breaking up the house. She broke the kitchen window. Then she broke the bathroom door. I had locked myself in, she kicked the door in."

Jade became quiet and sad after she told me what had happened. When the police arrived, they took Lacey to the emergency room, where she was hospitalized for psychiatric illness. The police connected Jade with a social worker who helped her make the decisions about whether to allow her daughter to move back in. They discussed whether she felt safe in her home. Jade replied that she did not feel safe when her daughter was living with her, but she could not imagine how she could keep her daughter from moving back in. The social worker explained that she could have her locks changed. When Jade told the social worker that she would not know how to do this, the social worker told her that it could be arranged for her the next day. It was her choice. Jade had the locks changed and applied for a legal order of exclusion, which forbid her daughter from reentering their home. At the urging of the social worker, Jade joined a support group for victims of elder abuse where she was able to talk openly about what had happened. She told the group that she had been having second thoughts about having had evicted her daughter. The women, who had had similar experiences, confirmed what the social worker had told her: Letting her daughter move back in could result in her being killed.

PARENT ABUSE

Parent abuse was first identified by clinicians working with violent teenagers who were emotionally and physically attacking their parents.[7] Yet calling it "parent abuse" hides the reality that while fathers are also attacked, it is primarily the mother who is the recipient of most abuse perpetrated by teenagers.[8] This abuse has been described as harmful acts of a child or adolescent intended to gain power and control over a parent—which can be physical, psychological, or financial. Commonly reported abusive behaviors targeting mostly mothers include name-calling, threats to harm self or others, attempts at humiliation, damage to property, theft, and physical violence. The data shows that it is predominantly single mothers and families under stress due to poverty and divorce who are likely to be the victims of their teenaged children.[9]

Mothers of teenagers are understandably reluctant to call the police and start actions that could criminalize their child. In addition, many police officers do not take seriously child-to-parent violence and will blame the parent for their child's behavior.[10] Called "the dark side of mothering," child-to-parent violence is underreported. Women are reluctant to acknowledge their children's aggression toward them due to embarrassment, shame, and a desire to protect their child.[11] Grandmothers who take on kinship care because of their adult children's substance abuse, mental health problems, or incarceration are also possible targets of their grandchildren's violence. They, too, are reluctant to report the abuse because of a desire to protect their grandchildren and a feeling of shame about their own parenting failures that led to their daughter or son's abdication of their parenting role.[12]

PROFILES OF ABUSE:
ADULT CHILDREN AND THEIR MOTHERS

Mothers of adult children, like mothers of violent teenagers, are reluctant to report or evict their aggressive adult children to authorities. Mothers do not want their troubled adult children incarcerated. They want them to get help for their psychiatric or substance abuse problems. They also fear that acknowledging the abuse will lead them to be categorized as a "bad mother." Vivian told me that one reason she didn't report Tony's abusive behavior was her fear that people would view her as weak for having tolerated the abuse for all of those many years. Tracy shared how horrible it felt to call the police and admit that her own daughter was violent—and violent toward her. One aspect of child-to-parent abuse that is different than an older parent being attacked by their adult child is that when the abuser is an adolescent, and the victim is their parent, that parent is legally responsible for the underage child and has no viable option to leave.[13] Parents of abusive adult children have no legal responsibility to continue caring for or living with their adult children. Yet most older parents who are abused by their adult children do not walk away. Many do not even report the abuse, fearing that this will only create more problems for the adult child and for themselves.

> Mothers of adult children are reluctant to report or evict their aggressive adult children to authorities because they do not want their troubled adult children incarcerated. They also fear that acknowledging the abuse will lead them to be categorized as a "bad mother."

No checklist has been created to identify persons who are likely to commit violent acts against their own families or which family members are more liable to become victims. We can, however, learn about the likelihood of elder abuse by reviewing the risk factors identified in previously reported cases.[14]

Dependent Adult Children

Adult children who live with their mothers or fathers, and are financially dependent upon them, are the most likely perpetrators of abuse. Having few, if any, resources increases the likelihood that adult children can feel helpless, perhaps angry or depressed. Upset at their own "off-time" dependency on their parents,[15] they may lash out. The risk is greater if the adult child has a substance use disorder or a serious mental illness. An adult child with both a mental health illness and substance use disorder presents the greatest risk when living with their family.[16] Another risk for committing abuse against a family member is having few friends or meaningful connections.[17] In addition, elderly people who themselves are isolated are more likely to be the victim of abuse.

A history of family violence can also be a factor in elder abuse. An adult who as a child was a victim of family violence—or witness to it—has a greater likelihood of committing elder abuse.[18] Violence can be learned as a way to resolve problems. Isolation plays a part in this too. Adult children who were victimized when they were younger may develop problems in forming relationships, leading them to become socially insulated and increasingly dependent on their families.

Elder Abuse Victims

Most studies, but not all, have identified women as the most likely victims of elder abuse.[19] But solid knowledge about the gender of the person committing the abuse, or the gender of the victim, is not yet available because many studies do not identify either the relationship between the victim and the perpetrator or their gender. Spouses and/or other family members, as the perpetrators, are often grouped together in many surveys.

Stress in the parent or their inability to cope can both precede and be the result of elder abuse. Women who have a history of being a victim of interpersonal or intimate partner violence are at increased risk for elder abuse victimization.[20] Having been traumatized earlier in life can be accompanied with feelings of fear and helplessness, which can rise to the surface later in life. Earlier experiences of abuse, either by a partner or by one's parent in childhood, can contribute to feelings of hopelessness and passivity when tension re-arises within the family.[21]

Mental health problems in the mother or father, particularly depression, make them more vulnerable to elder abuse. Mental health problems can cause the victim to avoid seeking help and can lead to isolation and self-blame. In turn, this seclusion reduces the likelihood that abuse will be noticed by others.[22] Parents with dementia, Alzheimer's disease, and reduced memory are extremely vulnerable[23] to being abused, especially if they are dependent on their difficult adult child for care. The parent's vulnerability may trigger violent feelings and stress in the adult child, who is also serving as a caregiver.[24]

Social isolation or lack of friends and relatives on whom the parent can depend on are also risk factors for abuse and victimization.[25] In all studies, low social support is associated with a greater likelihood for mistreatment of older adults. Poor physical health and having limited ability to care for oneself are risk factors for elder abuse. Physical limitations can in turn limit a victim's ability to escape harm, protect themselves, and obtain outside help.[26]

REBECCA AND BRANDON

I met Rebecca in a community center. A tall and stately woman, she seemed strong, despite needing to use a walker and carry a canister of oxygen. Rebecca began the interview by telling me about Brandon's abusive behavior, as well as his mental health history and use of alcohol and drugs. He was back living with his mother at age thirty-two. "Brandon has bipolar. He can be very verbally aggressive, physical . . . breaking things. When I correct him, I become his enemy." She shocked me when she continued and said, "Well, I have to separate myself from Brandon because if I don't, I'm either going to have a massive heart attack from the stress or maybe one day he might get so angry and choke me and kill me."

Interrupting the interview to express my concern about the danger that she was describing, I encouraged her to contact the social worker who had referred her to me. I told her that I also would reach out to the social worker, who was knowledgeable about elder abuse. I asked Rebecca what actions she had taken to date to ensure her safety, and she told me that she had made contact with social workers and with the police. She was holding an envelope addressed to the director of aging services in White Plains, in which she described her dilemma and need for help.

Her situation was "impossible." That was the word she used. Rebecca believed that because her son had been living with her in the apartment, he had tenant's rights. Therefore, she had to give him sixty days' notice before he could be formally evicted. She saw this as an impossible solution because if she told Brandon that he was going to be evicted, he would become enraged and hurt her. Instead, she was trying to locate a halfway house for persons with mental illness that he would voluntarily move into.

It is not easy for any person to report a family member's aggressive behavior to outside authorities. But the risks of not getting help may be much greater.

I did learn from the referring social worker that there were ways that Rebecca could keep herself safe, including getting a legal order of exclusion to remove Brandon from her home, which the police would have enforced immediately, with no warning period. Apparently, Rebecca had been told about this alternative to guarantee her safety but was not interested in following up. The social worker believed that Rebecca had her own mental health challenges that were affecting her inability to take action.

When applying the profile for family violence presented previously, Rebecca and Brandon meet several of the criteria: Rebecca is a senior living with her son who is dependent on her for his housing, he has a mental health history, and he uses substances. She also has mental health and health problems. Although there are legal interventions that could be instituted to keep Rebecca safe, she chooses not to use them. Because she is not cognitively impaired, she cannot be forced to evict her son.

WHY MOTHERS DON'T ASK FOR HELP

Seeking help for abuse by one's adult children is complicated. Typically, there are several barriers that people face when reporting elder abuse or intimate partner violence:[27]

- Fear of negative consequences for the adult child
  - Most mothers do not want their adult children to be treated as criminals.
  - They do not want them to be put in jail.
  - They do not want their children to become homeless.
- Belief that the abuse was not the adult child's fault
  - Particularly when the adult child has a mental illness or substance abuse problem, mothers may view their adult child as a victim to their illness and rationalize the emotional or physical abuse as caused by the illness and not by the person of the child.
  - The mother may blame herself for how she failed as a parent and is not able to accept her failing and also hold her child responsible.
  - The mother, knowing that her child was raised in an abusive family environment, witnessing domestic violence and/or experiencing child abuse, may not feel able to hold the child responsible.
- Fear of negative consequences for themselves
  - Mothers may fear that if they report their adult child to authorities, the adult child will turn their anger even more strongly onto their mother.
  - Mothers who are dependent on their adult child or spouse for financial help, physical help around the house, and/or direct caregiving may fear for their own safety if left alone. They fear not being able to provide adequate self-care.
  - Women who are immigrants or undocumented may fear danger in reaching out for help. A perpetrator may incorrectly tell their victims of domestic violence that if they report the abuse at home, they will be deported.
- Stigma, shame, and embarrassment
  - As in other types of intimate partner violence, being a victim of abuse can affect a woman's self-esteem and agency. She may believe that she is weak and bad for having allowed the abuse to occur. These internalized negative views can get in the way of seeking help.
  - Seeking help makes the problem public. Women may fear what will happen once others know about how their adult child has been treating them. Will she be labeled as a bad mother? Will family and neighbors disapprove of her and reject her? The anticipation of possible rebuke can interfere with getting help.
  - Cultural stigma within certain groups emphasizes the needs of the family over the needs of the individual. Prioritizing a woman's

safety over her child or partner, can be taboo—a violation of gendered norms.[28]

- Hopelessness
  - To reach out for help requires having a belief that long-standing problems can be fixed or changed. A woman may have had personal relationships that were abusive and/or unsatisfying, and she cannot imagine that change is possible. One author referred to feeling stuck in this status quo of hurtful relationships as "emotional gridlock."[29] Getting help with a situation of elder abuse requires having to interact with formal systems such as law enforcement, the courts, and social service agencies, which may feel beyond a woman's capacity who lacks a sense of civic empowerment.
- Not being aware of services that can offer help to them and their adult child
  - Women's commitment to protecting their adult children often conflicts with or overrides their need to safeguard themselves. Most victims are not informed that most elder abuse professionals will also provide information for parents on services that can help not only the mother, but the adult child as well.

It's not easy for anybody to report a family member's aggressive behavior to outside authorities. But the risks of not getting help may be much greater. Elder mistreatment is associated with psychological and emotional costs to victims and perpetrators. As Jade was told when she came to her support group, "you could have been killed." Although elder abuse often occurs in the privacy of the home, preventing abuse against older adults is now recognized as a public health and human rights issue. The field of elder abuse prevention has broadened to the promotion of *elder justice*—a term first introduced in the Elder Justice Act, which became law in 2010. The term "elder justice" is defined by law to mean: "From a societal perspective, efforts to prevent, detect, treat, intervene in, and prosecute elder abuse, neglect, and exploitation, and protect elders with diminished capacity while maximizing their autonomy; and from an individual perspective, the recognition of an elder's rights, including the right to be free from abuse, neglect, and exploitation."[30] There are now adult protection services available in every community, funded by the federal government, and an updated National Center on Elder Abuse. See Appendix A for how to find services in your community.

Chapter Eleven

The Pain of the Past

Gabriella suffers watching her daughter, Maria, make the same mistakes she did. When her two girls were young, Gabriella was fearful that her daughters would inherit their father's drug and drinking habits. "I was always on top of them," she said. Her way of trying to ensure they did not turn out like their dad was to run a tight ship at home, perhaps too tight. She realizes that now. "You could say I verbally abused them. And in today's world, I would have been arrested. I physically abused them. That's the way I was brought up. I got hit with the barbed wire strap. I used the strap, too, sometimes with the buckle." Gabriella told me that her mother was "aggravated" by her father, which I assumed meant that he beat her. Her mother would then hit Gabriella. Violence was not only something Gabriella witnessed as a child; it was also how she was treated.

When her oldest daughter started dating, Gabriella increased her surveillance. When she discovered that Maria had lied to her about where she was going one night, Gabriella got so angry that she threw her daughter out of the house. "She went to her girlfriend's house to live and that was the biggest mistake I ever made. That's how she met her husband, who had already been in prison."

Two years later, when Maria's husband was back in jail, Gabriella let her daughter move back in—with a small baby in tow. Gabriella tried to help. She wanted to protect her daughter from making even more poor choices. Maria wasn't having any of it. "Ma, you made your mistakes, let me make mine."

As the years went on, Gabriella became increasingly aware of the real problems in her daughter's marriage. "I saw the verbal abuse. I saw the physical abuse. As a parent, that's the biggest frustration. I couldn't do anything about it. *She* had to do something about it." Gabriella felt powerless knowing that her own daughter could be killed by her husband while she could do nothing to prevent it. The violence she had lived with as a child was now part of her daughter's life.

Sixteen years later, Gabriella fears that Maria's eighteen-year-old son will hurt his mother. The grandson hangs out with a tough crowd and has guns in the house. "I just hope she wakes up before her son hurts her. That's my fear. Ernie hurting her. I think I would go off the deep end. They would have to arrest me. Grandson or no grandson, you are not going to hurt my child. Even though he, too, is part of me."

Listening to her story, I could feel Gabriella's sadness, her deep sense of hopelessness and helplessness. This woman had watched her mother being beaten by her father. She, in turn, had been beaten by her mother. Having missed out on the lessons of loving parenting, she used harsh discipline to protect her children. "I wish I could go back and do things differently. Maybe if I had allowed them more freedom. Maybe if I hadn't been so stringent with the rules. Maybe if I had looked the other way. Maybe things would have been different."

> *Maybe.* It's a powerful word for a mother and it carries within it a world of regret.

Living with regret is part of many mothers' later life experience. As Gabriella tries to help her daughter Maria, she also revisits the problems in her own marriage and the difficulties of her past.

TRAUMA AND FEAR

Many of us, when we became parents, set out with the best of intentions. Our aim is to avoid every mistake that our own mothers and fathers made—to avoid becoming them. Yet, despite our best intentions, we often find ourselves sounding and acting just like our parents, especially in stressful situations. This is especially true for those who have experienced abuse and dysfunction in childhood.

Childhood trauma can create lifelong feelings of intense fear, helplessness, low self-esteem, or even horror.

For a child, being abused, witnessing domestic violence, or being abandoned at a very young age can become traumatic events that are stored in the brain. These traumatic memories, often forgotten, can be retriggered by stressful events. The unprocessed childhood experience of helplessness and fear can get in the way of an adult's ability to cope and protect herself. For some, early trauma in childhood creates lifelong feelings of intense fear, low self-esteem, or horror.[1] Common psychological problems that accompany a history of trauma are frustration, anger, hopelessness, and loneliness.

Psychological research has demonstrated repeatedly that early experiences impact the adult, as well as the parent, that we become. This is especially true where trauma is involved. The Adverse Childhood Experiences (ACEs) study described the connection between exposure to childhood abuse or household dysfunction and long-term health in adulthood.[2] You can calculate your own ACE score by adding up how many of the following events you experienced as a child. Having experienced any of the events counts as "1." Evidence from the study shows that if you experienced four or more ACEs, then you are living with the aftereffects of a traumatic childhood.

- Sexual abuse
- Emotional abuse
- Mental illness of a household member
- Problematic drinking or alcoholism of a household member
- Illegal street or prescription drug use by a household member
- Divorce or separation of a parent
- Domestic violence toward a parent
- Incarceration of a household member

While I didn't calculate the ACE score for any of the women I interviewed, many of their stories revealed the long-term effects that an early life of trauma and abuse had on their lives as mothers.

When I asked Sylvia what it was it like for her to be a new mother—what kind of baby her daughter Jasmine had been—she casually informed me that she gave birth in a large public psychiatric hospital and had been there during most of her pregnancy. In the hospital, she was able to tell people for the first time about the abuse she had experienced as a young teen. She had been abused by many of the adults in her mother's house: her grandmother's boyfriend, her aunt's boyfriend, her cousin's boyfriend. Sylvia's pathway into motherhood was filtered by years of having been frightened, taken advantage of, and traumatized. Her vulnerability made her "naïve," as she described it. The man who she married and who was the father of her children was an alcoholic. He and his family neglected her needs as a new mother. They housed her and her new baby in their apartment, but in a small room with no windows. No one in the family came in to talk to her or help her learn how to feed or diaper her daughter. Her own mother never came to visit. Finally, an aunt got the family to move Sylvia and the young child into a cleaner and brighter part of the home. With time, she and her husband moved into their own place.

Fifty years later, Sylvia had chosen to speak with me about her experiences as a mother of a difficult adult child. She was trying to understand the frustration and disappointments she felt with her grown daughters. The daughters and their two children, Sylvia's grandchildren, were all back living with Sylvia and her husband in the tiny rundown apartment where she had raised them. She was ashamed that neither of her daughters had succeeded in work or marriage. Their poverty, and her poverty, embarrassed her. "They have nothing," she said.

Now, ill with stage IV cancer, this poverty and her daughters' seeming indifference to their mother's suffering had created a Dickensian situation. Sylvia described having gone to the emergency room by subway and having no money to take a taxi home. When she phoned Jasmine to see if she could lend her money for a cab, the girl had not even realized that her mother and father had been missing all night. When Jasmine agreed to meet them when they arrived home and pay for the ride, Sylvia was overwhelmed with gratitude. She had acclimated to complete disregard by her children and their inability to show her any concern or assistance.

Sylvia's early years, as the recipient of neglect and abuse, were interfering in her later life. She didn't seem able to expect respect and caring from her daughters now that she was ill. When she was still young and healthy, Sylvia maintained her relationships with her daughters without having to ask for anything from them. She gave them as much time and money as she could. Now that she was no longer working and was physically unable to help them out, she felt that she had lost her value. Sylvia did not have the tools to negotiate for herself in a productive way. Her early trauma had set her on a trajectory to put herself last and to become the inevitable victim. She and Jasmine were constantly fighting. But these conflicts only created and let off tension in a seemingly endless circle of emotion with no resolution.

TRAUMA-INFORMED CARE

People who have experienced early trauma find it difficult to ask for help. Fortunately, health and mental health providers have become much more aware of how earlier traumatic experiences can influence a person's ability to accept help or feel safe. Trauma-informed care is being instituted in emergency rooms and by community mental health centers. Dr. Nancy Needell, a trauma-informed psychiatrist working in the emergency room at a New York hospital, had to sedate and put in restraints an older woman who was psychotic at the time of admission. The patient's chart noted that the woman had endured years of homelessness, poverty, and drugs. Her children were in the foster care system.

> People who have experienced early trauma find it difficult to ask for help.

Dr. Needell understood that this woman's life had been filled with danger and fear. For that reason, she assumed that being tied down to the bed could be retraumatizing as she had experienced so many incidents where she had been helpless. But the woman had to be put in restraints, otherwise she might have hurt herself or someone else while she came down from the drug-induced psychotic episode. Dr. Needell's understanding of trauma informed her decision that this woman needed a female soft presence to sit with her and calmly talk with her in order for her to not be triply traumatized by being in the restraints. Her male residents and interns all offered to free her of this responsibility, which was not part of her job as the chief psychiatrist. But she insisted that it had to be a woman.

More and more mental health providers are being educated to have the empathy and wisdom that Dr. Needell demonstrated in this example of trauma-informed care. Hopefully, if someone like Sylvia were to seek help, she too would be greeted by a health professional who could respond to her current and past hurts. Rather than berate her for not being more assertive with her daughters, a trauma-informed clinician would recognize how past events in Sylvia's life had interfered with her ability to stand up for herself. They would help her to gradually take small steps toward reclaiming her own voice.

Marsha's later-life mothering was also affected by her early life. Sixty-four years ago, when Marsha was eight years old, her mother had left her and her sister in North Carolina with their grandmother while her mother "got established" up north. Even though Marsha was well treated by her grandmother, this two-year absence broke her heart. "I wanted to be with my mother and we had to wait until she found a place for us here in New York, which she did. And it was hard. It was hard. . . . And I used to cry all the time because I wanted to be with her."

Now, Marsha's fifty-year-old daughter, Melanie, was unemployed and unable to motivate herself to find a new job. Marsha was using her savings to support Melanie and her grandson. Even though she was worried that she might have to foreclose on her home, she did not feel able to communicate the urgency of the situation to her daughter and force her to either move out or get a job. Perhaps Marsha's childhood experience of feeling vulnerable and abandoned by her own mother was getting in the way of letting her adult daughter know that she could not continue to protect or support her.

As mothers, we want to nurture and provide for our children. But as people, we each have internalized our unique histories that may contain vulnerability, pain, and/or resilience. When our adult children have difficulties, their issues awaken and interact with our own previously buried feelings. If you have had a very painful or traumatic early life in which you were overwhelmed by fear or harmed by others, you may benefit from examining with a clinician how these wounds are interfering with your ability to face current day stressors. Coming to terms with your own past may help you to see the way forward to a better future.

Part II

SMALL STEPS

There are no evidence-based models that you can use as guides to transform your relationship with your difficult adult child. There are, however, ways to evaluate your situation, and from there, learn how to instigate change, however small. The model of change presented in the next section will not require you to choose between yourself or your adult child. Instead, it offers a way of assessing your situation to determine what, if any changes, you want to make.

This section includes:

- Description of the Stages of Change model
- The significance of seeing (or not seeing) your current situation accurately
- Self-assessment of your readiness for making some (one) change or none at all

Change is hard and occurs in many increments. By acknowledging how tough it is for any of us to make meaningful changes in our lives—especially when those changes involve another person—the Stages of Change model encourages a gradual approach that respects both the individual and the challenges they face.[1]

Chapter Twelve

Stages of Change

Where do you begin to make changes in your relationship with your difficult adult child or in yourself? While there are no organizations that will give you a plan for changing family relationships in later life—something prescriptive to provide you with an action plan or a to-do list—there are support groups for family members with adult children with serious mental illness (the National Alliance on Mental Illness) and family members with adult children who are substance abusers (Al-Anon, Nar-Anon, etc.). But to avail yourself of help from any of these organizations, you have to be at a state of readiness to seek help. Even if you are already attending a support group or engaged in therapy, whether you will actually make any changes depends on your readiness, hopefulness, and motivation.

How ready are you?

Everyone reading this book is at a different place regarding how capable they feel about making a change, and how knowledgeable they are about the options available to them. That said, there are several barriers that may prevent you from reaching out for help. You may hold the belief that your adult child's problem is somehow your fault. Even if you know in your rational mind that your actions alone did not create the situation, you may feel in your heart that as a parent you are responsible and that it falls on you to fix things. To look for help for yourself as a mother can feel as if you are admitting failure and weakness. To acknowledge that you may have mixed feelings about your caregiving situation can feel like you are being a bad mother or are being disloyal to your loved one.

Few people want their problems with their adult children made public. How could a stranger ever understand your continuing love for this child who is hurting you? How can your friends whose lives are proceeding so smoothly ever be able to tune into yours? These are the questions that torment mothers of difficult adult children. Side by side with those thoughts is the fear that your attempt to get help will only bring more harm to your child—and perhaps to yourself.

> Putting a child's welfare first is a central tenet of mothering, one that's not easily put aside once the child is grown.

There are no models for transforming mothering in later life with difficult adult children, but there is value in adapting the Stages of Change model, which has demonstrable results in helping people change many kinds of behaviors. Also known as the TransTheoretical Model, the Stages of Change model was introduced in the late 1970s by researchers James Prochaska and Carlo DiClemente, two psychologists who were studying ways to help people quit smoking.[1]

> Change is hard and occurs in many gradations.

Changing your relationship with your difficult adult child is not the same as stopping smoking. With an addiction, the goal is to remove a problem such as cigarettes or alcohol from your life. As we have seen, none of the women who I spoke to wanted to completely cut-off from their adult child, although many had had passing thoughts that included a wish for an end to the stress of the relationship.

The Stages of Change model is a gradual approach that acknowledges how difficult it is for people to actually alter their lives. It is used in programs designed for clients suffering from interpersonal problems or depression, for alcoholics and alcohol abusers, to help delinquent adolescents and cocaine and heroin addicts, and to change behaviors of sedentary people and people with high-fat diets, for example.[2]

Using the Stages of Change model requires the ability to evaluate where you are in the change process and to assess the strength of your motivation for change. This is not like a quick fix weight-loss program or a twenty-eight-day fitness guarantee where you are expected to start the program immediately and move quickly toward your goal. Instead, built into this model is the assumption that most people are unwilling or resistant to change, especially during the early stages.

Each person's tolerance for discomfort is unique to them.

Change is hard. It occurs in many gradations. If you are a mother of a difficult adult child, reading this book, you are already contemplating change. Seeing yourself in the women's stories presented here may have brought you comfort. Now you may understand that you are not the only woman who is upset with or angry at her adult child's dependency. Reading about what other women have done, you might have told yourself that you are not willing or emotionally able to attempt similar actions. That's perfectly fine.

After reading this book, you might decide to learn more about the Stages of Change, more about support groups, or more about the problems that your adult child is facing. By doing this, you are gathering information about the issue.

What impels one person to take action while another may only be thinking about change depends on many factors. Consider how uncomfortable you are with the balance of how things are now for you. To borrow a popular quote: "We change our behavior when the pain of staying the same becomes greater than the pain of changing."
Each person's tolerance for discomfort is unique to them. Each mother's ability to let herself see what feels good or uncomfortable about her situation varies among women and can change within the same person over time.

THE STAGES OF CHANGE

The Stages of Change model guides people to move gradually from denying or minimizing the dangers of their situation to gradually acknowledging (seeing) the problem, to considering change, to taking action, to maintaining the change, with possible recycling back to earlier ways of being from each stage. The model can be broken down into five phases: pre-contemplation, contemplation, preparation, action, and maintenance.[3]

Stage 1: Pre-Contemplation

People in the pre-contemplation stage often feel resigned to their current state or believe that they have no safe way to make things different. They are not considering change. In fact, they're often described as being "in denial" because they don't believe they have a problem or don't understand that their situation is damaging.

While in this stage, women feel resigned to their current state and believe that they are making the best decision for themselves and their adult children by keeping the status quo. For example, a mother might tell herself that living with her difficult adult son who curses at her, screams at her, and who will not allow visits by extended family is what she chooses. She is doing this because she feels sorry for him and his illness (mental illness or substance abuse) and doesn't want to make his situation any worse. Or another mother may feel threatened by her grown daughter's behaviors but excuses them because the daughter is "dealing with a lot."

Prochaska, Norcross, and DiClemente[4] suggest asking yourself a few questions to determine if your situation is actually a life choice or a problematic behavior.

- Do you discuss your fears about living with your adult child with family or friends?
- Do you get upset when people tell you that they think you should have your adult child move out or get help for yourself, or do you appreciate their concern?

Prochaska, Norcross, and DiClemente have found that those who are actually in the pre-contemplation stage—who have a problem that they are trying to deny—get defensive when someone questions their situation, while those who have accepted their choice welcome the feedback as caring. How would you feel if a friend or relative asked you the following?

- Are you well-informed about the dangers you might be facing by allowing the relationship with your adult child to stay as it currently is?
- Are you aware of the short- and long-term effects of maintaining the status quo?

If you are in the pre-contemplation stage, you most likely rely on the defense mechanisms of denial, minimization, or internalization. Denial and minimalization allow people to tune out unpleasant aspects of their situations. A mother who is minimalizing might complain about the way her son can lose his temper and yell at her. Yet when a friend reacts with concern, she might reply, "I'm ok. It's not bad. He has a good heart." Internalization is how we can turn our upset inwards. Rather than seeing how others are causing our pain, we blame ourselves for the problem. In Vivian's situation, she blamed herself for Brandon's abusive and controlling behavior. She believed that her early mothering was the cause of his behavioral problems. This self-blame contributed to her avoiding getting help for herself.

For some of the mothers, the growing realization of her own aging, her health, and mortality served as a springboard for contemplating an alternative route. Doctors' warnings, or friends' concerns, might prompt a person to look more carefully at how they are living. Faith described herself at a crossroads—she had to decide whether to ask her adult children to move out. Her doctor had told her to limit the stress in her life; if not, she would be putting herself at serious risk. For others, it is time itself that serves as a warning signal. Jillian, Alana, and Rebecca all lamented that their ongoing involvement with their adult child was interfering with their ability to enjoy the last part of their lives.

Stage 2: Contemplation

During this stage, people are gathering information and considering how they might alter a situation that they now acknowledge is harmful to them. Journaling during this phase can be useful. Keeping a log of what your life is like every day with your adult child is one way to examine how you are being affected by your situation. Let's say you and your daughter have a fight. When you write about it, push yourself to be truthful and detailed. Who started the fight? What was it about? How did you respond when and if you felt hurt or attacked? Did you attack back? Did you walk away? Did you reach for a drink to swallow your upset? Was there anyone you could call to talk about your upset? This stage of contemplation is an opportunity to take stock of how you are living and your appraisal of your situation and your way of handling your problems.

Prochaska, Norcross, and DiClemente describe how people can remain in the contemplation stage for months or even years. Contemplators are often waiting for the "right" moment to begin a change. With mothers of difficult adult children, many rely on wishful thinking—hoping that things will miraculously turn around in the adult child's life and that they will be able to, for example, move out voluntarily without the mother forcing them.

During this stage, people become more and more aware of the potential benefits of making a change, but the cost and risks associated with it tend to stand out even more. A mother may want her adult son to move out and start imagining being more comfortable in her house without the daily commotion of living with another person, but she also fears the consequences for her son being on his own. This conflict creates a strong sense of ambivalence and uncertainty. Because of this, the contemplation stage of change can last months or even years.

Stage 3: Preparation

People in the preparation stage are planning to take action in the near future. A mother may decide that she needs input from others and searches for a support group. During the preparation stage she would be sharing with appropriate people her wish to change and seeking recommendations for possible groups. Or if she is tired of being afraid as a result of living with an abusive adult child, she would be looking on the internet to find elder abuse referral information and making phone calls and seeing what her options are to get concrete help. Preparation takes you out of the past and mourning the mistakes you think you might have made, to begin to look toward the future.

Stage 4: Action

The action stage is when a mother is directly involved in trying new ways of being with her adult child and/or with herself. Wendy had to move quickly into the action stage when her daughter told her that she had purchased a gun and was thinking of shooting people on the street. Up until then, Wendy, who lived far from her daughter, was trying to figure out if she should be very concerned and get involved or not. She had been in the contemplation stage and had been gathering information to understand mental illness. Suddenly, Wendy realized she had to act. She and her husband intervened within hours. They used the information they had been gathering during the preparation stage and used the courts to get their daughter committed to a psychiatric hospital.

Stage 5: Maintenance

There are great challenges at every stage, and the maintenance stage is no exception. It's during this stage that you work to consolidate the gains you made during the action and other stages, and struggle to prevent relapses.

The authors of the Stages of Change model recognize that maintaining a changed behavior takes work. Some of us may have to recycle back to an earlier way of handling a situation and try again. One woman went through months of interacting with social workers and lawyers to get her daughter legally evicted from her home. The police came and escorted the daughter out of the house. When the daughter phoned later in the day, crying, saying that she had no place to go, the mother let her come back. No person is to be blamed if she or he is unable to sustain the changes they themselves had wanted to institute. The assumption is that the process can begin, again, from wherever you are. The social worker working with this woman continued to help her and said if at a later point she wanted to begin the eviction process again, she was there to help.

Chapter Thirteen

Seeing and Not Seeing

Is love blind? Romantic love and maternal love can be exhilarating, but the scientific truth is that loving feelings can get in the way of seeing things clearly. Andreas Bartels, a neuroscientist in Tübingen, Germany, has shown that maternal love—with young children—can, in fact, be blind. He has pinpointed how a mother's connection to her young child deactivates the part of her brain that is responsible for negative emotions and critical assessment.[1] In other words, a mother's positive feelings that arise from her developing attachment to her child overrides the part of her brain that is responsible for more objective appraisals. Being hopeful and optimistic regarding your child's future is a good thing. But wearing rose-colored glasses with your adult child can be dangerous over the long run. Your filters may be blocking your ability to make a realistic assessment of their and your needs.

CLOSING MY EYES

Lucy, a dynamic sixty-nine-year-old woman, described how she discovered her blind spots. She laughed, telling me how frightened she got when she saw that her son Carlos, who had moved back in with her, had put a towel in front of his door. She worried that he might be trying to hurt himself. He was recently separated from his wife and children, and they were getting a divorce. Maybe, Lucy feared, he was depressed and trying to kill himself.

She called her daughter for help. "Ma, he's smoking pot in that room and that's why the towel is there—so you can't smell it." Lucy smiled as she described how, at her daughter's suggestion, she went into Carlos' room and found little pieces of a joint on the window, as well as a spray can that he was using to cover the odor. "I couldn't believe how long I had been blind to what was happening. I had smelled something sweet but I had told myself 'that's nice—it must be incense.'"

After this revelation Lucy started to pay more attention to what her son was doing. Money had gone missing from her drawer. "You know, I'd have maybe $180 dollars, I'd look and there'd be $140. I had been questioning myself, 'Where could I have spent that missing $40?'" Nevertheless, she kept asking Carlos to go to her bank for her so that she didn't have to walk up and down the five flights in their apartment building. "I'd tell myself I can trust him. He always gave me the receipt that showed the $200 that I asked him to get."

After realizing that he had been covering up the fact that he was smoking pot in her house and purposely trying to deceive her, she saw that on the very same day that there was a withdrawal for two hundred dollars, there would also be another transaction for forty dollars. Her first reaction was to assume that the bank had made an error. She called them to report the problem. "For some reason, I didn't want to believe what was going on." She paused for a long minute as she described how hard it was for her to really believe that her son would steal from her. She assumed that he respected her and appreciated all she had done for him, raising him as a divorced, single, working mother. She had done everything she could to make him a good man.

> It's hard for mothers to admit that their adult child is stealing from them. They're reluctant to admit what the evidence is telling them.

ONLY SEEING THE GOOD

Loretta's story illustrates how it can take fifteen years for a mother to move from contemplation to action. Loretta was eighty-two years old. Tall and thin, she spoke with a musical lilt in her voice, still maintaining her Jamaican accent. She was physically mobile and relatively cognitively sharp, although it was hard for me to follow the timeline of the stories about all the years of legal battles she had had with her son, Jason. When we met, it had been three years since she had had contact with him or her grandchildren. She had no idea where or how they were living. Last she knew, they were homeless.

Years ago, Loretta and her husband, Karl, had been able to purchase a small home in Brooklyn, where she still lived. Karl had died when Jason was just ten years old. Loretta had been a widow for many years when Jason, aged thirty, asked if he, his girlfriend, Zahra, and their one-year-old daughter could stay with her temporarily. She remembers thinking, "He's not a bad kid. Why not?" I was left speechless when she described the way that he and his wife had behaved toward her during the many years that they lived with her. Her daughter-in-law treated Loretta with disrespect, made no effort to clean the kitchen that they shared, and the parents seemed to instruct their kids to lie to Child Protective Services, accusing Loretta of having hurt them. Jason wanted to have Loretta evicted from her own home. Apparently, he believed that his father wanted him to have the house and that was why, according to Zahra, he felt justified in his attempts to use the law to challenge his mother's ownership of her home. As I listened, I kept trying to understand the timeframe. When had the problems begun? How had she allowed this to go on for so long? What had kept her from protecting herself earlier on from her son's continual aggressive behavior and disregard for her comfort?

Loretta told me stories about Jason as a young boy. She proudly recounted that at age eleven, when he was in sixth grade, he refused to follow the Board of Education's decision that he enter Special Education classes because of his behavior problems. He wrote a letter to the Chancellor of Education stating his case for why he believed he should be able to attend regular classes. His request was granted. Back then, Loretta and Jason's siblings admired his fighting spirit and perseverance. They believed this meant that he would go far in life. Loretta's maternal optimism was also evident when she told me what a great athlete Jason had been, how he had gotten a basketball scholarship to college, and about her and Jason's firm belief that he would soon be recruited for a national team in South America, even though it had been ten years since he had left college where he played ball.

Side by side with describing his talents, Loretta suggested that Jason had a way of fudging the truth. He claimed that he had graduated from a private four-year college, something Loretta knew not to be true. He would always present his leaving a job as his choice—not that he was let go. As Loretta described Jason's actions prior to her having him evicted, I heard her describe the same personal characteristics—pushy, perseverant, and determined—that she had valued in him at age eleven. Yet, now in his forties, living with his mother, his goal was not to avoid Special Education classes, but to gain ownership of his mother's house which he believed he was entitled to.

Loretta finally got help from a legal center for seniors. They offered her free legal help to respond to Jason's constant use of the courts in his efforts to take her home away from her. It wasn't simple to have him evicted. He was very savvy and had taught himself how to use the law to harass his mother. One judge got so annoyed at his endless trumped up charges that he forbade Jason from ever coming into his court again. After what seemed like years of attempts to stop his abuse and legal attacks, Loretta secured an exclusionary order of protection forbidding Jason or his family to enter her home. But Jason was not to be stopped. He managed to go to another court and find a second judge, who issued a warrant for Loretta's arrest unless she allowed him entry.

When the police arrived, Loretta did what the public attorney had instructed her to do. She told the police officers that she had obtained an exclusionary order of protection against her son and would not allow him back into the house. Instead of understanding the situation, the police arrested Loretta and took her away in handcuffs. She sobbed as she described to me what it was like for her to be in jail for two nights. The cell smelled of urine, there was no working toilet, and no one gave her anything to drink for hours on end. Telling me, three years later, about this experience, she reexperienced the humiliation and cried. However, it was the sting of her son having had her arrested that became a turning point for Loretta. Sitting in the jail cell, she fully acknowledged that there was something wrong with him, "if he could be ok with his mother being put in jail."

Loretta had been using what mental health professionals call the defense mechanism of "minimization" or filtering out the negatives in a situation and only letting herself focus on the positives. This generosity of spirit, or seeing only one side of a situation, was likely at play when she accepted her son's request that he move into her small one-family home with his new baby and girlfriend. When she told herself "he's a good kid," she was discounting what she also knew about his difficulty with authority and his inability to get along with people, as well as his history of lying or distorting the truth for his own ends. Loretta's capacity to tune out the problematic effects of Jason's behavior can explain how she had allowed him and his expanding family (he had six children when they were finally evicted) to continue to live with her, all those years. Her wish that things would eventually go well for Jason took priority over acknowledging her own discomfort.

NOT WANTING TO SEE

Rosanne described herself as someone who could never talk about or address upsetting things. She had stayed in a very unhappy marriage for years. When her son, Derek, cut off all contact with her several years back, she never discussed the situation even with her daughter, who she saw every week. She lived her life squashing down all discomfort. Soon before she had chosen to be interviewed by me, Rosanne learned that Derek might be in serious trouble. Derek was living on his own, unemployed, supported by a monthly allowance from a family trust, that was administered by a lawyer and did not require his parents' involvement. Derek had maintained some contact with his father, Michael, from whom Rosanne was divorced. It was Michael who told Rosanne that he had gotten a troubling call from Derek demanding that he give him five thousand dollars immediately. Michael and Rosanne feared that Derek might be involved in drugs or gambling debts and that explained why he needed the additional money. Perhaps someone was after him. Rosanne was scared. She considered hiring a detective to find out how serious the situation was. She was afraid for her son's safety.

To have hired a detective sounded to me like a metaphor for changing her lifelong mode of not allowing herself to acknowledge the things that upset her. If she had followed this idea and had hired someone to investigate what was happening with Derek, she would have been trying out a new way of being. Instead, she decided against getting involved. She told her ex-husband to give their son the money with no questions asked. Her rationale was that she did not feel strong enough or savvy enough to know what to do if she were to learn that her son was in serious trouble with mobsters or drug dealers. She did not believe that she had the capacity to help.

SEEING AND INTERVENING

In contrast, Wendy allowed herself to act on her worries about her daughter's safety. She had thought that her mothering tasks were done, that she and her husband could enjoy their retirement and engage with their grown kids during vacations and through email. But when her forty-year-old daughter Mindy started making changes in her life that seemed out of character, Wendy—with time—allowed herself to acknowledge her concerns.

The first surprise came when her daughter announced "out of the blue" that she was leaving her engineering job to become a yoga instructor. She explained her job change as part of a larger evolution into a more spiritual existence, and that she was also changing her name, legally, to Vishnu. The name change really bothered Wendy, and she even refused a birthday present Mindy had sent because it was signed from "Vishnu." Several months later, Mindy reported that she was getting a divorce from her husband. Wendy and Robert, very surprised, asked many questions to be sure that Mindy was making the right decision, but accepted that she knew what was best. They had always had full confidence in their daughter's choices up until then. They figured that Mindy was going through a spiritual crisis which would lead to something new for her. Yet, as they noticed more and more odd changes in their daughter, they started to make more frequent calls and visits with Mindy in the hopes of monitoring more closely the changes that seemed confusing and surprising.

With time, their unease with Mindy's erratic behavior motivated them to seek out information about symptoms of mental illness and possible treatment options. Neither of them had ever had any contact with the mental health system. First, they relied on the internet for information, then they went to local doctors and started to network with everyone they knew to understand their daughter's situation. They were able to face the situation, as well as their lack of knowledge. They got educated quickly enough so that they could intervene and protect their daughter when that became a necessity.

Seeing clearly an adult child's difficulties, or acknowledging the impact of their behavior on themselves or on you, is the first step in a mother's change process.

SEEING LEADS TO ACTION

Seeing an adult child's difficulties, acknowledging the impact of their behavior on themselves or on you, is the first step in a mother's change process. There are two kinds of changes that mothers may make. One is to more clearly see how an adult child's life may need a parent's intervention, even though this will require getting involved as a helper when you believed that active parenting was already over. The second kind of change is related to removing or changing your adult child's ability to hurt you, as in the case of Loretta. Loretta's filtering out the ways in which she felt pushed around and taken advantage of by her son were her way of holding onto her image of her son as a "good boy." Wendy and Robert took a while to see that their daughter's surprising and erratic behavior was, in fact, mental illness. But once they saw that she was in trouble, they acted and did something that was hard: committing their daughter against her will to a psychiatric hospital. But this saved her life. Seeing is the first step in the change model for dealing with a difficult adult child.

Chapter Fourteen

Readiness

Self-Assessment

Feelings of anxiety and depression are known to interfere with people's ability to make changes. Before deciding what kind of help might be for you, or before deciding that any change is impossible to even consider, please take a short assessment quiz that will measure your level of current depression and anxiety, on page 152. If you discover that you are very depressed, bring the results of the assessment to your physician and talk to her or him about it. Depression is treatable. Depression and/ or anxiety can make you feel overwhelmed and unable to take small steps toward improving your situation.

Add up your score on the Patient Health Questionnaire. The higher your score, the greater indication that you are experiencing depression and should be consulting with a health care professional or a mental health counselor. If your score is five to fourteen, you are considered to have moderate depression. If your score is fifteen to nineteen, your depression is moderately severe. Finally, if your score is over twenty, your depression is severe, and it is definitely recommended that you talk to a health care professional.

To understand your score on the General Anxiety Disorder scale, total your answers. Scores can range zero to twenty-one. A score of five represents mild anxiety, ten represents moderate anxiety, and fifteen or more refers to severe anxiety. Bring these results to discuss with your physician.

Another way to evaluate the pros and cons of making changes or of continuing with things as they are is to create decisional worksheet.[1] Ask

Table 14.1. Patient Health Questionnaire-8

Over the *last two weeks* how often have you been bothered by any of the following problems?	Not at all	Several days	More than half the days	Nearly every day
1. Little interest or pleasure in doing anything	0	1	2	3
2. Feeling down, depressed, or hopeless	0	1	2	3
3. Trouble falling or staying asleep, or sleeping too much	0	1	2	3
4. Feeling tired or having little energy	0	1	2	3
5. Poor appetite or overeating	0	1	2	3
6. Feeling bad about yourself—or that you are a failure or have let yourself or your family down	0	1	2	3
7. Trouble concentrating on things, such as reading the newspaper or watching television	0	1	2	3
8. Moving or speaking so slowly that other people could have noticed; or the opposite—being so fidgety or restless that you have been moving around a lot more than usual	0	1	2	3

Developed by Drs. Robert L. Spitzer, Janet B. W. Williams, Kurt Kroenke, and colleagues, with an educational grant from Pfizer Inc. No permission required to reproduce, translate, display, or distribute.

Table 14.2. General Anxiety Disorder-7

Over the *last two weeks* how often have you been bothered by the following?	Not at all	Several days	More than half the days	Nearly every day
1. Feeling nervous, anxious, or on edge	0	1	2	3
2. Not being able to stop or control worrying	0	1	2	3
3. Worrying too much about different things	0	1	2	3
4. Trouble relaxing	0	1	2	3
5. Being so restless that it is hard to sit still	0	1	2	3
6. Becoming easily annoyed or irritable	0	1	2	3
7. Feeling afraid as if something awful might happen	0	1	2	3

(For office coding: Total Score T____=____+____+____)

Developed by Drs. Robert L. Spitzer, Janet B. W. Williams, Kurt Kroenke, and colleagues, with an educational grant from Pfizer Inc. No permission required to reproduce, translate, display, or distribute.

yourself *how important is it for you to change your current situation with your adult child.* On a scale from 0 to 10, where 0 is not at all important and 10 is extremely important, where do you see yourself, now?

Table 14.3.   How important is it for you to change your relationship with your adult child?

1	2	3	4	5	6	7	8	9	10
Not at all important									Extremely important

The next question that you want to ask yourself is *how confident are you that you could make a change?*

Table 14.4.   How confident are you that you can make changes in your relationship with your adult child?

1	2	3	4	5	6	7	8	9	10
Not at all confident									Extremely confident

If you rated your desire to seek change as somewhat or extremely important, but saw yourself as having little confidence in your ability to change things, then you might want to start speaking with others to find out how they went about making changes. You might decide to seek professional support from a counselor or to join a support group to see how others found the courage to try.

Another way is to examine where you are in the change process is to think about the advantages and disadvantages of doing, versus not doing, anything to change. Using the Decisional Worksheet (on page 154) as a guide, think about your current situation with your adult child and what are the potential gains and losses from taking action.

While this may look like an easy exercise, it is not. Articulating the plusses of keeping the status quo with your difficult adult child will be much harder than you imagine. Yet we heard from so many of the women's stories how torn they felt about prioritizing their own needs over their adult children's. For example, Alana, Sylvia, and Rebecca expressed that keeping things as they were, regardless of their own fears or discomfort, were necessary for each of them. They expressed that they would not be able to tolerate the anticipated negative outcomes

Table 14.5.   Decisional Worksheet: Pros and Cons of Change

	Plusses	*Minuses*
Keep my social support system exactly as it is		
Add one thing to my life that gives me pleasure		
Change one way that I interact with my adult child		
Ask my adult child to make one change in their behavior with me		
Make major changes in my situation		

that would come to their adult child if they were to try something new. They chose to stay "torn in two."

Perhaps the women's stories presented here have helped you to consider aspects of your own situation that you usually don't let yourself acknowledge. We saw how Vivian could not reflect on how frightened she had been of her son until she was completely safe and separated from him. Taking off blinders and acknowledging your hurt is hard. Not everyone has the strength to openly explore their choices or to risk making some changes if their adult child might be hurt. Being connected to adult children and grandchildren provides essential support and meaning to mothers, whether or not this relationship includes pain and disappointment.

Part III

HELPING YOURSELF

This section of the book describes actions mothers can take to get help for themselves and/or for their adult children. It is based on recommendations from professionals in the fields of mental health, social services, aging, and elder abuse prevention. In addition, examples are provided of how some of the mothers were successful in changing their situations. The material is organized by four central aspects of well-being for women with difficult adult children:

- Getting social support
- Engaging in self-care
- Staying safe in your own home
- Helping your adult child

There is no dedicated place where mothers of difficult adult children can share their strategies and get advice. But these chapters come close.

Chapter Fifteen

Social Support

Mothers told me they often felt judged by their closest relatives, many of whom held negative opinions about the way they had raised their difficult adult child. Alana believed that her brother blamed her for the problems with her daughter. Sylvia didn't feel that she could turn to her older son because he had already helped her out of so many messes with her daughter, Jasmine. Durene's other children were fed up with her because of her decision to allow Caleb to continue to live with her, despite his abusive behavior. And Jillian described how her friends were bewildered by her continued commitment to engage with Celia, regardless of the strain on her health.

If women feel alienated by their closest family and friends, who do they turn to for social support when crises emerge—again?

Social support is the assistance and comfort that we receive from others in difficult times. It may take the form of practical help (offering advice or taking on chores), emotional support (helping the individual to feel valued and understood by listening), or even material help (lending money or a place to stay). Social support is an essential buffer to stress.

Social support is the provision of assistance or comfort to others, typically to help them cope with biological, psychological, and social stressors. Support may arise from any interpersonal relationship in an individual's social network, involving family members, friends, neighbors, religious institutions, colleagues, caregivers, or support groups. It may take the form of practical help (e.g., doing chores, offering advice), tangible support that involves giving money or other direct material assistance, and emotional support that allows the individual to feel valued, accepted, and understood.[1]

OUR SOCIAL NETWORKS

As we age, the size of our social networks usually shrinks. Gone are the watercooler conversations, the college cafeteria, or hanging out at bars. When our kids get older, the hustle and bustle of family life and the connections with other families who also had children quiets down. For those who have retired from work, there are fewer "peripheral" interactions with people who, before retirement, formed part of the fabric of daily life. No fellow commuters, lunch counter staff, grocery store clerks, or co-workers to interact with—however briefly. Older people come to rely more often on the people with whom they have a long history and close emotional ties, usually family or long-term friends.

But these lost peripheral interactions may be more important than we realize. While most people prefer to spend their later years with those that they feel close to, rather than holding onto or developing more superficial relationships, sociologists have found that these "weaker" or nonfamily connections are also very important. Weaker ties include acquaintances or people one meets in an organization or club—people to whom you may not feel quite that close but are still in your peripheral social network. When they tested whether there was any measurable value in maintaining or developing what they call "weaker ties" in later life, researchers were surprised to find that in fact the number of more peripheral ties that a person reported was strongly related to their positive well-being and decreased depression. In fact, the number of weaker ties a person reported was more predictive of well-being than the number of close ties.[2]

One of the risks of both getting older and parenting a difficult adult child is that you may have cut off from extended family and many of your prior social connections. If you are feeling lonely or socially isolated, you are not alone. A recent study found that more than one-third of adults aged forty-five and older feel lonely, and nearly one-fourth of adults aged sixty-five and older are considered socially isolated.[3] Loneliness and social isolation are not only painful, but they can negatively affect your physical and mental health. Social isolation can become deadly, especially if you have an adult child who is volatile or aggressive. The tendency to not tell your neighbor about problems at home or to not tell your sister about your son (once again) stealing money for drugs can leave you unprotected. Especially if you live with someone who can get angry, you want as many people as possible to be watching out for you.

If you are feeling lonely or socially isolated, you are not alone. A recent study found that more than one-third of adults aged forty-five and older feel lonely, and nearly one-fourth of adults aged sixty-five and older are considered to be socially isolated.[4]

Many mothers told me that they chose not to share their feelings of disappointment or anger about their adult children with family or close friends. They felt embarrassed and ashamed. They feared that revealing what was happening might lead to gossip or undermine how others viewed their child—or them. But by keeping the upsetting situation a secret, these women are missing the chance to connect with someone who might be able to offer much-needed social support. There is extensive research to show that when people feel supported by others, their feelings of self-worth increase, which then increases their overall sense of well-being.[5] Researchers from Columbia University found that confiding in others decreases the secret keeper's feelings of shame. Keeping things secret from others has been shown to lead to unexpected negative effects on yourself. The researchers showed that within people who kept secrets, their mind would continually wander back to the secret, and this then increased the person's feelings of shame.[6]

Many older women have lost the support of friends and their partners who have passed away. Marsha wouldn't share the details of the financial strain she was experiencing because of her daughter's unemployment with anyone, including her own sister. She used to share the burden of her daughter's situation with one girlfriend, but that friend has since died. Now Marsha keeps her troubles to herself. Loretta wondered if she would have ended up in the same predicament if so many of the people who supported her early life had not died. Her other children believe that if their father had still been alive, Jason could never have acted the way he did toward his mother, trying to steal the house out from under her.

Some of the women I spoke with did have support within their family circle. Wendy had seven living brothers and sisters. Although she at first was reluctant to tell them about her daughter's mental illness, once she did, they mobilized and formed a prayer circle for Wendy and her husband. Every day at 3 pm, Wendy's phone alarm would remind her to get on the call. Not only did the whole family pray for Mindy, but they also shared advice based on research that they had recently done on mental illness.

Lucy had a group of friends she could call on when she was exasperated with her son, Carlos. She had had these friends for a lifetime. After her divorce, she moved to lower Manhattan and her kids were school-aged, she met and connected with a group of women friends who bonded around the challenges of being single parents. They helped each other then and continue to be there for each other now. "It's a group of strong independent self-sufficient women who just do what they gotta do because they got to do it." One friend, Claudia, had a daughter who would mistreat her in a similar way that Lucy felt Carlos acted toward her. Both Lucy and Claudia had voluntarily taken custody of a grandchild when their own son or daughter was younger and unable to manage the responsibility of parenting. Instead of feeling appreciated for all that she had done for him, Lucy felt that Carlos took advantage of her, especially now that he was successful in his own small business. Lucy did not tell many friends or even family members about her disappointment in Carlos. But with Claudia, she was able to speak honestly. They used humor to laugh and vent. Lucy reported getting a call from Claudia saying, "Lucia, you got money for my bail? Because I'm going to need it. I'm going to jail. I'm gonna kill this one." They could laugh with each other at their common situation.

Psychologists from Stanford University demonstrated through a research study that "If you are able to teach people to be more playful, to look at the absurdities of life as humorous, you see some increase in wellbeing."[7] Lucy and Claudia were able to bond and support each other's coping by using humor and empathy.

Consider looking beyond your close ties and joining organizations devoted to educating families of adult children with mental illness or substance abuse.

SUPPORT FROM FORMAL SOURCES

Support is also available from more "formal" sources. Several of the women interviewed had looked beyond their close ties by joining organizations devoted to educating families of adult children with mental illness or substance abuse. Many of the mothers had sought out these groups during the early part of their adult child's struggle. But one can get support from these groups at any time in your parenting journey. Durene stayed in the group she found for many years as she found the leader particularly helpful. "It was fantastic. And I stuck with that group and stuck with that group. But that group really carried me through. I didn't have any parents to lean on. I didn't have any friends to lean on because they knew nothing about mental illness." When Hope discovered that Samantha had been stealing from her and was on drugs, she took Samantha with her to a meeting of Al-Anon. As a newcomer, Hope was asked to speak about why she had come. "I pretty much told them the whole thing with stealing and the drugging and the shock that it was to me because I was unconscious about everything that had been going on. I hadn't picked up on any of it." When they left the meeting, Hope felt positive about meeting other people in the same situation. Samantha, however, was shocked that her mother had just told all these strangers "everything." Samantha did not want the help and never went back to an Al-Anon meeting.

Hope stayed involved in Al-Anon for over ten years. She described the meetings as attracting vital and engaged people who were very open and honest. She felt supported and liked the mix of people who came to the meetings. She found it extremely helpful when a young person/addict would come and share their perspective and their successes. Hope purchased several of the Al-Anon–authored books and has learned concepts that she has used, including "don't enable" and the three "Cs" of addiction: "I didn't cause it. I can't cure it. I can't control it." She has tried to integrate the concept that parents need to separate themselves from the problems that are making them feel guilty or at fault. Al-Anon stresses that parents must give up the idea that they can control the child who has the problem. "Surrender can be a very powerful tool when there's nothing in fact that you can do," Hope reflected. "So, surrendering isn't a bad thing."

Family members whose adult children are struggling with mental health issues may find support by joining one of the family-to-family classes offered by the National Association of Mental Illness. America's largest grassroots mental health organization, the National Association of Mental Illness offers these classes to help you better understand mental illness and to provide tools which can then lessen your level of frustration and confusion about your adult child's behavior. Similarly, Al-Anon and Nar-Anon can also help with strategies. Your adult child may not be ready to tackle their substance use disorder or take their psychiatric medications, but your learning how to cope with the situation will be in your best interest—and theirs.

Organizations like Al-Anon and the National Association of Mental Illness provide women an opportunity to share their experiences with others in a nonjudgmental environment.

When she was seventy-three years old, Ada entered the support group at the Jewish Association for the Services for the Aged/Legal Social Work Elder Abuse Program. Ada had never been in a support group before. Going to the first session of the group, she did not know what to expect. She was uncomfortable about having to talk to strangers about her son's mental illness. She was embarrassed that he had once thrown a soda bottle at her during an argument, causing her to need to be hospitalized. In the first session, she heard the group members sharing experiences not unlike what had happened to her, which caused her to relax and speak about her situation. She kept going back to the group. She told me that has learned new ways to respond to her son, Harris. Rather than feeling like the helpless victim or angry parent, she feels much more confident. She sees herself as less reactive to his moods. She can now think about the best way to respond, and their communication has improved. In the group, participants share incidents that happen at home and help each other brainstorm about how they could have handled the situation in a better way, "rather than being bitter, rather than lashing out." She feels a greater sense of calm. An additional benefit for her from being in the group is that it gets out of her house and she has met new people. Her mood has improved, and she no longer feels the shame that she did about her situation.

Being in a support group with others who are "in the same boat" can be transformative.

Getting advice and practical help from people who have lived through similar situations as you has been demonstrated in numerous studies to be emotionally, psychologically, and practically useful.[8]

Chapter Sixteen

Self-Care

Women are used to putting their own needs on the back burner. We attend to infants, young children, and teenagers, all the while telling ourselves that there will be time enough for ourselves when our kids are grown. But what happens when our beloved child turns out to have mental health concerns, substance abuse disorders, or financial or employment issues? What then?

Caring for, living with, or worrying about a family member—whether that's a troubled adult child, a frail older parent, or both—can result in a woman ignoring her own needs. Carving out the time to look after herself is difficult. Being able to do something pleasurable or just go to a doctor may feel unimportant, even impossible. That was certainly true for the women I interviewed, all of whom felt torn between their own needs and those of their adult children.

The phrase *self-care* is a buzzword these days, used by people who want to sell body lotions and bath products, yoga mats, and weighted blankets. It can be off-putting to hear it used so often in marketing promotions and social media campaigns—#Self-care! But the fact is, self-care is essential to everyone, especially those who are looking after the needs of others.

At its most basic level, the notion of self-care is contained in the words themselves: care for the self. Think of it as the act of focusing on your own physical and mental well-being. The word *act* is important here. We must act for ourselves, do things for ourselves, include ourselves in the decisions we make for others. This, for a mother, can be revolutionary.

Caring for, living with, or worrying about a family member can result in a woman ignoring her own needs.

There are mothers who cannot envision feeling better—at peace—while their adult child lives with them or has such a dominant presence in their lives. Yet at the same time they do not want to cut ties. Rebecca, for example, wanted to evict her son, but believed there was no way she could without risking her own life. She couldn't imagine resuming her own life—"having a chance to live" is how she put it—until he was out of her home. It's a no-win situation. "I can't—I don't want to die. I haven't even had a chance to live. I've been caring for people all my life. I haven't had a chance to do anything that I really like. When will I get to do that? When will I get to walk in my apartment and feel good about my home? When will I have that?"

While your commitment to your adult child may be your priority, you can match that with a commitment to yourself. Mental health professionals who help women living in demanding situations, including those living with a difficult or even abusive adult child, urge us to understand that this is not an all or nothing choice. Change focused on self-care is possible without abandoning your commitments as a mother.[1] There's room in the lifeboat for both of you.

TAKING CONTROL OF YOUR PHYSICAL AND MENTAL HEALTH

Several mothers shared with me their feelings of despair because they saw no way out of their situation. They were unhappy living with their adult children but could not envision a way out of their current bind in providing residential support for their adult child. But you do not have to evict your adult child in order to take better care of your physical and mental health. Seeing your physician regularly (and finding one who is respectful toward older people) is an important place to begin, especially if you are suffering from depression or anxiety. You might not be aware that depression can show itself in other ways than feeling sad. Signs of depression can include trouble falling asleep, having a poor appetite, not being able to concentrate, as well as feeling down or hopeless. If you did not do it already, I suggest taking the self-assessment to see if you are perhaps suffering from depression or anxiety. (These forms are available on page 152.) After you fill out these appraisals, bring the results to your family doctor and use them to start a conversation about your situation. Depression can be treated. You do not have to accept your hopelessness or low mood.

MAKING TIME FOR YOURSELF

What gives people pleasure varies from person to person. For some, it may be listening to music, cooking a meal, or doing a jigsaw puzzle. For others, it may be taking a walk every day when the weather is good. One study on depression found that you will get more emotional benefit from this walk, or other activities, if you ask a friend to join you.[2] Consider going to the library with a neighbor or meeting someone for a casual cup of coffee.

Another option is to take a class—painting, writing, dancing. Regular exercise has been proved to be another antidote to depression. Senior centers are another resource—often overlooked. Most senior centers, realizing the emotional and physical value of maintaining bone strength and flexibility as we age, now offer chair yoga, Tai Chi, and ballroom dancing. If senior centers are not for you, making a date with someone to walk with, or go to the gym with, can improve both your mood and your health. And you don't have to join a gym to get the benefits of adding movement into your life: the internet has an endless supply of exercise programs geared toward women over fifty, a great number of them free of charge. Meditation has been shown to reduce stress and anxiety. There are many links on the internet to help you get started with a meditation-like practice.

For Jade, going to church was a positive and social experience. She felt welcomed and supported there. Respected. While at home she may, at times, have felt depressed and tired, she knew that when she arrived, there would be people to say hello to and many of the younger people would still come to her for advice. Even when her physical strength lessened and getting there was difficult, the church group found congregants to pick her up and drive her back home.

TAKING CONTROL OF YOUR SPACE

Many women felt upset when their homes were not treated with care and respect by their adult children who have been invited back to live with them. Faith, at eighty-two, felt violated by her daughter and grandson's inability to respect her wish when they were living in her home that all the cooking and eating was done by 7:30 pm. She told me that she didn't expect her house to be spotlessly clean all the time, but she did want her daughter to be more considerate. After two years of living with her daughter and grandson, the problems had still not been resolved.

There are some innovative programs that might have helped Faith negotiate with her daughter regarding her goal to have them share the kitchen in a more respectful manner. Weill Cornell Hospital in New York City offers home visits and short-term counseling to women struggling with abusive family members. The program encourages women to set goals and engage in meaningful, pleasurable activities to address anxiety and depression, while improving self-esteem. Had Faith been assisted by a clinician, she might have learned how to break down her ultimate goal of a clean kitchen and a regular schedule by putting in place smaller, more achievable goals—chosen by Faith.

Perhaps if Faith had been asked to break down her goals into smaller steps, she might have said that she wanted at least two nights a week when she could count on having quiet in the house after 7:30 pm. If she could not get her kids to agree to this limit, or if she could not find a way to tell them about it, she and the clinician would have brainstormed other ways to achieve her goal. That could have included Faith making a smaller request. Or it could have meant that with the clinician, together, they would have found the language to best express her needs. Regardless of the specifics, the worker and Faith would have set out a new action plan together.

Breaking down goals into smaller steps makes them more manageable.

Lenore was helped by the staff at Weill Cornell Hospital. Her daughter, who was using drugs, had been stealing from her. Each time Lenore's daughter came to visit, she'd wander through the house taking clothes, checks, and toiletries. Only after her daughter had left did

Lenore realize that these items were missing. She did not want to use the courts to prohibit her daughter from visiting her, but she also didn't want her daughter to steal from her. Working with her clinician, Lenore learned how to tell her daughter to stay only in the living room on her next visit. The daughter, while surprised, did not question this limit. There was an unspoken acknowledgment between them of her daughter's past behavior. Lenore was glad that she had figured out a way to protect herself and still allow her daughter to visit.

Then there is Noella, whose very large extended family would call to complain for hours about their worries and multiple problems. Overwhelmed by these calls, Noella's goal was to have more time to herself, more time to devote to her self-care. She and her clinician brainstormed and came up with the idea of designating a time each day when she would not pick up the phone. When it turned out that Noella wasn't comfortable letting the phone ring—in essence, ignoring her family— she and her counselor decided that she would limit the amount of time she spent on each phone call. She got herself a timer and would set it for five minutes. Soon, the family members got used to the timers and with humor remark, "Oh my God, is that the bell, already?" This was a big first step for Noella to feel a sense of control.

CHALLENGING YOUR GUILT AND SHAME

How many times a day do you think, "If only I had . . ." regarding your parenting decisions. Nearly every mother I spoke with believed that she was the cause of her child's problems, that she was to blame for the way she had raised her child. The mental health professionals who I interviewed echoed this. They told me that women's feelings of guilt and shame are universal obstacles to their getting help.

A social worker at the Jewish Association Serving the Aging/Legal Social Work Elder Abuse Program (JASA/LEAP) in New York, Miriam Goldberg facilitates groups for older people who have been abused by their adult children or grandchildren. She described the powerful moment that can occur if a group member is able to hear and empathize with another woman as she describes her feelings of guilt: "Being able to see how another person tried everything, like she really did, can become the road into self-forgiveness," she reported.

Miriam also helps mothers (and fathers) understand that what their adult children may need is more than any one person can provide. "Your child needs a team. They need supportive housing. They need to learn how to budget, how to buy a MetroCard. You cannot solve this all on your own."

> Very often what an adult child needs is more than any one person can provide.

Some mothers, however, provide believable evidence on how they had failed their children earlier in life. Francine, a client in Project Protect, had a daughter who at age forty had many emotional problems. She was making her mother's home uninhabitable. She had a terrible temper and had physically struck her mother on many occasions. Francine shared with the social worker that her daughter was sexually abused by a family member when she was younger, and that Francine had not intervened to protect her daughter. Her feelings of guilt and self-blame were getting in the way of her protecting herself in the present.

The clinician asked Francine to imagine what she would think if her neighbor had revealed to her that she had failed her daughter much earlier in life. Would Francine feel that it was acceptable, therefore, for the child, now an adult, to be physically attacking her mother for this past injury? In other words, one way to handle your self-blame for your parenting limitations when you were younger is seeing your situation in another person's skin. Do they really deserve to be beaten?

SELF-CARE IS NOT EASY: THE ROLE OF COUNSELING

Guilt, shame, grief, depression, anxiety, chronic sorrow—these are complex feelings. Many people have found a way to swallow these feelings and try to convey a "stiff upper lip." While the wish to push away pain is understandable, denial does not lead to emotional health or the resolution of mixed feelings. Without an open exploration of conflict, most people remain depressed, ruminating about their situation. They stay stuck. Talking to a trained counselor or psychotherapist can help. Talk therapy, whether one-to-one or in a group, has been proven to alleviate emotional distress. An empathic and knowledgeable professional—someone who can help you disclose your pain and encourage you to tell your story—is at the core of therapy.

Loving a difficult adult child is a complex matter. You may have to first challenge your own biases against mental health treatment as something that only "sick" or "weak" people do. I hope that reading all of the stories presented here will remind you that you are not alone. You deserve to be supported in your journey.

The appendix provides information on how to find a counselor in your area.

Chapter Seventeen

Staying Safe

If you have an adult child who has been, or you fear may be, physically or verbally assaultive toward you or others, you are not alone. Mother abuse and elder abuse are both documented social problems that are occurring in homes like yours across the nation and across the world. It may be frightening or embarrassing to reach out for help when it is your own child, but I hope the following information—from lawyers, social workers, elder abuse specialists, and mental health professionals—will prepare you should you need to call for help. Being informed about your choices regarding who to call, what to say, and what to expect can make the experience less intimidating.

GAINING A SENSE OF CONTROL
AND SAFETY IN YOUR HOME

Many mothers of difficult adult children have already found ways to keep themselves safe. One mother told social worker Takai Forde, from the Jewish Association Serving the Aging/Legal Social Work Elder Abuse Program, "I'll get up in the morning, and John will usually be downstairs in the living room—cursing, drinking, and smoking. I've asked him countless times not to drink and smoke but when I do, he becomes very angry. He usually starts yelling and cursing, threatening me, and sometimes I'll just leave and go upstairs to my room and try not to be in the same space as him." Forde praised the woman for knowing how to remove herself from the situation without having a confrontation.

But there may be times when a mother's strategy of quietly removing herself from the situation may not work. She needs to have other options. Forde, a social worker who specializes in protecting older people from being abused, begins her work with new clients by requesting that they "Paint me a picture of what it is like living in your home."

How would you answer this question?

If a woman describes feeling unsafe all the time, Forde will suggest how she could obtain legal protection, which could include having the adult child removed from the home. If the mother is not interested in this legal route, Forde will work with her until she feels more empowered and can find a way to support her own safety.

"You provide for your kids no matter if they're adults or not." That's what many women say to Forde. But she helps them do more than this impulse to provide; she helps them to set boundaries and learn to say "no." She understands that mothers have an "instinctual reaction . . . to comply with whatever they the [adult] child asks for." That's why she'll help women experiment by saying "no" to small demands.

To the mother whose son or daughter is living with her and they may watch television together, she might suggest, "Mrs. M, do you think you could try—instead of immediately giving in to your son's requests—to try something new? Like when you and he are watching TV if he asks you to hand him the clicker when he's just as close to it as you are, could you try and say 'no'?" Helping Mrs. M start small, Forde is preparing her to become more comfortable in standing up for herself. This is a skill they will build on together.

Forde also helps her clients prepare for safety emergencies. She reminds them about the need to call 911 when they are at risk, but also inquires how comfortable they are with calling emergency services. She knows that many people do not trust the police. She has been told by families how they fear officers barging into their homes, or even worse, using lethal weapons to quiet a situation, at times ending in tragedy.

Forde also recommends that one way to become less frightened of having to call the police is to form a relationship with an officer at your local precinct. An elder abuse social worker can arrange for you to have the name of an officer you could call, if and when a problem arises. If you are not working with a social worker, get in in touch with the domestic violence unit in your local precinct. If you are not comfortable doing this on your own, consider having a friend or neighbor help you.

COMMUNITY-BASED SERVICES

Adult Protective Services

Adult Protective Services (APS) agencies are available to help in every area across the United States. If you are concerned about your safety, contacting APS will lead to a relatively rapid investigation into your situation. A trained professional will visit you in your home and evaluate the safety of your circumstances and your need for assistance. In addition, they will help you determine how they can best help and what services may best suit your circumstances. Unless you are in dire physical danger or unable to cognitively assess the danger of your situation, APS will not take any action without your consent.

Calling 911

If your life is at risk or if you have been hurt, you must call 911. Please do *not* tell your adult child that you are about to call. If you can, go into a separate space and privately place the call.

If your adult child has a psychiatric or substance abuse history (or both), provide this information to the person who answers. Tell the dispatcher that your loved one is having a mental health crisis and explain her mental health history and diagnosis. Many counties have crisis response teams or crisis intervention teams, so ask for an officer from one of those teams if possible.

Be ready to share the following information:

- Your name, address, and phone number.
- Whether you feel threatened or unsafe.
- The name of the person in crisis and your relationship with them.
- A description of the individual in crisis, including their age and gender, and what clothing they may be wearing.
- Any medication being used by your child, whether prescribed or self-medicated. Also, let the dispatcher know if your child is currently

taking their medication. If they have stopped, let them know when they last took the medication (to the best of your knowledge).
- Are any substances, including alcohol, involved? Is this use current or in the past?
- History of interactions of your child with the police. Have you called 911 before?
- Does the person in crisis hear voices?

After making the call, you might want to take a note pad into a private space to prepare. Write down exactly what transpired before making the call. One woman who called the police wrote down the following.

> Today around noon, I was making lunch, my son barged in, he threatened me and told me I needed to give him money for drugs. I told him no. He kept going. He said he would kill himself and kill me if he didn't give him the money. I felt frightened and came into my bedroom to call the police. He continued to yell at me behind the closed door.

You will likely feel anxious and frightened when the police arrive. Communicating clearly may be hard. This is natural. Take a deep breath. Stay as calm as you possibly can. Do your best to focus and speak calmly. Talk to the police face-to-face. Inform them of your child's psychiatric history, even if you have already told the dispatcher.

Your son or daughter may try to divert the police by telling them that everything is okay. If this happens, do not get into an argument. Instead, just tell the officers, "My child has one perspective and I have another. Can I speak with you over here? I'd like to tell you my side of the story."

Not all officers are well-trained, and you may have to take the lead. If you sense that the officer is unsure of how to proceed and is more comfortable talking to your adult child, politely request to speak to the officer. You might say, "I know you just got here, but I'm pretty stressed out, and I'd just like to get a record of who was here. Can you tell me your name and badge number, please?" Write the information down. If the officer is rude to you or dismisses the danger of your situation, having their name/badge number will be useful when you follow-up with the precinct, if you need to make a complaint.

If you are a person of color and fear that the officer's racial prejudices and/or lack of training regarding mental health crises might endanger your adult child, you can prepare for this situation by connecting with alternative community services. But if you have not yet made these alternative plans, and you are in danger, try and be the first person the officers meet at the door. Ask your son or daughter to go into their room while you talk to them.

Once you have explained the situation, the officers will decide whether they will take the person to the psychiatric emergency room or to jail. Hopefully, if no one has been hurt, and if your child has a mental illness or substance use disorder, they will be taken to the emergency room. If you are not hurt, and if you change your mind and do not want to have your child taken from the home, you still have the option to not press charges or not have them taken to the hospital.

If the police determine that your child needs to be removed from your home and that they are a threat to themselves or others, they will be placed in the hospital on a seventy-two-hour hold, during which time they will be evaluated by mental health professionals who will then decide on next steps. An emergency hold (also called a seventy-two-hour hold, a pick-up, an involuntary hold, an emergency commitment, a psychiatric hold, a temporary detention order, or an emergency petition) is a brief involuntary detention of a person presumed to have a mental illness. An emergency hold will help determine whether the individual meets the criteria for involuntary civil commitment. It does not necessarily entail involuntary treatment. Even if your adult child is involuntarily committed, this does not mean that your child will then be forced into treatment. In the United States, no one can be forced into taking antipsychotic drugs. A plea bargain deal can be made post-arrest if your adult child chooses to go into treatment in exchange for being released from prison.

If your child is taken to the emergency room or to jail, you may have conflicting feelings: guilt for calling 911 and relief that the situation has been diffused. Both feelings are understandable.

Mobile Crisis Unit

If your adult child has a history of mental illness or substance use disorder, you may find it helpful to connect with a mobile crisis unit. Available in many areas across the country, these teams are comprised of nurses, social workers, and psychiatrists who will provide mental health evaluations, primarily in your home. If you become a client of a team, the mobile crisis unit will provide crisis intervention, supportive counseling, and information and referrals to community-based mental health services. You can request help from a crisis team for a family member, or for yourself. Any of the national helplines listed in Appendix A can route you to a local mobile crisis team. A mobile crisis team is able to provide transport to the emergency room if the person in crisis needs further psychiatric or medical attention. They can only take someone to the emergency room against their will if they are a danger to themselves or others.

Mental Hygiene Warrant

In some states it is also possible to get a mental hygiene warrant, which is an order from a judge for police to transport the mentally ill person to a psychiatric emergency room. This warrant does not necessarily mean that your adult child will be hospitalized. The advantage of getting a mental hygiene order is that even though the police are involved, there is no possibility of the person being charged with a crime.

To obtain a mental hygiene order, you need to file a petition in mental hygiene court. It is a court order to direct the police to escort a person with suspected mental illness to appear before a judge. (You do not have to be related to the person to obtain the warrant.) Depending on the jurisdiction, once you have received the mental hygiene order, you must bring the document to your local police precinct. The police will come (it will look like an arrest) and take the person to the judge to see if they can be mandated for admission into an emergency psychiatric hospital for assessment.

The Court System

Every state allows you to apply for an order of protection to maintain your safety from someone who is harassing you or putting your life in danger. There are *exclusionary orders of protection* and *limited orders of protection.*

An *exclusionary order of protection* prohibits the alleged abuser from entering your home, your place of worship, or your place of work. Mothers of adult children with mental health issues or substance use disorders often are not ready to take this step, as they fear that excluding their adult child from the home may bring about more harm, perhaps even homelessness.

The other alternative, a *limited order of protection*, allows the person to remain in your home under terms stipulated by the court. If your adult child drinks or takes drugs, the order can state that they cannot be under the influence of these substances when in your house. If your son or daughter breaches these conditions, they may be arrested for violating the order of protection. This will depend, in part, on the officers who arrive on the scene. With an exclusionary order of protection, if the person violates the terms—by, for example, entering your home—it automatically becomes a criminal matter.

You may apply for an order of protection or order of exclusion and later decide that you are not ready to use it. Most social workers who will be assisting you in this process will respect your wishes. Forde, a social worker, tells the women she works with, "Whatever road you wish to go down, we're here to support you. We will work out the pros and cons of each action, but ultimately it is your decision. Today you may not be ready, but in three months from now, you can give me a call, and we'll continue to work with you to keep you safe." One psychiatrist expressed this in another way. "People have the right to make bad decisions." The only time this right is taken away from U.S. citizens is if they are at risk of hurting someone else or hurting themselves.

IMPROVING YOUR SAFETY AT HOME

Simply putting a lock inside your bedroom door may bring about some peace of mind.

You may want to also develop a safety plan for yourself in case your son or daughter becomes menacing. There are several different options:

- Ask a neighbor to call the police if they hear a disturbance coming from your home.
- Devise a code word or phrase with your neighbors, for example: Calling your neighbor and saying, "I need some milk" could be a signal that you are in trouble. Upon hearing this, the neighbor will know to call the police.

- Plan where you will go and what you will take with you if you must leave your house or apartment in an emergency. Think about where you will stay and how you will get there.
- Be ready to leave in a hurry if something dangerous happens. Visualize how you would get out of your home safely and quickly, and practice that escape route. Identify the best doors, windows, elevator, or stairwell, and familiarize yourself with this route. If something dangerous happens, you will be ready.
- Have a packed bag ready with any essentials such as medication, identification, and an emergency credit card. Consider leaving the bag at a neighbor or a friend's if the person abusing you routinely searches your things.

EVICTING YOUR CHILD

This is the hardest safety measure to enact. Evicting your child can feel "heartless," as if you are "throwing them away." A little voice may be telling you that taking this step is against everything that a "good" mother would do. There may come a time, however, when this is the only option.

One social worker told me about a woman whose son was living on the street after being evicted from her home. She tolerated the pain of her decision by keeping in mind "the utter chaos and damage that he had caused . . . along with her love for him . . . along with her desire to not live in that chaos and terror and miserable situation anymore." The woman was able to arrive at the difficult decision to evict her son after participating in a support group with other mothers who were living with the same kind of chaos and danger as she was. She saw how these women had survived the eviction of their sons or daughters. With time, she felt okay about having to draw the line. She used the analogy of a box she had drawn: "This is me and he is not here."

The eviction process is not easy, and it is not quick. Bear in mind the laws vary by state. Housing evictions are complicated, and you will need help. If you can hire an attorney, do so. There may be free legal services available in your community for housing problems. If you cannot locate an attorney—or do not want to hire one—many jurisdictions have a housing court help desk where you can get free legal advice. It's advisable to bring along a friend to help you learn all the steps that will be necessary to carry out an eviction.

In California and many other states, if you initially welcomed an adult child to live in your home and never asked him or her to pay rent, then he or she is a guest. If the welcome has worn out, you can demand that the child leave. If they refuse to leave, they are considered a trespasser. Generally, eviction is only for "tenants" or an adult child who has paid rent in the past. If your adult child has been a tenant, then you need to serve them with a "notice to quit." A parent who has been receiving rent from her adult child should also *not* accept any rent after this notice to quit is served. If the notice period has expired and the adult child has *still* not left, then the parent must file an unlawful detainer, also known as an eviction proceeding. These proceedings can be contested by your adult child and may go on for a year or more.

IF YOUR ADULT CHILD IS ARRESTED

Tragically, jails have become the de facto mental health institutions in many areas. If your loved one with a mental illness is arrested, there is conflicting advice about whether you should connect with a lawyer. Your child will be assigned a lawyer. Hopefully that lawyer will help them negotiate with the district attorney to move their case to a mental health or drug court. These courts link people who would ordinarily be prison-bound to long-term community-based treatment. You can suggest this option to your son or daughter.

A mental health or drug court seeks to address the underlying problems that contribute to criminal behavior. These specialized criminal courts for defendants with substance abuse disorders and mental illness seek to prevent future incarceration and facilitate community-based treatment, while at the same time protecting public safety. The one caveat of these courts is that your son or daughter—who is now a defendant—will have to agree to meet with the judge and abide by any plea deal that may be worked out.

A defendant who agrees to the plea deal can then be released from jail to begin court-ordered treatment. For people with mental illness, this can be injectable antipsychotic medication along with weekly counseling sessions. For persons with substance use disorders, this could be mandated treatment in a rehabilitation center for drug or alcohol use. While no mother or father wants to see their child go to jail, knowing that one positive outcome that might occur from the arrest is mandated treatment may soften guilt.

Every suggestion offered here is based on your ability to put aside your internalized blame and shame about your adult child's problems. As long as you blame yourself, as long as you allow shame to get in your way, you will be endangering yourself. You are not alone in not wanting to report the harmful situation in your home. One study found that only one out of twenty-three abusive incidents get reported. That means that twenty-two out of twenty-three incidents of older people being abused in their home are not being reported by the victims.[1]

What is standing in your way?

Chapter Eighteen

Helping Your Adult Child

Mothers of difficult adult children hope that their offspring will get the help they need to live healthy, happy lives. For some, that might take the form of court-ordered antipsychotic medication. For others, it could mean vocational training, anger management, or a drug rehab program. A mother might hope that her son will seek counseling and complete his education, that a daughter will find a good job and a safe place to live.

But where do you find that help?

And how do you get your child to accept it?

Pat Deegan, a psychologist and advocate for a recovery-based approach to treating serious mental illness, was once a sixteen-year-old girl diagnosed with "incurable" schizophrenia. She felt hopeless, withdrawn, without a future. After Pat's diagnosis, her grandmother would stop by the house each day and open the door to Pat's smoke-filled room. "Patricia, would you like to go food shopping?" she'd ask. It was a no-strings-attached invitation, simple and small. Each day her grandmother asked, and each day Pat said, "No."

> Hope looks different for everyone, but it holds within it the promise that your son or daughter will, in time, discover a better future for themselves.

Pat's grandmother would leave with a soft, "okay," and would return the next day and the day after that, always with the same question. "Patricia, would you like to go food shopping?" She was telling her granddaughter that there was a world out there and that she was a part of it. There was never any pressure, never an ultimatum. She couldn't carry Pat out the door, but she could keep reminding her of the world outside her room. A world that would be there when she was ready to face it. And one day she was ready. When her grandmother popped her head in the door and asked the now familiar question, Pat said, "Okay, but I'm not going to push the cart." That trip to the supermarket marked her re-entry into the world. It marked the start of her recovery.

Fifty years later, Dr. Pat Deegan tells family members to keep showing up with hope. This hope looks different for everyone, but it holds within it the promise that your son or daughter will, with time, discover a better future for themselves. As encouraging as that message is, family members must also live with the reality that they do not have the power to change their loved one.[1]

Recovery is about attending to the person underneath the diagnosis. Recovery occurs when a person is able to discover and cultivate "their own personal medicine," Deegan advises. The personal medicine is something that a person cares about. For Pat Deegan, her personal medicine became changing the mental health system and first becoming a psychologist. Her grandmother's quiet prodding helped her begin to see that she was more than a "schizophrenic." She was also someone who could enjoy going shopping. She had to get out of her room and start living. Personal medicine does not take the place of traditional drugs, but it is also essential.

LOCATING HELP

You can't talk your adult child into something they're not ready for. You cannot tell them what you think they should *do* and you certainly can't make your adult child *do* anything. You can, however, prepare for your child's decision to change their situation, by looking for suitable resources. Regardless of where you live, there are social services available for adults who want to be helped. If you don't know where to begin your search, there are many services listed in Appendix A. Making a call and gathering information can allow you to feel less helpless. It might also lead you to find resources and support for yourself.

Once you have gathered your information, the trick is in figuring out when to offer the resource—to recognize if your adult child might be interested or ready. The strategy used by Pat Deegan's grandmother might be a model. When sharing a pleasant lunch or television show with your son or daughter, finding a moment to casually mention in a nonconfrontational manner information you found out about—a nearby drug treatment center or counselor that a friend thought was very good. Let your son or daughter know that you are willing to share the information if they are interested. Be supportive. Be nonjudgmental. Be casual. Be prepared for them to say "no." Don't push. Just let the matter go, saying, "Okay, if you change your mind—I have the information." Then, like Pat Deegan's grandma, you can wait for another opportunity and gently try again.

Keeping the lines of communication open, regardless of how alienated or rejected you may feel, is important. You're throwing your child a lifeline, but only they can grab it.

ORGANIZING MEDICAL INFORMATION

You can help your child by acting as their advocate if they require medical treatment or hospitalization. Leslie maintained a detailed folder documenting each of her son's psychiatric and drug abuse treatments. The list included all medications that were tried and how they worked (or did not work). She made sure that when he was admitted to a new facility that the staff had this full history and understood the most recent medications he had been prescribed. Although visiting her son during psychiatric hospitalizations was always difficult—Leon would be hostile and at times violent—she continued to show up. Leslie kept the visits short; nevertheless, they let her son know that she was there for him. The visits also helped with her own peace of mind.

HOUSING

Most mothers cannot afford to provide separate housing for their adult child. With this level of financial support out of their reach, we have seen now many women open up their homes in what they believe will be a temporary solution. But sharing your home with a difficult adult child is rarely easy and can lead to numerous problems. If living with your son or daughter will be too dangerous for you, there are alternatives to inviting your adult child into your home. Options range from emergency shelters through transitional housing, to permanent housing options—supportive or otherwise. There are also group homes for people with psychiatric disabilities that are managed by the residents, community-based, and coordinated by centers for community living. Of course, as with all other solutions, your adult child has to agree to pursue these ideas, no matter how good they are. But if your home is not (or is no longer) an option, some adult children will choose a supportive housing situation if the only other options are homelessness or jail.

FINANCIAL SUPPORT

All parents question how much financial assistance to offer their adult child. "Will my helping hurt?" they ask. While it was common in the past to expect children to become financially independent at adulthood, many families today actively subsidize their adult children. Even parents of well-functioning children make temporary or even ongoing contributions to living expenses.

But when an adult child is not able to hold a job or support themselves, financial assistance is likely to be long-term and significant. Despite your wish to provide help in the form of money, there is likely to be a limit as to how much you can afford to give—and for how long. Women still lag behind men in terms of their financial security. This is particularly true in later life when events like the loss of a spouse, divorce, major health issues, limited retirement income, low-wage jobs, or unexpected expenses may leave women with limited resources. As you figure out how much, if any, financial help you can offer your adult child, you should also explore whether they might be eligible for government support.

In the United States, the Social Security Disability Insurance (SSDI) program provides income to people with documented mental illness, substance use disorder, and other disabilities, regardless of family income status. Often people get turned down upon first applying for SSDI, but persistence will pay off. There are several organizations that specialize in disability services and offer free, expert representation in helping individuals navigate the process of applying for and appealing SSDI decisions.

Adult children who have substance use disorders often pressure their mothers to provide money. This pressure can include threats of bodily harm. Takai Forde, a social worker with the Jewish Association Serving the Aging/Legal Social Work Elder Abuse Program, shared how mothers will report to her fights that have occurred between them and their substance-using adult child that have resulted in their giving in to their son or daughter's hostile demand for money for drugs. She helps the older parents to not berate themselves for giving into hostile demands for money. She empathically tells parents who feel embarrassed that they gave into their child's demand for money by telling them that many parents, like them, can get frightened and want the dispute to end. She also goes on to help them learn other ways to cope with these situations in the future.

Parents face similar dilemmas when their kids are in jail. "Do I give them money?" Each person decides this in their own way. Hope regularly deposited a small amount of money into Samantha's commissary account so that she could use it for phone calls. When Eric was incarcerated for selling drugs, however, Brenda and Anthony had given up providing any financial help to their son. They were surprised and pleased to see that while in jail, Eric was able to use his skills as a writer and a chef as bartering tools to acquire things from other inmates.

Aside from providing financial support, another way a parent can be extremely helpful to their child who is incarcerated is to engage a lawyer to help arrange an alternative to incarceration. For example, a referral to drug and mental health court may provide an opportunity for the adult child to access treatment for the issues that they are struggling with in addition to, or instead of, serving time in prison. A lawyer can be hired privately or through the public defender's office with no charge. Drug and mental health courts are available to people with mental illness and substance use disorders (post-arrest) in most states.

Forde describes how one mother was able to use this option to get her son mandated court-ordered treatment for his substance abuse. Christina had allowed her son Richard to move in with her, after his wife insisted that he move out. Richard, a drug user who had also been diagnosed with bipolar disorder several years earlier, was behaving erratically and his wife felt that he was threatening their children's safety. Once he had moved in with his mother, Richard, still using drugs, began threatening her. He threatened her for money, he threatened to burn down the apartment, and he threatened to harm himself. He blamed his mother, Christina, for his inability to interact with his kids as well as for his own drug use. Through it all, Christina gave her son the benefit of the doubt hoping he would change. She did not notify anyone in authority of Richard's violent threats. Finally, there was an incident where Richard, armed with a gun, threatened a repairman who had come into their home. In this case, Christina didn't have to call the authorities; the repairman did.

Richard was arrested, but he was released from jail the next day. He returned to his mother's house in a rage, blaming her for the arrest. He was stoned and physically assaulted her, leaving bruises on her face, arms, and shoulders. This time Christina did call the police, who took pictures of her bruises, and her son was rearrested. Because Richard had two arrests, one right after the other, he was remanded to do prison time and a bail was set that was more than he was able to pay. Christina had to acknowledge that her son had done something wrong. But she was not okay with her son merely staying in prison. She wanted him to get treatment for his mental health and addiction issues.

Christina and Forde worked with the district attorney to get Richard a hearing by a judge in the drug and mental health court. The judge was willing to offer Richard a reduced sentence if he would agree to mandated treatment for both the mental illness and the drug usage. Richard agreed, which was a positive step.

In drug and mental health court, the defendant has the right to accept the proposed plea deal and treatment plan or not. Many people refuse, but Richard agreed. He began receiving antipsychotic medication while he was in prison. After three months, his wife (who had excellent health insurance) was able to arrange a transfer for Richard from prison to a long-term drug treatment center that specialized in helping people with both mental illness and addictions. Forde was able to help Christina see that although it was upsetting to her that her son had to be put in prison, ultimately the incarceration in conjunction with the referral to mental health court had led to a positive outcome.

Helping an adult child is filled with contradictions. They are adults. You also thought you were done with active parenting. It's critical that you accept that you cannot provide everything that your now adult child needs. He or she must want to take help. Once this happens, there are many services available to help both you and your adult child.

Chapter Nineteen

What Comes Next?

When I told people that I was writing a book about older mothers, everyone assumed I meant women who gave birth when they themselves were older. This, to me, was proof that the concept of mothering adult children is not yet part of the public dialogue. Not when discussing family relationships. Not when discussing women's roles.

This is the first book to focus on older mothers with difficult adult children, a term I coined and which I hope you and others will find useful and start using. I hope to inspire a shared appreciation for and among mothers of difficult adult children, regardless of the fact that their children have different types of problems, each requiring their own unique solutions.

We've covered a lot of territory in this book. We have come to feel and know the pain and resilience of thirty-two mothers, most of whom are over sixty years old. Some are over eighty. One is fifty-seven. Their stories illuminate how aging, elder abuse, and adult children's mental illness, substance abuse, and unemployment overlap, how they can determine the trajectory of a woman's later years. It's hardly a discovery that mothers sacrifice their own needs for the sake of their children. What is news is how this sacrifice continues to affect the lives of older mothers. The women I spoke to had become the safety nets for their adult children. Regardless of their adult child's problem, they displayed a commitment to do all that they possibly could to protect their adult child and put their own needs aside. In other words, to be a "good mother."

> The concept of mothering difficult adult children must become part of the public dialogue.

Few of the women profiled in this book conform to the current depiction of "successful aging" in which women "retire" from work and parenting responsibilities and develop new hobbies, exercise more, and volunteer in their communities. Most mothers of difficult adult children do not have the energy to focus on themselves. Side by side with the relationship tensions between themselves and their struggling adult children, many of the mothers are living with feelings of disappointment and sorrow in the loss of their child's potential due to the effects of mental illness or drug/alcohol use.

WHO ARE THE MOTHERS?

The sample for my work is not a nationally representative sample, but I did intentionally include low-income, middle-income, and affluent mothers. Differences among the women include financial resources, mental health literacy, social support resources, as well as the severity of their adult children's problems. Families with large financial resources were able to house their struggling or ill daughter in a separate apartment, thus providing the parent with a day-to-day respite that other mothers did not have. Most of the mothers I spoke to face the tension of sharing a small space with grown adult children and their children who were not necessarily easy or grateful roommates.

The women's early life experiences in their families of origin and their early childrearing and work/family conflicts were also diverse. Some had raised their children in neighborhoods that were safe, filled with resources like parks and good schools, while others had lived in areas where crime and shootings were a given. Some of the mothers didn't fear calling 911 if their child became violent, while others dreaded that such a call for help could lead to the death of a daughter or son.

All had been married when they had their first child, but many have since become widowed or divorced, which meant they had to meet their adult children's struggles on their own. Despite the class and racial differences between the mothers, and the differences in their adult children's problems, I have focused on the issues that are similar and cut across these differences.

What became clear to me as I analyzed the women's journeys as mothers in later life was that it was not a reasonable question to ask if they had taken on this new responsibility out of sense of obligation versus out of love. This is a false dichotomy.[1] The mothers saw no alternative. Their children had no money. They couldn't work. Who else was going to take them in? Even if their child was thirty or forty years old, none of the women who talked with me was willing to see her child become homeless, at least in the short run.

A STRUCTURAL PROBLEM

Most everything we have witnessed in these families seems to be muddled with what seems like insoluble problems. But in my recent conversations with experts in the fields of psychiatry, aging services, elder abuse, and social services, I see glimmers of hope for the future. We have already made progress, but there is still much to be done. Throughout time, every society has struggled with the questions of what should be done for those who cannot find work. Who should take care of the mentally ill? And what about those who turn to alcohol or other drugs? What is the role of the government and of the family?

In 2021 in the United States, the richest country on the planet, mothers with difficult adult children are attempting to solve on an individual basis problems that are really structural and affect us all. Many of the mothers were providing subsidized (rent-free) housing and attempting to be the ad hoc caregivers for their mentally ill, problematic, substance-using, and unemployed adult children. Is it fair or appropriate for a twenty-first-century advanced industrial nation to be depending on older women for all this care?

Each of the women explained her "choice" to prioritize her adult child's needs over her own as based on her role as a mother. But what kind of choice is it when there are few available alternatives to house or care for dependent adult children? Yes, there are government policies aimed at serving the homeless and providing housing for the mentally ill, but these are limited and need to be expanded. The women saw themselves as the only lifeline protecting their adult children.

IF NOT ME—WHO?

Many of the women felt "if not me, who?" in terms of who else will care for and protect their vulnerable and unemployed adult children. It is important to make a distinction between caring for and caring about. *Caring about* involves affection and perhaps a sense of psychological responsibility, whereas *caring for* encompasses both the performance and supervision of concrete tasks and a sense of psychological responsibility.[2] The older mothers who have taken in their adult children are doing this because they care about them—but also having to do the caring for, when older themselves, becomes a burden and health risk for them. They are part of a larger group of unpaid and often invisible family caregivers who are providing long-term care to frail and dependent family members. This unspoken social policy of relying on women to continue to be the unrecognized and unpaid safety net promotes the oppression of women. Unpaid female caregivers do not feel valued or recognized by others for the contributions they are making. There are no subsidies for their caregiving work; nor are they being given access to family psychoeducation on mental health, drug use, or access to employment opportunities.

> The experiences and needs of family caregivers have been ignored for too long.

In several European countries, including the United Kingdom, there are hopeful changes in social policy around addiction that include government provision of services for the family members affected by their loved one's addiction, rather than just providing services for the person with the substance use disorder.[3] Here in the United States, the National Alliance of Mental Illness is growing as a support system for families with a mentally ill child, parent, or sibling. Their membership of six hundred thousand in no way yet represents the thirty-nine million family members who have a relative with a serious mental illness. The numbers of family members who have a relative with a substance use disorder are ten times that number.

ACKNOWLEDGING THE ISSUE

There is no way to know how many women are struggling with challenging adult children. There's no place where mothers with difficult adult children can gather. It's not a question on any questionnaire, and it's certainly not a topic discussed freely, without stigma or judgment. It's my hope that having a name to describe their situation will help women seek help openly and explain their struggles to friends and family. Because only by speaking out will a woman be able to dismantle her feelings of isolation and find relief—even empowerment.

> It's time to recognize those older women who are still caring for and taking care of others, despite their advanced years.

By using the term "difficult adult child," I am hoping that women family caregivers who are experiencing "difficult mothering" can come together for both emotional support and to advocate for policies that will support them and their adult children. While this book has been addressed to women because my research sample was only mothers, I am fully aware that fathers are also impacted by these same dilemmas. I hope that you, too, have been able to learn and feel acknowledged. Similarly, siblings, neighbors, and friends of mothers and fathers of difficult adult children are all part of the needed solution to change societal supports for these families.

I close this book hoping that you are now feeling less alone. Each woman who took the time to share her story with me (and with you) in the hope that someone else might be helped by her lived experience. Mothering an adult child who has significant problems is difficult. You cannot do this alone.

Resources for Mothers and Adult Children

GETTING HELP FOR YOURSELF AND YOUR ADULT CHILD

General Resources

A good starting point if you are looking for services for yourself or another older adult in your state is your local state office on aging. They are federally funded and provide grants and funding to Area Agencies on Aging (AAA) that will be local to you, and thus can provide you guidance for who to contact in your area.

To locate your nearest AAA, you can go to https://eldercare.acl.gov /Public/Index.aspx.

Hotlines and Helplines

The 988 Lifeline is a direct connection to immediate support and resources for anyone in crisis. 988, previously known as the National Suicide Prevention Lifeline, offers 24/7 call, text and chat access to trained crisis counselors who can help people experiencing suicidal, substance use, and/or mental health crisis, or any other kind of emotional distress. People can also call, text or chat 988 if they are worried about a loved one who may need crisis support. You can also visit https://suicidepreventionlifeline.org.

SAMHSA's National Helpline—1-800-662-HELP (4357)—is a free, confidential, twenty-four/seven, 365-day-a-year treatment referral and information service (in English and Spanish) for individuals and families facing mental and/or substance use disorders. Visit online at https:// www.samhsa.gov/find-help/national-helpline.

FindHelp (formerly known as Aunt Bertha) has a nationwide search tool that enables you to find resources in your area such as employment assistance, food assistance, education assistance, etc. Visit online at https://www.findhelp.org/.

Mental Health Services

This step-by-step guide created by the National Alliance on Mental Illness gives an excellent overview of how to find a mental health professional: https://www.nami.org/Your-Journey/Individuals-with-Mental-Illness/Finding-a-Mental-Health-Professional.

Community mental health clinics: Resources will vary depending on where you live. Many cities and large towns have community mental health clinics that focus on serving their local population. If you are unsure of how to find one nearby, community centers or local organizations like the YMCA are often able to connect you with what's available near you.

Here are two directories for clinics in the United States:
https://findtreatment.samhsa.gov/
https://www.nafcclinics.org/clinics/search

Psychotherapy: Here is a helpful guide on how to find a therapist: https://www.nytimes.com/2017/07/17/smarter-living/how-to-find-the-right-therapist.html.

A directory that is useful for finding therapists near you: https://www.psychologytoday.com/us/therapists.

Many therapists take insurance, but not all do. Cost can vary widely, but a therapist may charge on a sliding scale if there is financial need. You should always discuss the cost with the therapist before your first session takes place.

Online therapy: There are now many counselors that offer online-only therapy, which can sometimes be more affordable as well as easier to fit into your lifestyle. This article is a good primer on services that offer online therapy right now: https://www.nytimes.com/wirecutter /reviews/online-therapy-services/. Post-COVID 2020, many more online therapy services were created and are not reviewed in this article.

Most therapists in private practice also may offer online therapy and you can locate professionals in your area through the *Psychology Today* directory. You can also check with your insurance company for any partnerships they might have with online mental health providers, as many insurance companies have established relationships with specific telehealth and mental health providers.

SERVICES FOR PARENTS

Self-Help and Support Groups

Self-help and support groups are not psychotherapy, per se, unless they are run by a therapist in a formal group therapy structure. But they can have therapeutic qualities and help you to process your experiences while receiving mutual support.

You can do a general search for support groups in your area through *Psychology Today*: https://www.psychologytoday.com/us/groups.

Here are some support groups that are established nationally and/or worldwide:

- NAMI Connection Recovery Support Group is a support group for adults who have experienced mental illness. There are groups all over the United States, and you can find your closest group here: https:// www.nami.org/Find-Your-Local-NAMI/Affiliate/Programs?classke y=a1x36000003TN9TAAW.

- NAMI Family Support Group is a support group for adults with a loved one who has experienced mental illness. There are groups all over the United States and you can find your closest group here: https://www.nami.org/Find-Your-Local-NAMI/Affiliate/Programs?c lasskey=a1x36000003TN9LAAW.

- *Al-Anon* is a support group for parents, family, and friends of alcoholics, regardless of whether their child or loved one is in recovery. It is a worldwide organization with meetings available in every

state. You can find meetings online at https://al-anon.org/al-anon
-meetings/find-an-al-anon-meeting/ or by calling 1-888-4AL-ANON
(1-888-425-2666).

• Alcoholics Anonymous and Narcotics Anonymous are twelve-step
groups for people recovering from alcohol or drug addiction. Be sure
to find a group that understands the role of mental health treatment in
recovery. You can find listings for meetings near you at https://www
.aa.org/pages/en_US/find-aa-resources or by calling (800) 839-1686
for twenty-four-hour assistance.

• Smart Recovery is a sobriety support group for people with a va-
riety of addictions that is *not* based in faith. (Alcoholics Anonymous and Narcotics Anonymous believe in surrendering to a "higher
power"; members can choose how they define their higher power.)

• Double Trouble in Recovery is a twelve-step fellowship for people
managing both a mental illness and substance use disorders. Many
states have agencies that support these peer groups . See Kentucky,
for example; https://dtrky.org/.

• Depression and Bipolar Support Alliance offers many online support
groups, including specialized ones for friends, family, and caregivers.
You can find more information here: https://www.dbsalliance.org
/support/chapters-and-support-groups/online-support-groups/.

You can also start your own support group based on needs and af-
finities. Finding other participants who might be interested can happen
through word of mouth, community organizations, senior centers, or
online message boards.

Advocacy Groups: Changing the Mental Health System

There are many ways you can get involved and connect with other
families who are engaged in efforts to improve the US mental health
system. Here are a few.

• Schizophrenia and Psychosis Action League https://sczaction.org/
• Shattering the Silence https://www.nationalshatteringsilencecoalition
.org/
• Treatment Advocacy Center https://www.treatmentadvocacycenter.org/

STAYING SAFE

Adult Protective Services: At some point you may need to contact Adult Protective Services (APS) on your or someone else's behalf to get services and prevent further abuse. To find your local APS, you can use this interactive map: https://www.napsa-now.org/get-help/help-in-your-area/.

National Domestic Violence Hotline at 1-800-799-7233 or or https://www.thehotline.org/.

The National Domestic Violence hotline also has a list of domestic violence resources by state: https://www.thehotline.org/get-help/domestic-violence-local-resources/.

Elder abuse shelters: In New York City, The Weinberg Center for Elder Justice has a shelter dedicated to victims of elder abuse. For more information, you can go here: https://theweinbergcenter.org/. The Spring Alliance is a network of elder abuse shelters across the United States. https://www.springalliance.org/.

Legal assistance: The federal government provides grants to many states for the provision of free legal assistance to seniors. In New York City, the Department for the Aging can connect seniors to free legal services. See NY State, for example, https://www1.nyc.gov/site/dfta/services/legal-help.page. A useful guide for legal resources for women in need, state-by-state, can be found here: https://www.womenslaw.org/find-help.

Legal Aid societies across the United States provide pro bono legal services. A directory of those societies can be found at https://www.lsc.gov/what-legal-aid/find-legal-aid.

The American Bar Association has a Free Legal Answers virtual clinic, which can be found here: https://abafreelegalanswers.org/.

Fraud

If you have been the victim of financial abuse or fraud, here are agencies to contact for information: https://www.womenshealth.gov/relationships-and-safety/other-types/financial-abuse.

This article describes the problem of financial abuse along with a list of resources for getting help: https://www.wiserwomen.org/fact-sheets /women-retirement-the-facts-and-statistics/women-and-financial -fraud-abuse/.

Drafting Powers of Attorney to Deter Exploitation: https://www .findlaw.com/legalblogs/estate-planning/how-to-prevent-power-of -attorney-abuse/.

Protecting Your Home: If you are in need of legal services related to housing, there is free legal help in most states. https://www.stateside legal.org/lso. In NYC you can contact Legal Aid: https://www.legal aidnyc.org/get-help/housing-problems/.

There are housing laws that protect survivors of abuse which vary state by state, here is a compendium of those laws for each state: https://nnedv.org/resources-library/h_state-housing-laws-survivors/ or call 1-800-994-9662.

LGBTQ Resources

Sage is an advocacy organization for LGBTQ older adults. Their website is https://www.sageusa.org, and they have a national helpline: 877-360-LGBT.

Callen-Lorde has a crisis text line for the LGBTQ community. You can text callenlorde to 741741 or go here for more information: https:// callen-lorde.org/helpnow/.

Centerlink has an interactive map of LGBT centers in the United States and worldwide: https://www.lgbtcenters.org/LGBTCenters.

The *Trans Lifeline* provides peer support for the trans community. Their helpline is 877-565-8860 and their website is translifeline.org.

Senior Centers

Senior centers can be a conduit for resources in your community, and they often have trained social workers on staff who can help connect you to people and programs in your community and beyond. Many also have support groups and/or offer counseling onsite.

A directory of senior centers in the United States can be found here: https://seniorcenter.us/.

Many senior centers are a part of a local AAA (Area Agency on Aging), which receive federal, state, and/or municipal money to administer services to older adults. In order to find an AAA or senior services near you, you can use the Eldercare locator: https://eldercare.acl.gov/Public/Index.aspx or call (800) 677-1116.

Yoga and Exercise

Yoga and exercise can be effective interventions for stress management and relief, as well as help elevate your mood. The YMCA has a comprehensive YouTube channel with free videos guiding you through all kinds of exercise: https://www.youtube.com/channel/UCnMjjYuia JZT7JilnXPo7jQ.

Long-Term Planning for Dependent Adult Children

How do I create a long-term care plan for my loved one who is living with a serious mental illness?
What are the considerations when developing a life care plan?

- https://www.specialneedsalliance.org/special-needs-101/life-care-planning/
- https://www.nami.org/Blogs/NAMI-Blog/December-2020/What-Is-a-Pooled-Special-Needs-Trust

Some other useful resources are:

- Legal and Financial Planning Resources Special Needs Alliance: www.specialneedsalliance.org https://www.specialneedsalliance.org/special-needs-101/life-care-planning/
- National Academy of Elder Law Attorneys: www.naela.org
- ABLE National Resource Center: www.ablenrc.org
- The Arc's Center for Future Planning: https://futureplanning.thearc.org/

(Please note that while it is a website designed to assist the families of those with intellectual and developmental disabilities, many of the tools can be of assistance to the families of those with severe mental illness)

RESOURCES FOR ADULT CHILDREN

Government Financial Benefits

Applying for Supplemental Security Income

Social Security Disability Insurance (SSDI) and Supplemental Security Income (SSI) provide needed financial assistance to people in the United States who have mental health conditions. Both programs are run by the Social Security Administration (SSA).

SSDI provides monthly income to individuals who are limited in their ability to work because of a physical or mental disability. The SSA uses its own definitions of disability and its own diagnostic criteria for determining whether an individual has a certain disability. SSI provides financial assistance to low-income, disabled individuals. While SSDI requires a disability and minimum past work requirements, SSI requires disability and financial need, determined by income and current assets.

While you may not be able to collect Social Security retirement income as a noncitizen, you may still be able to qualify for SSI or SSDI as a noncitizen if you fulfill other eligibility requirements. You can look up eligibility on the SSA website, www.ssa.gov, or or inquire with a local community organization that can help facilitate your application.

Resources for Applying for Supplemental Security Income

SSA: SSA is an agency that administers and manages Social Security application process (SSI and SSDI). Applicants are often denied the first time they apply and should file an appeal if they feel they are eligible. Contact at (800) 772-1213 or www.ssa.gov.

National Organization of Social Security Claimants Representatives: Provides referrals to (fee for service) representation for persons (twenty-one and older) seeking SSDI and SSI. Contact at (845) 682-1880 or www.nosscr.org.

National Association of Disability Representatives: Offers referral services for (fee for service) lawyers and nonlawyer representatives who can assist in accessing SSI/SSDI. Contact at (800) 747-6131 or www.nadr.org.

Help with Medical Bills

Many hospital bills are negotiable if you are unable to pay them. A good place to start is with calling the hospital's billing or finance department and tell them that you are in need of financial assistance, then find out what paperwork they have that you can fill out to prove this. While it will not make your bills go away, it could help to reduce them substantially.

Applying for Medicaid

Eligibility for Medicaid, and how you apply, can vary state by state because of variations in the application of the Affordable Care Act within each state. The best way to find out if you are eligible is by visiting Medicaid.gov or your state's Healthcare Exchange website. Many states have serviced Medicaid plans, and those providers can help facilitate your Medicaid application.

This page has a list of Healthcare Exchange websites by state: https://www.healthcare.gov/marketplace-in-your-state/.

This page has a calculator which will show you if you are eligible for Medicaid in your state: https://www.healthcare.gov/lower-costs/.

Supportive Low-Cost or Government-Supported Housing

The National Alliance on Mental Illness has a useful online guide for finding supportive housing, focusing on what to look for in supportive housing and where to find it: https://www.nami.org/Your-Journey/Individuals-with-Mental-Illness/Finding-Stable-Housing.

If you are in need of immediate housing or shelter, a national directory of homeless shelters can be found here: https://www.homelessshelterdirectory.org/.

Section 811 is a government program with low-cost supportive housing program for people living with disabilities: http://portal.hud.gov/hudportal/HUD?src=/program_offices/housing/mfh/progdesc/disab811.

The Department of Housing and Urban Development Resource Locator displays an online network of affordable housing options, housing for individuals with special needs, homeless resources, and many other housing-related options in your area. You can go to https://resources.hud.gov or call (800) 569-4287.

You can find your local Public Housing Agency by using the Department of Housing and Urban Development Public Housing and Resource Center. Your Public Housing Agency provides referrals for subsidies, information, and guidance for Section 8 voucher holders and public housing residents. Contact at https://www.hud.gov/program_offices /public_indian_housing/pha/contacts or call (800) 955-2232.

Food Assistance

United Way operates a twenty-four-hour help line that connects callers to local food programs, housing assistance, health care resources, and mental health support. You can dial 211 from your phone or go to https://www.unitedway.org/local/united-states.

Food Finder is a directory of food pantries and soup kitchens across the United States: https://foodfinder.us/.

FoodPantries.org also has a similar list: foodpantries.org.

MENTAL HEALTH SERVICES AND JOB PROGRAMS

Individual Counseling or Psychotherapy

Assertive Community Treatment

Assertive Community Treatment is an intensive, integrated approach to community mental health service delivery. Mental health services are provided by a team of mental health professionals in a community setting (rather than a more restrictive residential or hospital setting) to people experiencing serious mental illness. You will need a referral which can be obtained at a local mental health clinic, community organization, or psychiatric hospital. The SAMHSA Treatment Locator can help you find an ACT team: (800) 662-4357 or https://findtreatment .samhsa.gov/.

Court-ordered Treatment (Assisted Outpatient Treatment; AOT) is for persons with serious mental illness who are in danger to themselves or others and are refusing treatment. A court order is issued for involuntary hospitalization. AOT can be difficult to obtain and the process varies from state to state. See https://www.treatmentadvocacycenter.org/aot

Clubhouses for Persons with Mental Illness

A Clubhouse is a voluntary day program organized to support people living with mental illness. Many large cities have Clubhouses. Members gain access to opportunities to socialize, find employment, and education. https://clubhouse-intl.org/what-we-do/what-clubhouses-do/

Job Counseling

The National Alliance on Mental Illness has an excellent page with guidance on how to succeed at work while living with severe mental illness. You can find it here: https://www.nami.org/Your-Journey /Individuals-with-Mental-Illness/Succeeding-at-Work.

SourceAmerica is a leading source for job opportunities for those with disabilities. They have many affiliated agencies, and you can use this tool to find the closest one to you: www.sourceamerica.org/nonprofit-locator.

abilityJOBS is also a source for job opportunities. www.abilityjobs.com.

Getting Hired is a search engine connecting people with companies looking to hire people with disabilities: www.gettinghired.com. They can also be reached by phone at (866) 352-7481.

JobsForFelonsHub offers information and resources for former felons, including expungement services, employment services, housing, legal representation. www.jobsforfelonshub.com.

Career One Stop: A service of the U.S. Department of Labor that provides resources and guides for career exploration, training, as well as jobs availability sorted by location and job type. Call 877-872-5627 or go to www.careeronestop.org.

Goodwill Services: Many local Goodwill Care centers provide job training/career services and employment opportunities by location: www. goodwill.org/jobs-training/find-a-job.

Consumer-Driven Services

National Mental Health Consumer's Self-Help Clearinghouse is a nationwide directory to locate local consumer-driven mental health services, including resources such as clubhouses, crisis prevention/respite services, drop-in centers, employment resources, housing, and peer case management and support: http://www.mhselfhelp.org/.

Guardianship

It is possible that at some point you may need to obtain guardianship and/or conservatorship over your loved one in order to guide their care. Guardianship is a legal process utilized when a person can no longer make or communicate safe or sound decisions about their person and/ or property or has become susceptible to fraud or undue influence. Because establishing a guardianship may remove considerable rights from an individual, it should only be considered after alternatives to guardianship have proven ineffective or are unavailable. Guardianship laws vary by state, and in many cases by the locality in which you may be seeking Guardianship.

You can find more information on the guardianship process here: https://www.guardianship.org/what-is-guardianship/

The Special Needs Alliance is an organization that provides additional information on the guardianship process as well as legal referrals to attorneys skilled in this area: https://www.specialneedsalliance.org/.

Each state's process and laws surrounding civil commitment differ. You can find information on civil commitment laws in each state here: https://www.treatmentadvocacycenter.org/component/content /article/183-in-a-crisis/1596-know-the-laws-in-your-state.

Substance Use Treatment

Treatments for substance abuse vary. In general, they fall into the following categories: long-term and short-term residential treatment, outpatient treatment, individualized drug counseling, group counseling, and twelve-step programs. Many treatment programs incorporate the twelve-step model, but not all. Some information on how to differentiate these programs can be found here: https://www.drugabuse.gov/publications/ principles-drug-addiction-treatment-research-based-guide-third-edition/ drug-addiction-treatment-in-united-states/types-treatment-programs.

Often the best way to find a rehabilitative treatment program that works for you is through referrals from your primary care doctor, psychiatrist, or therapist as they will be familiar with programs in your community as well as what your health insurance might cover. Here are some general resources for substance abuse and intervention:

- *SAMHSA Treatment Locator:* SAMSHA is a federal agency that provides referrals for the different treatment facilities across the United States. They offer a search tool that allows you to narrow your search by insurance, cost of treatment, and type of treatment. Good for low cost/sliding scale mental healthcare, substance abuse and dual diagnosis facilities. Spanish-language calls accepted. (800) 662-4357 / https://findtreatment.samhsa.gov/

- *AddictionResource:* Website providing information and resources and a treatment finder to help those recovering from addiction and their loved ones to find the highest quality care. (844) 905-0277 / www.addictionresource.com

- *In the Rooms:* Online social network for the global recovery community—for those already in recovery or seeking immediate help from addiction, and for families and allies of those individuals. Free to join; members have access to over 129 live online meetings, weekly. www.intherooms.com

- *SMART Recovery:* A substance use self-help program using cognitive behavioral therapy approaches to recover from addictive behaviors. Provides free, peer-led online and in-person support groups for individuals and family members/allies of those living with addiction. (440) 951-5357 / www.smartrecovery.org

- *Start Your Recovery:* Offers information about the signs, symptoms, conditions, and treatment options for people who are dealing with substance use issues, as well as resources for others who know someone struggling with addiction and a treatment locator tool. Website offers a "Find a Local Rehab Center," counseling and in-person support groups function. www.startyourrecovery.org

Alcohol

NIAA Alcohol Treatment Navigator: Website provides extensive information on alcohol use, how to help someone with an alcohol addiction, treatment facility finder, and guidance on how to find and choose the best treatment options. www.alcoholtreatment.niaaa.nih.gov

Alcoholics Anonymous: Twelve-step program for individuals who believe they are living with an alcohol addiction; website offers daily reflections, videos, and a find an in-person support group meeting feature as well as online intergroup/support groups. https://www.aa.org/

Al-Anon/Al-Ateen: Offers support and hope for family and friends of individuals (including teen-specific resources) abusing alcohol. Website offers find an in-person support group meeting feature; also offers phone and online meetings. (888) 425-2666 (Meeting Line) / www.al-anon.alateen.org

Partnership for Drug-Free Kids: Supports families and caregivers in a supporting role in the life of a young person struggling with drug or alcohol use. The organization offers information, resources, peer support (parent coaching, phone-based support) and a HelpLine (855-378-4373). www.drugfree.org

Therapy Insider's Sober Living Homes Locator: Mental and behavioral health directory website with access to sober living homes—independently owned and operated homes designed for young people who are serious about sobriety. These homes are an aftercare stage of rehabilitation providing enhanced support. The best sober living homes charge a fee for rent, food, and counseling. Each home has its own unique set of house rules, shared responsibilities, and member expectations. www.therapyinsider.com/g/Sober-Living-Homes/

Narcotics

Narcotics Anonymous: Offers recovery from the effects of narcotics addiction through twelve-step program, including regular attendance at group meetings. Website offers a find an in-person support group meeting feature. (818) 773-9999 x771 / www.na.org

Nar-Anon: Designed to help relatives/friends of addicts recover from the effects of coping with a narcotics-addicted relative or friend. Website offers find an in-person support group meeting feature. (800) 477-6291 / www.nar-anon.org

Dual Recovery Anonymous Resource Center: A twelve-step self-help membership organization for individuals with a dual diagnosis. Their website helps people find an in-person support group meeting search function on its website. www.draonline.org

Centers for Independent Living is a consumercontrolled, community-based, crossdisability, nonresidential private nonprofit agency that is designed and operated within a local community by individuals with disabilities and provides an array of independent living services. https://www.ilru.org/projects/cil-net/cil-center-and-association-directory

Advocacy organizations to influence substance use policies. Here are a few:

* Community Anti-drug Community Associatons of America; CADCA https://www.cadca.org/
* Drug Policy Alliance https://drugpolicy.org/about/
* Shatterproof https://www.shatterproof.org/

Appendix B

Research Methodology

Difficult: Mothering Challenging Adult Children through Conflict and Change is based on an empirical qualitative research study. The research was conducted as part of my work at Fordham University. The study was approved by the Fordham University Intuitional Review Board. The women's confidentiality is protected. All identifying information has been omitted unless specific permission was granted to use actual names. Several professional articles have been published from this study.[1] For the book, I expanded my focus and did additional interviews beyond the initial study sample. All the key ideas in the book are drawn from, and based on, the findings of the research study.

Recruitment for the research study was carried out in two parts, locating first low-income women and then nonpoor, middle-class, and affluent women. The first part targeted low-income women (less than 150 percent of the official poverty threshold; $21,960 for family of three in 2021 dollars) and the second wave sought out nonpoor women (greater than 300 percent of the poverty threshold; $65,880 for a family of three in 2021 dollars). The low-income women were recruited in senior centers and in trade union associations for retired workers in the New York City metro area. Nonpoor and affluent women for the study were recruited through outreach done in both the New York area and on a national basis, using personal contacts and outreach to mental health professionals, in addition to a nationally broadcast radio interview and a webinar for elder abuse professionals.

The in-person recruitment included my giving a ten-minute talk to the seniors about my study. I asked who in the audience was a parent and what they remembered about the problems of parenting their children when they were one year old, three years old, and fifteen years old. The audience shouted out various things such as teething, sleep, drugs, and problems in school (for the adolescents). I then asked what kinds of problems do their forty-year-old kids have? Fewer folks were vocal about their adult children but some suggested drug problems and unemployment. I then explained that I was doing a research study that hoped to understand from mothers the kinds of problems that their older "kids" face.

In each site, a small group of women chose to share their contact information. Follow-up phone screenings were conducted to determine if each interested woman met the study's eligibility requirements: Willing to share income data, sixty-two years of age or older, parent of at least one biological child and the self-identified mother of a child who the mother saw as "difficult," but who had some period of independence from parents.

The interviews I conducted were open-ended dialogues about the woman's experience with mothering her adult child who she believed was having problems. All the interviews were carried out by me. I prefaced the interviews by talking about myself as an older woman/mother and my realization that mothering did not end when the child was twenty. As the women shared their often-painful stories, I was careful to separate out my own experiences as a mother from what I was learning from the interviewees—I did this by writing memos about the issues that could bias the interviewer's (i.e., my own) analyses.[2]

Based on the literature that has shown how mothers feel stigmatized or blamed for their adult children's problems, the women were interviewed two times. The first interview focused on women's early mothering when their children were young to allow the women to discuss less conflictual material before focusing on the problems that emerged in adulthood. This also was a way for me to learn the possible timeline of the mother's ambivalence in her feelings about her child and maternal role. The second interview focused exclusively on the current situation with the "difficult" adult child. I used prompts based on themes that emerged in the first interview. (A few women [three] were only interviewed one time and their interviews were included in the analysis.) I began the second interview with a more open-ended question: "Pretend you are creating a movie—Tell me the story of your relationship with _____ since right before the first time he/she moved out of your house. What have been the high points and what have been the low points." This question is based on McAdams's life story approach and allowed the women to narrate the development of stress between themselves and their children in the way that presented how they saw the timing or chapters in their parenting career without the researcher imposing an order.[3]

After interviewing and analyzing the transcripts of the first eight women subjects, based on theoretical sampling,[4] I recruited additional women for the study who had contacted elder services for legal or supportive counseling to manage situations with their adult children. This decision was made after analyzing the second interview conducted with a woman from the senior center population that revealed that this mother's needs were being seriously neglected by her children and Adult Protective Services (APS) had been called in to help her. I had coded her upset with her daughter as "role violation," a code that had emerged in many of the previous interviews related to the women's upset that her children did not treat her with the respect that she believed she was due as the mother. Upon learning that APS had been called to investigate this woman's situation with her adult daughter, I realized that there was an overlap between mothers who were potentially at risk for abuse or neglect and those who were not. Based on this discovery, a decision was made to include a sub-sample of women who had reported being abused by their adult children to compare the two groups. Analysis and subject recruitment were concluded once meaning saturation was achieved.[5]

ANALYTIC METHOD

The data was analyzed using constructivist grounded theory.[6] Initial codes were created that identified the mother's positive or negative feelings about her child, her role, and their relationship, as well as her presentation of the adult child's problematic behaviors. Vignettes that illustrated mixed, conflicting, or back-to-back positive and negative feelings were coded as ambivalent. Initial codes led over time to focused coding. Comparisons across cases and within cases was done.

Memos were written throughout the project on emerging theoretical ideas. Several research questions guided the coding and analysis. The first was how does the woman describe her role as a mother of an adult child? What situations create conflict for her in this role? The second question was what types of situations are linked with the mothers' expressions of negative (and/or positive) appraisal or negative (and/or positive) emotions when talking about their adult child. A third question was how do the mothers' stories convey their personal explanations for their adult children's problems.

RESULTS

Twenty-nine American women were interviewed: 40 percent were poor (total income less than 150 percent of the poverty threshold) and half were minority (three Hispanic and eleven Black). Racial differences were associated with income and education. Among those who were poor, 75 percent were Black or Hispanic. Among those who were nonpoor, 16 percent were Black or Hispanic. Within the group of poor women, 70 percent had experienced some form of abuse, compared to 50 percent of the nonpoor women. Median age of the low-income mothers was sixty-seven and 66.5 for the nonpoor. The median age of the adult children among the low-income women was forty-two compared to 32.5 for the nonpoor. A third of the final sample had sought help from the elder abuse service community.

While all the adult children had left the parental home in late adolescence or early adulthood, problems or transitions in the adult child's life led to a change in the mother's life when she responded to her adult child's renewed need for support. All the women (except for two) had willingly reopened their home to provide shelter to their adult children for some period of time. The issues in the adult children's lives that had led to their need for shelter included mental health and substance abuse problems, and/or relationship break-ups or loss of employment that interfered with the adult child's ability to afford housing. Many of the adult children had remained living with their mothers for many years once they returned home.

Using the theoretical model of intergenerational ambivalence, three types of structural ambivalence were discovered: mothers' reactions to their adult children's behaviors that violate expectations for reciprocity, women's dismayed reactions to their adult children's aggressive behaviors toward themselves as their mothers, and the women's struggle regarding balancing their role as a mother to protect their adult children alongside their wish and identified needs for self-care. All the conflicts were expressed within the frame of their role of mother. The internalized mandate to be a "good mother" resulted in many experiencing shame, self-blame, and guilt, and this self-blame was an obstacle to reaching out for help.

Appendix C

The Mothers

Ada (eighty; African American; high school graduate; *son, Harold*). Ada and her husband had been living with and struggling with the behavior of their adult son, Harold, who was diagnosed with schizophrenia in his late twenties. Their lives changed course when Ada was taken to the hospital, after she was injured by a bottle Harold had thrown at her during a disagreement. Harold was taken off to Rikers Island. A few months later, a social worker helped Ada and Harris connect with the district attorney to have Harold's sentence lifted if he agreed to enter court-ordered treatment, which he did. Ada also agreed to attend an elder abuse workshop and counseling services, which she did.

Alana (sixty-four; Caucasian; graduate studies; *daughter, Deborah*) was living again with her daughter Deborah, with whom she has been fighting since primary school. Deborah had attention-deficit/hyperactivity disorder and a bad temper, according to Alana. While Alana has investigated moving away from New York City in order to afford herself some "peace and quiet" away from the constant mother-daughter fights, she does not feel that she can abandon her daughter who she believes will not survive without her.

Brenda (sixty-seven, Caucasian; graduate studies; *son, Eric*), a schoolteacher, was getting ready to retire. She had lived her entire life with her husband in a small suburban community where she and her husband raised her two boys. Surprised when their son informed them that he and the mother of his child were separating, they agreed that he and his young son could come back to live with them. Everything changed when they learned that he was shooting heroine. After two years of supporting him through methadone treatment, they were shocked to learn that he was using again. This time, they evicted him from their home. Their grandson returned to live with his mother. They tolerated the shame of having Eric's addiction become public, as he was living downtown dealing drugs. She told me, "Eric is still my child. I haven't given up on him," but added that her hope was that he would eventually use his excellent brain and deal with his addiction. Brenda got lucky. In prison, Eric "saw the light" and was able to give his drug life.

Corrine (seventy-eight; Hispanic; graduate studies; *daughter, Alyssa*) was a successful lawyer, as was her daughter, Alyssa. Corrine's family history included a father, grandfather, and husband, who all were alcoholics. Her daughter's law career was being ruined by her drinking problem. When she could not support herself, Corrine allowed her daughter to move back in with her. Alyssa, on several occasions, intoxicated, became violent and struck out at her mother. Corrine received help from elder abuse services and obtained legal orders of protection form her daughter. But each time Alyssa became ill again, without a place to live, Corrine opened her home as a refuge for her daughter.

Durene (seventy-two; African American; college graduate; *son, Caleb*) brought her her son back home to live with her after he had his first psychiatric break while in college. Caleb has lived in his mother's house now for more than twenty years, except for brief periods of homelessness when Durene insisted he move out. He has had several hospitalizations. When he threated Durene with a knife, during an altercation, she called the police, which connected her with help from elder abuse services. They helped her arrange wellness checks from the police department. Her friends and family wished that she would throw him out because they fear for her safety, but she fears more for her son's safety. She does not believe he will survive being homeless.

Ellen (sixty-two; Caucasian; graduate studies; *daughter, Sarah*) interrupted her professional career in finance to be available to her daughter who suffered from extreme anxiety starting in middle school. Despite her daughter's intellectual promise, her emotional and perhaps cognitive processing issues interfered with her ability to stay in college or to develop a profession in which she could be fully self-supporting. Sarah works part-time at minimum wage jobs. Her parents pay her rent. The parents continue to search for new therapies that they hope might help Sarah to have a more satisfying life.

Esther (sixty-three; African American; high school graduate; *son, Reginald*) had moved from the West Indies to New York City for work twenty years ago and now wanted to move back home. She is delaying this move until her son, Reginald, gets back on his feet and obtains a green card. He had moved in with her after a romantic relationship ended. Reginald was out of work, smoking marijuana, and seemed depressed. She was embarrassed that her son, at older than thirty years, was dependent on her and had not succeeded in forming his own family as an independent person. She saw his dependency on her as violating scripture which stress that the child should become separate from his parents.

Faith (eighty; African American; some college; *daughter, Ebony; grandson, Lester*) described herself as at a "crossroads." Her blood pressure was too high, and her doctor believed she had to change her lifestyle to include less stress. Faith knew that continuing to live with her adult daughter and grandson was becoming too much for her. Both of them had mental health challenges. Negotiating living in a small space together was very demanding for everyone. Faith worried that if she prioritized her own health and asked them to leave before they could stand on their own two feet she would not be able to forgive herself if anything happened to them.

Francine (seventy-five; African American; some high school; *daughter, Lillian*) had three children, two of whom were living with her, as well as her grandson. Her daughter, Lillian, had serious emotional problems and would become argumentative and even physically attack her mother, leaving bruises and scars. While Francine had sought help from an agency for seniors, she would not consider having her daughter evicted from her home. She felt tremendous guilt that she had not been a good enough mother to Lillian when she was a girl. Instead of protecting her daughter from sexual abuse, she had ignored the situation.

The social worker, mindful of how hard it was for Francine to protect herself from Lillian, was willing to work with her on small steps to keep herself safe.

Gabriella (sixty-six; Caucasian; high school graduate; *daughter, Maria*) grew up in a strict home where she witnessed domestic violence. She married someone who was mentally ill and used drugs. As a mother, she also used harsh discipline when raising her daughters. Gabriella felt enormous sadness that her daughter had "followed in my footsteps" and married a man who also had many problems. He was abusive and involved in criminal behavior. Gabriella's grandson, Maria's son, at age eighteen also used violence when upset. Gabriella fears that he may hurt his mother, her daughter.

Georgia (seventy; African American; some high school; *son, Desmond*) had allowed both of her sons to move back in with her when they became unemployed. Disrespectful toward her, they would "say whatever came into their heads." Neither was paying rent, even though they worked on and off. She had asked them to leave numerous times but did not want to use legal means of eviction because of her fear that something "bad" might happen to them if they had to live on the streets. One day in anger, she obtained a reverse mortgage on her co-op apartment, which later she realized had been a scam and a financial mistake.

Greta (sixty-six; Caucasian; high school graduate; *son, Anthony*). Greta's son started having behavioral problems at a very young age. She described her husband as a "bum." They divorced early on. While raising her son, Greta had to miss many days of work taking Anthony to therapists and special schools. He started using and selling drugs in his teens, got arrested, and has been in and out of prison ever since. Last year, when released from prison, Greta allowed him to come back to live with her. Within one week, he had stolen from her, broken his parole, and was back in prison, now serving a very long sentence.

Hope (sixty-eight; Caucasian; graduate studies; *daughter, Samantha*), an artist and art teacher, described her struggle as trying to stop herself from continually getting hurt and disappointed by her daughter, Samantha. Hope had lived through periods during which her daughter was using drugs and living on the streets, alternating with her being in jail, and times when she was free from using drugs. Hope participated in self-help groups sponsored by Al-Anon and Nar-Anon, which are similar to Alcoholics Anonymous, but for the relatives of people with drug and alcohol problems. In Al-Anon Hope learned the importance of letting go of unrealistic expectations regarding the relationship with her daughter.

Iris (sixty-eight; Caucasian; some college; *daughter, Fern*) regretted that she had not realized the seriousness of her daughter's teenaged behavioral problems. At twenty-one, Fern left home, married, had children, but soon became very ill with serious mental illness. Her illness interfered with being able to stay married, and she moved back home with Iris. One day, Fern struck her mother during an altercation. Iris, shocked and hurt, told her to leave and never come back. Now homeless, Fern continued to live in the same small community as her mother. Iris felt helpless witnessing her daughter's destructive lifestyle. She made the decision to move away. She wanted to enjoy the last part of her life in peace.

Jade (eighty; African American; some college; *daughter, Lacey*). Jade's daughter had been diagnosed with schizophrenia and had been living with her on and off. A year ago, Lacey became violent and attacked her mother, including trying to choke her. Jade was able to lock herself briefly into a bathroom and call for help. The police took Lacey to the hospital and connected the mother with an elder abuse social worker, who helped her assess whether she felt safe having her daughter return home after the hospitalization. She said that she would only feel safe if her daughter was no longer living with her. Jade decided to have the locks changed and get a legal order prohibiting her daughter from moving back in.

Jillian (seventy-seven, Caucasian; graduate studies; *daughter, Celia*) reported that she was "bleeding inside" from the twenty-plus years of rescuing her daughter from one crisis after another. Celia had her first psychiatric break after completing college. Her husband of fifty years was a supportive partner and a successful lawyer. They always had the financial resources to rent or purchase an apartment near them for Celia to live in that was safe. Being able to afford housing Celia in her own apartments allowed them to avoid the strains of having to live with her. Despite these financial resources, Jillian described her life, at age seventy-seven, as being on a rope, forever tied to her daughter's crises.

Lenore (sixty; Caucasian; some high school; *daughter, Cinda*) had an abusive relationship with her daughter's father. After he died from an overdose, her daughter, Cinda, also became volatile and abusive toward Lenore. Two years ago, after being hurt during one of their fights, Lenore sought legal and counseling help from an agency supporting seniors. Cinda moved out into a boyfriend's apartment. Lenore contacted the agency again when she felt at a loss about how to handle her daughter's stealing from her each time that she would visit.

Leslie (fifty-seven; Caucasian; graduate studies; *son, Leon*). Leslie's son had his first depressive episode when he was sixteen. The next twelve years of Leon's and the family's life included twenty-one psychiatric hospitalizations, three residential drug treatment centers, and four different group homes. Leslie does not foresee her son ever recovering from his psychiatric illness. Leslie's life was transformed when she attended a National Association for Mental Illness workshop, six years into her son's illness. There, she was asked what types of advocacy work she might like to do. This question inspired her. She now works full-time educating politicians and their staff on the types of mental health care policies that are needed in order to protect people with serious mental illness. She has turned her grief into a life based on public service, building a better future for others.

Loretta (eighty-two, African American; high school graduate; *son, Jason*) is still an active member of her church and her local community association. These two organizations were important supports to her during the years in which her son was trying to evict her from her own home. Jason believed that the house should be his, despite having no legal grounds for his claim. Loretta's story illustrates how hard it is on both a legal and personal level to have one's adult child removed form one's home.

Lucy (sixty-five; Hispanic; college graduate; *son, Carlos*) felt proud about the way she had raised her children, for many years as a divorced single parent. She had a strong support network of friends, one of whom became her confidant with whom she could share her anger and disappointment with about her son, Carlos. The "difficulty" she reported to me with her son was about her disappointment in the man that her son had become. She called him "selfish." It angered her that now that her son was successful financially, he still would not help his mother, financially, while she supported his daughter.

Margie (sixty-three; Caucasian; college graduate; *son, Jeremy*) was a recent widow. Her son, twenty-eight years old, lost his job during the COVID pandemic. Depressed and without a way to pay for his own apartment, he returned to live with his mother. Living together in a very small apartment, the tensions between them kept growing. Jeremy threatened to both kill his mother and kill himself. Margie, terrified, called 311, not knowing what to do or where to turn. She connected with an elder abuse agency, where she learned ways to keep herself safe if similar incidents reoccurred. She had never considered herself an "elder" nor a victim of abuse.

Marsha (seventy; African American; college graduate; *daughter, Melanie*). Marsha's youngest daughter Melanie had been laid off from her job for two years. Melanie lived in a rental apartment that was part of Marsha's home. Until losing her job, she had paid her mother rent every month and this allowed Marsha to meet her mortgage payments. Now, without Melanie's contribution, Marsha feared that she might have to go into foreclosure on the house. Marsha did not want to let Melanie know about the gravity of their financial situation. Marsha hoped that by having supportive conversations with Melanie, she would eventually get the courage to push herself to find a job, which she did. Long-term unemployment of adult children in multigenerational families can have serious economic consequences on the older mother.

Natalie (sixty-eight; Caucasian; graduate studies; *son, Chip*) had three adult children all living on their own when her husband had an unexpected heart attack and died. Not only did Natalie lose her partner of forty-five years, with whom she had shared everything, she also lost "the heart of the family." He had been very helpful to Chip who had developed a serious speech problem at age six. As a young mother of a child with a speech disability, Natalie had felt her son's vulnerability. Chip graduated college but was unable to find a job. Depressed, he returned home, and his drinking problem became evident when he developed chronic pancreatitis. Natalie's story illustrates the lengths a mother may go to make sure her adult child gets the best possible life-saving care and the unintended resentment this attention may create among siblings.

Noella (sixty-two; African American; high school graduate; *son, Phillip*) had been helped by an elder abuse agency to evict her abusive and drug-using son from her apartment. Feeling empowered by the success of the eviction, she and the social worker started looking at other areas of her life in which she had difficulty setting limits and taking better care of herself. They worked on how to create better boundaries with her large circle of relatives, who all wanted a piece of her time.

Noreen (sixty-four, Caucasian, some high school; *son, Nevin*) lived in a rural area and relied on her son, Nevin, for help with activities of daily living. Nevin administered her pain medications for her serious chronic pain. However, it was discovered that he would often take the opiates for himself. Noreen did not want to report her son and instead continually changed her doctors so that his criminal neglect of her care could be hidden.

Paulette (sixty-four; African American; primary school; *son, Raul*) remembers when her father put her on the airplane from Jamaica to live with her mother in New York. She was just ten years old. He told her "make me proud of you." She believes she had fulfilled this promise. But her son, Raul, is not yet making his three daughters proud of him, which distresses and disappoints Paulette. Although he has been trained as a welder, he refuses to use his skills and seems to have no direction in his life. Paulette adores her grandchildren. Looking into their eyes, she says, feels like butter melting. She works full-time as a home attendant but has always arranged her schedule so that she can see her grandkids for at least one afternoon a week and one sleepover.

Priscilla (seventy-three; Caucasian; *two grown sons*) posted a short note on my blog reporting her feelings of shame because she had allowed her two grown "middle-aged" sons to live with her again. She had surprised herself by talking openly on the blog about her mixed feelings. When asked if she had joined a support group to talk with other women who were in the same position, she replied that she could never do this. Her embarrassment was preventing her from getting any help.

Rebecca (sixty-two; African American; college graduate; *son, Brandon*) uses a walker and is currently on disability. She worked as an administrator for the New Jersey State government for thirty years. She desperately wants some peace in her later years—specifically she wants to be free of her son's abusive treatment of her. Brandon was diagnosed with mental health problems at age sixteen. Rebecca worries that Brandon still needs his mother's protection, despite his being forty-two years old and having been self-supporting and having lived on his own. Living together, they constantly fight; recently, he punched her and broke her nose. She is convinced that she will be killed by her son but also fears evicting him. Her story illustrates the dangers a mother may live with when she believes there are no viable solutions.

Rosanne (sixty-eight; Caucasian; graduate education; *son, Derek*). Rosanne's son had cut off all contact from her several years back with very little explanation given. Despite Rosanne's grief about this loss, she was not able to discuss her feelings about the cutoff, even with her own daughter. Rosanne realized that she had spent much of her life pushing away an acknowledgment of the things that upset her, including an unsatisfying and controlling marriage. This pattern of denial had gotten in her way of allowing herself to try and reach out to her son, even when she was worried that he might be in trouble.

Sylvia (sixty-eight; African American; some college; *daughter, Jasmine*) and her husband were living with their two adult daughters and their two children in a small, rundown, crowded apartment. They had taken their grown daughters back in years ago, when they each had no place to live. Jasmine and her sister seemed unable to show their mother any love or help her out in the house as she coped with stage IV cancer. For Sylvia, the hardest part of her illness was having to face how neglectful and uncaring her daughters were to her. Adult Protective Services were called in to investigate the neglect and get help for Sylvia.

Tracy (sixty-three; Caucasian; college graduate; *daughter, Jeannie*), a widower with three grown children, had always looked forward to an "empty nest" when she could actualize her lifetime hope to travel, write, and start a new business. Her daughter's diagnosis of schizophrenia had been followed by ten years of decline—including violent attacks on her mother. Tracy described herself to be in an unresolvable conflict. She could not separate from her very ill daughter, but she also could not give up on her own dreams.

Vivian (sixty-seven; Caucasian; high school graduate; *son, Tony*) will spend the rest of her life living in an elder abuse shelter in Bethesda, Maryland. She described that on the first night she slept in the shelter (which is part of a nursing home), it was the only time she had felt safe in thirty years. Her son's problems began when he was four years old. By his teens, he was homeless, using drugs, and harassing Vivian and his grandmother for money. Vivian did not have the inner strength to stop her son from bothering her, even when the harassment became physical and sexual. She only found safety and refuge through the intervention of others who got her the help she needed.

Wendy (sixty-six; Caucasian; high school graduate; *daughter, Mindy*) was a traditional "stay-at-home" mom who raised four children, each of whom was flourishing professionally and personally. Her only daughter, Mindy, was a successful environmental engineer who surprised her parents one day by announcing that she was leaving her job to become a yoga instructor. Because they had confidence in Mindy, they accepted the new path she was choosing to follow. However, within months, they became concerned that something was "not right." Wendy and Ralph had no experience with the mental health system. Nevertheless, they used the internet and neighbors' friends of friends to educate themselves. Within a short time, Ralph was knowledgeable enough to know what he had to do to have his daughter committed to a psychiatric hospital to protect her from suicide and/or homicide. Wendy's life in retirement now includes the daily worry that her daughter might experience a relapse. She hoped to write a book about what she learned about mental illness.

Notes

CHAPTER 1

1. C. Henry Kempe, Frderic N. Silverman, and Brandt F. Steele, et al, "The Battered-Child Syndrome," *JAMA*, 181, no. 1 (1962).

2. Report of House of Commons debate Parliament of the United Kingdom by Jack Ashley in 1973.

3. A. A. Baker, "Granny Battering," *Modern Geriatrics*, 5 (1975): 20–24; G. R. Burston, "Granny-battering," *British Medical Journal*, 3 (1975): 592.

4. C. Wright Mills, "The Promise," in *The Sociological Imagination* (Oxford: Oxford University Press, 1959).

5. J. Choi, J. Zhu, and L. Goodman, *Young Adults Living in Parents' Basements: Causes and Consequences* (Washington, DC: Urban Institute, 2019).

6. Jeffrey Jensen Arnett, *Emerging Adulthood: The Winding Road from the Late Teens through the Twenties* (Oxford: Oxford University Press, 2014).

7. Kristin Myers, "Study: Parents Skimp on Retirement to Support Adult Children," *Yahoo Finance* (2019).

8. J. O. Prochaska, J. C. Norcross, and C. C. DiClemente, *Changing for Good* (New York: Morrow, 1994).

CHAPTER 2

1. S. Hays, *The Cultural Contradictions of Motherhood* (New Haven: Yale University Press, 1998); J. Coleman, "Parents Are Sacrificing Their Social Lives on the Altar of Intensive Parenting," *The Atlantic* (2021).

2. Yangtao Huang, Francisco Perales, and Mark Western, "The Long Arm of Parental Advantage: Socio-Economic Background and Parental Financial Transfers over Adult Children's Life Courses," *Research in Social Stratification and Mobility*, 71 (2021); M. Silverstein and V. Bengtson, "Intergenerational Solidarity and the Structure of Adult Child–Parent Relationships in American Families 1," *American Journal of Sociology*, 103, no. 2 (1997).

3. K. Luscher and K. Pillemer, "Intergenerational Ambivalence: A New Approach to the Study of Parent-Child Relations in Later Life," *Journal of Marriage and Family*, no. 2 (1998).

4. K. Pillemer and K. Luscher, *New Perspectives on Parent-Child Relations in Later Life* (Amsterdam: Elsevier Science, 2004).

5. Anna Bahney, "The Bank of Mom and Dad," *New York Times*, April 20, 2006.

6. Jenna Goudreau, "Nearly 60% of Parents Provide Financial Support to Adult Children," *Forbes*, May 20, 2011.

7. G. Hagestad and V. Bengston, "Reflections on Continuity and Discontinuity from an Illness Process," in *Adulthood and Aging: Research on Continuities and Discontinuities* (New York: Springer, 1996).

8. G. Bouchard, "How Do Parents React When Their Children Leave Home? An Integrative Review," *Journal of Adult Development* 21 (2014).

9. Ellen Galinsky, *Six Stages of Parenthood* (Addison-Wesley Pub. Co., 1987).

10. J. Gross, "Mothers Are the 'Shock Absorbers' of Our Society," *New York Times*, October 14, 2020.

11. Glen Elder, H. Jr., "Time, Human Agency, and Social Change: Perspectives on the Life Course," *Social Psychology Quarterly* 57, no. 1 (1994).

12. H. Avieli, Y. Smeloy, and T. Band-Winterstein, "Departure Scripts and Life Review of Parents Living with Abusive Adult Children with Mental Disorder," *Journal of Aging Studies* 34 (2015); A. Mitchell Barbara, V. Wister Andrew, and M. Gee Ellen, "The Ethnic and Family Nexus of Homeleaving and Returning among Canadian Young Adults," *The Canadian Journal of Sociology / Cahiers canadiens de sociologie*, no. 4 (2004).

13. A. Rossi and P. Rossi, *Of Human Bonding: Parent-Child Relations across the Life Course*, Social Institutions and Social Change (A. de Gruyter, 1990).

CHAPTER 3

1. J. Kahn, G. Goldscheider, and J. Garcia-Manglano, "Growing Parental Economic Power in Parent-Child Households: Co-Residence and Financial

Dependency in the United States, 1960-2010," *Demography*, 50 (2013); J. Choi, J. Zhu, and L. Goodman, *Young Adults Living in Parents' Basement: Causes and Consequences* (Washington, DC: Urban Institute, 2019).J. Zhu, and L. Goodman, "Young Adults Living in Parents' Basement: Causes and Consequences," (Washington D.C.: Urban Institute, January, 2019).

2. E. Courtin and M. Avendan, "Under One Roof: The Effect of Co-Residing with Adult Children on Depression in Later Life," *Social Science & Medicine*, 168 (2016).

3. Jeffrey Jensen Arnett, *Emerging Adulthood: The Winding Road from the Late Teens through the Twenties* (Oxford University Press, 2014).

4. Hardie Jessica Halliday and A. Seltzer Judith, "Parent-Child Relationships at the Transition to Adulthood: A Comparison of Black, Hispanic, and White Immigrant and Native-Born Youth," *Social Forces*, 95, no. 1 (2016); Judith A. Seltzer, Charles Q. Lau, and Suzanne M. Bianchi, "Doubling up When Times Are Tough: A Study of Obligations to Share a Home in Response to Economic Hardship," *Social Science Research*, 41, no. 5 (2012); Marcus L. Britton, "Race/Ethnicity, Attitudes, and Living with Parents During Young Adulthood," *Journal of Marriage and Family*, 75, no. 4 (2013).

5. E. M. Davis, K. Kim, and K. Fingerman, "Is an Empty Nest Best?: Co-residence with Adult Children and Parental Marital Quality before and after Recession," *J Gerontological B Psychol Soc Sci*, 73, no. 3 (2018).

6. K. Pillemer and J. Suitor, "Exploring Mothers' Ambivalence toward Their Adult Children," *Journal of Marriage & Family*, 64 (2002).

7. L. P. Kennedy and P. Farrell, "What to Do When Adult Children Want to Move Back In," in *Under One Roof Again: All Grown up and Re (Learning) to Live Happily Together*, edited by S. Newman (Guilford CT: Lyons Press, 2010).

8. K. Appiah, "My Adult Son Moved In. It's a Nightmare. Can I Kick Him Out?" *NY Times*, October 30, 2020.

CHAPTER 4

1. Nancy Chodorow, *The Reproduction of Mothering* (University of California Press, 1978); Martha McMahon, *Engendering Motherhood: Identity and Self-Transformation in Women's Lives* (Guilford Press, 1995), 8.

2. Miriam Liss, H. Schiffrin, and K. Rizzo, "Maternal Guilt and Shame: The Role of Self-Discrepancy and Fear of Negative Evaluation," *Journal of Child and Family Studies*, 22, no. 8 (2013).

3. D. Jackson and J. Mannix, "Giving Voice to the Burden of Blame: A Feminist Study of Mothers' Experiences of Mother Blaming," *International Journal of Mental Health Nursing*, 10 (2004).

4. Rozsika Parker, *Torn in Two: The Experience of Maternal Ambivalence* (Virago, 1995).

5. K. Korabik and A. K. McElwain, "Work-Family Guilt," in *Work and Family Encyclopedia*, edited by E. Kossek and M. Pitt-Catsouphes (Chestnut Hill, MA: Sloan Work and Family Research Network, 2005); M. Silfver and K. Helkama, "Empathy, Guilt, and Gender: A Comparison of Two Measures of Guilt," *Scandinavian Journal of Psychology*, 48 (2007).

6. Ellen I. Goodman, "Guilt Gap," *The Washington Post*, 1990.

7. A. Rotkirch and K. Janhunen, "Maternal Guilt," *Evol Psychol*, 8, no. 1 (2010).

8. Miriam Liss, H. Schiffrin, and K. Rizzo, "Maternal Guilt and Shame: The Role of Self-Discrepancy and Fear of Negative Evaluation," *Journal of Child and Family Studies*, 22, no. 8 (2013).

9. R. Nemzoff, *Don't Bite Your Tongue: How to Foster Rewarding Relationships with Your Adult Children* (New York: St. Martin's Press, 2008).

10. C. Ryff, P. Schmutte, and Y. Lee, "How Children Turn Out: Implications for Parental Self-Evaluation," in *The Parental Experience in Midlife*, edited by Carol D. Ryff and Marsha Mailick Seltzer (Chicago, IL: University of Chicago Press, 1996); K. Pillemer and J. Suitor, "Explaining Mothers' Ambivalence toward Their Adult Children," *Journal of Marriage and Family*, 64, no. 3 (2002).

11. Stella Chase, "The 'Blame the Mother' Ideology," *International Journal of Mental Health*, 11, no. 1-2 (1982): 95–106.

12. A. Henderon, S. Harmon, and H. Newman, "The Price Mothers Pay, Even When They Are Not Buying It: Mental Health Con Sequencwes of Idealized Motherhood," *Sex Roles*, 74 (2016).

13. Sharon Hays, *The Cultural Contradictions of Motherhood* (Yale University Press, 1996); Joan B. Wolf, "Is Breast Really Best? Risk and Total Motherhood in the National Breastfeeding Awareness Campaign," *Journal of Health Politics, Policy and Law*, 32, no. 4 (2007): 595–636.

14. Erin N. Taylor and Lora Ebert Wallace, "For Shame: Feminism, Breastfeeding Advocacy, and Maternal Guilt," *Hypatia: A Journal of Feminist Philosophy*, 27, no. 1, (2012): 76–98.

15. Joan B. Wolf, "Is Breast Really Best? Risk and Total Motherhood in the National Breastfeeding Awareness Campaign," *Journal of Health Politics, Policy and Law*, 32, no. 4 (2007): 595–636.

16. Erin N. Taylor and Lora Ebert Wallace, "For Shame: Feminism, Breastfeeding Advocacy, and Maternal Guilt," *Hypatia: A Journal of Feminist Philosophy*, 27, no. 1, (2012): 76–98.

17. D. Seccombe, D. James, and K. Walters, "'They Think You Ain't Much of Nothing': The Social Construction of the Welfare Mother," *Journal of Marriage & Family*, 60, no. 4 (1998).

18. P. Leach, *Your Baby and Child* (New York: Knopf, 2010).

19. Karen Bullock, "Get Thee Behind Me: African-American Grandparents Raising Grandchildren who Experienced Domestic Violence," in *Interpersonal Violence in the African-American Community* (Boston, MA: Springer, 2006), 149–63; Emily A. Greenfield and Nadine F. Marks, "Linked Lives: Adult Children's Problems and Their Parents' Psychological and Relational Well-being," *Journal of Marriage and Family*, 68, no. 2 (2006): 442–54; Karl Pillemer and J. Jill Suitor, "'Will I Ever Escape My Child's Problems?' Effects of Adult Children's Problems on Elderly Parents," *Journal of Marriage and the Family* (1991): 585–94; Carol D. Ryff, Pamela S. Schmutte, and Young Hyun Lee, "How Children Turn Out: Implications for Parental Self-Evaluation," *The Parental Experience in Midlife* (1996): 383–422.

20. Einat Peled, Keren Gueta, and Nili Sander-Almoznino, "The Experience of Mothers Exposed to the Abuse of Their Daughters by an Intimate Partner: 'There Is No Definition for It,'" *Violence Against Women* 22, no. 13 (2016): 1577–96; Jeffrey Jensen Arnett, *Emerging Adulthood: The Winding Road from the Late Teens through the Twenties* (Oxford University Press, 2014).

21. D. Jackson and J. Mannix, "Giving Voice to the Burden of Blame: A Feminist Study of Mothers' Experiences of Mother Blaming," *International Journal of Mental Health Nursing*, 10 (2004).

22. Paula J. Caplan and Ian Hall-McCorquodale, "Mother-Blaming in Major Clinical Journals," *American Journal of Orthopsychiatry*, 55, no. 3 (1985).

23. D. Jackson and J. Mannix, "Giving Voice to the Burden of Blame: A Feminist Study of Mothers' Experiences of Mother Blaming," *International Journal of Mental Health Nursing*, 10 (2004).

24. V. Phares, "Where's Poppa? The Relative Lack of Attention to the Role of Fathers in Child and Adolescent Psychopathology," *American Psychologist* 47 (1992).

25. Collins, W. Andrew, Maccoby, Eleanor, Steinberg, Laurence, Hetherington, E. Mavis, and Bornstein, Marc H. "Contemporary Research on Parenting: The Case for Nature and Nurture," *The American Psychologist*, volume 55, no. 2 (2000).

García Coll, C., Lamberty, G., Jenkins, R., McAdoo, H. P., Crnic, K., Wasik, B. H., and Vázquez García, H. "An Integrative Model for the Study of Developmental Competencies in Minority Children" *Child Development*, volume 67, no. 5. (1986).

Leventhal, Tama and Jeanne Brooks-Gunn. "The Neighborhoods They Live in: The Effects of Neighborhood Residence on Child and Adolescent Outcomes" *Psychological Bulletin*, volume 126, no. 2. (2000).

Smith, Judith R., Brooks-Gunn, Jeanne. & Klebanov, Pamela. "Consequences of Living in Poverty for Young Children's Cognitive and Verbal Ability and School Readiness." In G. Duncan & J. Brooks-Gunn (Eds.). *Growing Up Poor* (pp. 132–189). NY: Russell Sage. (1997).

26. A. Waldman, *Bad Mother: A Chronicle of Maternal Crimes, Minor Calamities, and Occasional Moments of Grace* (New York: Doubleday, 2009).

27. R. Counter, "Mom Shaming Is Running Rampant During the Pandemic," *New York Times*, September 10, 2020.

28. Terri Peters, "Mom Responds to Stranger's Phone-shaming at Costco in a Viral Letter," Today.com, 2019.

29. Terri Peters, "Mom Responds to Stranger's Phone-shaming at Costco in a Viral Letter," Today.com, 2019.

30. H. Harbin and D. Maddfen, "Battered Parents: A New Syndrome," *American Journal of Psychiatry*, 136 (1979); J. R. Smith, "Expanding Constructions of Elder Abuse and Neglect: Older Mothers' Subjective Experiences," *Journal of Elder Abuse & Neglect* (2015); A. Holt, *Adolescent-to-Parent Abuse: Current Understandings in Research, Policy and Practice* (Briston England: Policy Press, 2013); M. Lachs and J. Berman, *Under the Radar: New York State Elder Abuse Prevalence Study* (New York: Lifespan of Greater Rochester, Inc., Weill Cornell Medical Center, New York City Department of Aging, 2011).

31. J. R. Smith, "Expanding Constructions of Elder Abuse and Neglect: Older Mothers' Subjective Experiences," *Journal of Elder Abuse & Neglect* (2015).

32. Jennifer Paff Ogle and Juyeon Park, "Maternal Experiences of Parenting Girls who are Perceived as Overweight or at Risk for Becoming So: Narratives of Uncertainty, Ambivalence and Struggle," *Children & Society*, 32, no. 4 (2018): 325–40.

CHAPTER 5

1. M. Silverstein and V. Bengston, "Intergenerational Solidarity and the Structure of Adult Child–Parent Relationships in American Families 1," *American Journal of Sociology*, 103, no. 2 (1997).

2. K. Luscher and K. Pillemer, "Intergenerational Ambivalence: A New Approach to the Study of Parent–Child Relations in Later Life," *Journal of Marriage and the Family*, 60, no. 2 (1998).

3. K. Pillemer and J. Suitor, "'Will I Ever Escape My Child's Problems?' Effects of Adult Chldren's Problems on Elderly Parents," *Journal of Marriage & Family*, 53 (1991).

4. R. van Gaalen, P Dykstra, and A. Komter, "Where Is the Exit? Intergenerational Ambivalence and Relationship Quality in High Contact Ties," *Journal of Aging Studies*, 24, no. 2 (2010).

5. Gunhild O. Hagestad, "On-Time, Off-Time, Out of Time? Reflections on Continuity and Discontinuity from an Illness Process," in *Adulthood and Aging: Research on Continuities and Discontinuities*, edited by Vern L. Bengtson (New York, NY: Springer Publishing Co, 1996).

6. Elizabeth A Carter and Monica McGoldrick, *The Family Life Cycle: A Framework for Family Therapy* (Halsted Press, 1980).

7. K. Pillemer and J. Suitor, "Exploring Mothers' Ambivalence toward Their Adult Children," *Journal of Marriage & Family*, 64 (2002); J. Suitor, Megan Gilligan, and Karl Pillemer, "Conceptualizing and Measuring Intergenerational Ambivalence in Later Life," *The Journals of Gerontology: Series B: Psychological Sciences and Social Sciences*, 66, no. 6 (2011).

8. C. Beck and P. Indman, "The Many Faces of Postpartum Depression," *Journal of Obstetric Gynecological Neonatal Nursing*, 34, no. 5 (2005).

9. S. Hays, *The Cultural Contradictions of Motherhood* (New Haven: Yale University Press, 1998); Sara Ruddick, *Maternal Thinking: Toward a Politics of Peace* (Beacon Press, 1989).

10. C. Beck and P. Indman, "The Many Faces of Postpartum Depression," *Journal of Obstetric Gynecological Neonatal Nursing*, 34, no. 5 (2005).

11. C. Beck and P. Indman, "The Many Faces of Postpartum Depression," *Journal of Obstetric Gynecological Neonatal Nursing*, 34, no. 5 (2005).

12. A. Henderon, S. Harmon, and H. Newman, "The Price Mothers Pay, Even When They Are Not Buying It: Mental Health Con Sequencwes of Idealized Motherhood," *Sex Roles*, 74 (2016).

13. Rozsika Parker, *Torn in Two: The Experience of Maternal Ambivalence* (London, UK: Virago Press, 1995).

14. Jantien Van Zeijl, Judi Mesman, Marinus H. Van Ijzendoorn, Marian J. Bakermans-Kranenburg, Femmiw Juffer, Mirjam N. Stolk, Hans M. Koot, and Lenneke R. A. Alink, "Attachment-Based Intervention for Enhancing Sensitive Discipline in Mothers of 1- to 3-Year-Old Children at Risk for Externalizing Behavior Problems: A Randomized Controlled Trial," *Journal of Consulting and Clinical Psychology*, 74, no. 6 (2006).

15. NBC10, "Walter Wallace Jr. Struggled With Mental Health Issues, Family Says," https://www.nbcphiladelphia.com/News/Local/Walter-Wallace-Jr-Struggled-with-Mental-Health-Issues-Family-Says/2575493/.

16. Megan L. Dolbin-MacNab, "Just Like Raising Your Own? Grandmothers' Perceptions of Parenting a Second Time Around," *Family Relations*, 55, no. 5 (2006); Antoinette Y. Rodgers-Farmer, "Parenting Stress, Depression, and Parenting in Grandmothers Raising Their Grandchildren," *Children and Youth Services Review*, 21, no. 5 (1999).

CHAPTER 6

1. G. Gibson Hunt, R. Greene, and J. G. Whiting, *On Pins and Needles* (Washington D.C.: National Alliance for Caregivers, 2016).

2. A. P. Hyde, "Coping with Threatening, Intimidating, Violent Behaviors of People with Psychiatric Disabilities at Home: Guidelines for Family Care-

givers," *Psychiatric Rehabilitation Journal*, 21 (1997); H. P. Lefley, *Family Caregiving in Mental Illness* (Thousand Oaks, CA: Sage Publications, 1999).

  3. A. P. Hyde, "Coping with Threatening, Intimidating, Violent Behaviors of People with Psychiatric Disabilities at Home: Guidelines for Family Caregivers," *Psychiatric Rehabilitation Journal*, 21 (1997).

  4. P. Gibson, "Intergenerational Parenting from the Perspective of African American Grandmothers," *Family Relations*, 54, no. 2 (2005).

  5. N. Hooyman and J. Gonyea, *Feminist Perspectve on Family Care: Pleas for Gender Justice*, volume 6 (Thousand Oaks: Sage, 1995); L. Funk and K. Kobayashi, "Choice: In Filial Care Work: Moving Beyond a Dischomy," *Canadian Sociological Review*, 46, no. 3 (2009).

  6. H. Thorning and L. Dixon, "Caregiving for Individuals with Serious Mental Illness: A Life Cycle Perspective," in *The Spectrum of Family Caregiving for Adults and Elders with Chronic Illness*, edited by L. D. Burgio, J. E. Gaugler, and M. M. Hilgeman (Oxford University Press, 2016), 173–211; Helle Thorning, *Grief: The Psychological Consequence of the Caregiving Dynamic on Family Caregivers of Persons with Severe Mental Illness* (New York University, 2004).

  7. National Institute for Mental Health, "Transforming the Understanding and Treatment of Mental Illnesses," https://www.youtube.com/watch?v=Nin4V1MeFds.

  8. Ellis D. Evans and Luann Warren-Sohlberg, "A Pattern Analysis of Adolescent Abusive Behavior toward Parents," *Journal of Adolescent Research*, 3, no. 2 (1988).

  9. B. Brent and A. Giuliano, *Harvard Review of Psychiatry*, 15, no. 4 (2007).

  10. K. Aschbrenner, J. S. Greenberg, S. A. Allen, and M. M. Seltzer, "Subjective Burden and Personal Gains among Older Parents of Adults with Serious Mental Illness," *Psychiatric Services*, 61 (2010).

  11. Kenneth J. Doka, "Disenfranchised Grief," *Bereavement Care*, 18, no. 3 (1999).

  12. Amy Patrick-Ott and Linda D. Ladd, "The Blending of Boss's Concept of Ambiguous Loss and Olshansky's Concept of Chronic Sorrow: A Case Study of a Family with a Child who has Significant Disabilities." *Journal of Creativity in Mental Health*, 5, no. 1 (2010): 73–86; Pauline Boss, *Ambiguous Loss: Learning to Live with Unresolved Grief* (Harvard University Press, 2009).

  13. H. Avieli, Y. Smeloy, and T. Band-Winterstein, "Departure Scripts and Life Review of Parents Living with Abusive Adult Children with Mental Disorder.," *Journal of Aging Studies*, 34 (2015).

  14. T. Labrum and P. Solomon, "Safety Fears Held by Caregivers About Relatives with Psychiatric Disorders," *Health in Social Work*, 43 (2018).

15. A. P. Hyde, "Coping with Threatening, Intimidating, Violent Behaviors of People with Psychiatric Disabilities at Home: Guidelines for Family Caregivers," *Psychiatric Rehabilitation Journal*, 21 (1997).

16. Sarah L. Desmarais, Richard A. Van Dorn, Kiersten L. Johnson, Kevin J. Grimm, Kevin S. Douglas, and Marvin S. Swartz, "Community Violence Perpetration and Victimization among Adults with Mental Illnesses," *American Journal of Public Health* 104, no. 12 (2014).

17. Sarah L. Desmarais, Richard A. Van Dorn, Kiersten L. Johnson, Kevin J. Grimm, Kevin S. Douglas, and Marvin S. Swartz, "Community Violence Perpetration and Victimization among Adults with Mental Illnesses," *American Journal of Public Health* 104, no. 12 (2014): 2342–49; Krishna S. Vaddadi, Chris Gilleard, and Helen Fryer, "Abuse of Carers by Relatives with Severe Mental Illness," *International Journal of Social Psychiatry*, 48, no. 2 (2002): 149–55; Edward W. Gondolf, Edward P. Mulvey, and Charles W. Litz, "Characteristics of Perpetrators of Family and Nonfamily Assaults," *Psychiatric Services*, 41, no. 2 (1990): 191–93; Raymond W. Swan and Melissa Lavitt, "Patterns of Adjustment to Violence in Families of the Mentally Ill," *Journal of Interpersonal Violence*, 3, no. 6 (1988).

18. Jens Henrichs, Stefan Bogaerts, Jelle Sijtsema, and Fanny Klerx-van Mierlo, "Intimate Partner Violence Perpetrators in a Forensic Psychiatric Outpatient Setting: Criminal History, Psychopathology, and Victimization," *Journal of Interpersonal Violence*, 30, no. 12 (2015): 2109–28.

19. T. Labrum and P. Solomon, "Safety Fears Held by Caregivers About Relatives with Psychiatric Disorders," *Health in Social Work*, 43 (2018).

20. T. Labrum and P. Solomon, "Safety Fears Held by Caregivers About Relatives with Psychiatric Disorders," *Health in Social Work*, 43 (2018); Abin Varghese, Deeepika C. Khakha, and Rakesh Kumar Chadda, "Pattern and Type of Aggressive Behavior in Patients with Severe Mental Illness as Perceived by the Caregivers and the Coping Strategies Used by Them in a Tertiary Care Hospital," *Archives of Psychiatric Nursing*, 30, no. 1 (2016): 62–69; Byoung-Hoon Ahn, Jeong-Hyun Kim, Sohee Oh, Sang Sub Choi, Sung Ho Ahn, and Sun Bum Kim, "Clinical Features of Parricide in Patients with Schizophrenia," *Australian & New Zealand Journal of Psychiatry*, 46, no. 7 (2012): 621–29.

21. S. E. Estroff, J. W. Swanson, W. S. Lachiotte, M. Swartz, and M. Bolduc, "Risk Reconsidered: Targets of Violence in the Social Networks of People with Serious Psychiatric Disorders," *Social Psychiatry and Psychiatric Epidemiology*, 33, Suppl. 1 (1998).

22. Kenneth Tardiff and Harold W. Koenigsberg, "Assaultive Behavior among Psychiatric Outpatients," *The American Journal of Psychiatry* (1985).

23. E. Fuller Torrey, H. Richard Lamb, Carla Jacobs, D. J. Jaffe, and John Snook, *Raising Cain: The Role of Serious Mental Illness in Family Households* (Washington, DC: Treatment Advocacy Center, 2016).

24. E. Fuller Torrey, H. Richard Lamb, Carla Jacobs, D. J. Jaffe, and John Snook, *Raising Cain: The Role of Serious Mental Illness in Family Households* (Washington, DC: Treatment Advocacy Center, 2016).

25. Gibson Hunt, R. Greene, and J. G. Whiting, *On Pins and Needles* (Washington D.C.: National Alliance for Caregivers, 2016).

26. Shin Ho Park, Yun Ju C. Song, Eleni A. Demetriou, Karen L. Pepper, Ian B. Hickie, Nick Glozier, Daniel F. Hermens, Elizabeth M. Scott, and Adam J. Guastella, "Distress, Quality of Life and Disability in Treatment–Seeking Young Adults with Social Anxiety Disorder," *Early Intervention in Psychiatry*, 15, no. 1 (2021).

27. D. Karp, *The Burden of Sympathy: How Families Cope with Mental Illness* (Oxford University Press, 2001).

28. Shaun M. Eack and Christina E. Newhill, "Racial Disparities in Mental Health Outcomes after Psychiatric Hospital Discharge among Individuals with Severe Mental Illness," *Social Work Research*, 36, no. 1 (2012): 41–52.

29. K. Park and M. Seo, "Care Burden of Parents of Adult Chldren with Mental Illness: The Role of Associative Stigma," *Comprehensive Psychiatry*, 70 (2016).

CHAPTER 7

1. N. Dain, "Critics and Dissenters: Reflections on Anti-Psychiatry in the United States," *Journal of the History of the Behavioral Sciences*, 25, no. 1 (1989).

2. Larry Davidson, Maria J. O'Connell, Janis Tondora, Martha Lawless, and Arthur C. Evans, "Recovery in Serious Mental Illness: A New Wine or Just a New Bottle?" *Professional Psychology: Research and Practice*, 36, no. 5 (2005): 480.

3. "Recovery from Mental Disorders, a Lecture by Patricia Deegan," *YouTube*, https://youtu.be/jhK-7DkWaKE.

4. E. J. Novella, "Mental Health Care in the Aftermath of Deinstitutionalization: Aretrospective and Prospective View," *Health Care Analysis*, 18 (2010).

5. Steven P. Segal and Leah A. Jacobs, "Deinstitutionalization," in *Encyclopedia of Social Work* (Oxford University Press, 2013); Michael J. Dear and Jennifer R. Wolch, *Landscapes of Despair: From Deinstitutionalization to Homelessness*, volume 823 (Princeton University Press, 2014); H. Richard Lamb and Leona L. Bachrach, "Some Perspectives on Deinstitutionalization," *Psychiatric Services*, 52, no. 8 (2001): 1039–45.

6. J. Rowe, "Great Expectations: A Systematic Review of the Literature on the Role of Family Carers in Severe Mental Illness, and Their Relationships and Engagements with Professionals," *Journal of Psychiatric and Mental*

Health Nursing, 19 (2012); E. Landeweer, "Sharing Care Respnsibilities between Professionals and Personal Networks in Mental Healthcare: A Plea for
Inclusion," *Ethics and Social Welfare*, 12, no. 2 (2018).
   7. Catherine Hungerford and Fiona Richardson, "Operationalising Recov-
ery-oriented Services: The Challenges for Carers," *Advances in Mental Health*,
12, no. 1 (2013): 11–21.
   8. D. Karp and V. Tanarugsachock, "Mental Illness, Caregiving and Emotional Management," *Qualitative Health Research*, 10, no. 1 (2000); D. Karp,
The Burden of Sympathy: How Families Cope with Mental Illness (Oxford
University Press, 2001).
   9. D. Karp and V. Tanarugsachock, "Mental Illness, Caregiving and Emotional Management," *Qualitative Health Research*, 10, no. 1 (2000); Megan
A. Pope, Gerald Jordan, Shruthi Venkataraman, Ashok K. Malla, and Srividya
N. Iyer, "'Everyone Has a Role': Perspectives of Service Users with First-
Episode Psychosis, Family Caregivers, Treatment Providers, and Policymakers
on Responsibility for Supporting Individuals with Mental Health Problems,"
Qualitative Health Research, 29, no. 9 (2019).
   10. D. Karp, *The Burden of Sympathy: How Families Cope with Mental
Illness* (Oxford University Press, 2001); D. Karp and V. Tanarugsachock,
"Mental Illness, Caregiving and Emotional Management," *Qualitative Health
Research*, 10, no. 1 (2000).
   11. Sarah E. Bledsoe, Ellen Lukens, Steven Onken, Jennifer L. Bellamy,
and Lauren Cardillo-Geller, "Mental Illness, Evidence-Based Practice, and Recovery," *Best Practices in Mental Health*, 4, no. 2 (2008): 34–58; Benjamin K.
Brent and Anthony J. Giuliano. "Psychotic-Spectrum Illness and Family-based
Treatments: A Case-based Illustration of the Underuse of Family Interventions," *Harvard Review of Psychiatry*, 15, no. 4 (2007): 161–68; E. Lukens and
H. Thorning, "Psychoeducational Family Groups," in *Psychosocial Treatment
of Schizophrenia*, edited by A. Rubin, D. W. Springer, and K. Trawver (Wiley,
2011).
   12. Megan A. Pope, Gerald Jordan, Shruthi Venkataraman, Ashok K. Malla,
and Srividya N. Iyer, "'Everyone Has a Role': Perspectives of Service Users
with First-Episode Psychosis, Family Caregivers, Treatment Providers, and
Policymakers on Responsibility for Supporting Individuals with Mental Health
Problems," *Qualitative Health Research*, 29, no. 9 (2019).
   13. D. Karp, *The Burden of Sympathy: How Families Cope with Mental Illness* (Oxford University Press, 2001); Megan A. Pope, Gerald Jordan, Shruthi
Venkataraman, Ashok K. Malla, and Srividya N. Iyer, "'Everyone Has a Role':
Perspectives of Service Users with First-Episode Psychosis, Family Caregiv-
ers, Treatment Providers, and Policymakers on Responsibility for Supporting
Individuals with Mental Health Problems," *Qualitative Health Research*, 29,
no. 9 (2019).

14. Erica Eassom, Domenico Giacco, Aysegul Dirik, and Stefan Priebe, "Implementing Family Involvement in the Treatment of Patients with Psychosis: A Systematic Review of Facilitating and Hindering Factors," *BMJ Open*, 4, no. 10 (2014).

CHAPTER 8

1. Whalen (1953, 634), as cited in Jim Orford, Guillermina Natera, Alex G. Copello, and Carol Atkinson, *Coping with Alcohol and Drug Problems: The Experience of Family Members in Three Contrasting Cultures* (Routledge, 2005).

2. Yannine Estrada, Tae Kyoung Lee, Shi Huang, Maria I. Tapia, Maria-Rosa Velázquez, Marcos J. Martinez, Hilda Pantin, et al., "Parent-centered Prevention of Risky Behaviors among Hispanic Youths in Florida," *American Journal of Public Health*, 107, no. 4 (2017): 607–13; Sandra Kuntsche and Emmanuel Kuntsche, "Parent-based Interventions for Preventing or Reducing Adolescent Substance Use—A Systematic Literature Review," *Clinical Psychology Review*, 45 (2016): 89–101; Karol L. Kumpfer and Cátia Magalhães, "Strengthening Families Program: An Evidence-based Family Intervention for Parents of High-risk Children and Adolescents," *Journal of Child & Adolescent Substance Abuse*, 27, no. 3 (2018): 174–79.

3. D. Jackson and J. Mannix, "Then Suddenly He Went Right Off the Rails: Mothers' Sotires of Adolescent Cannabis Use," *Contemporary Nurse*, 14 (2002); A. Holt, "Adolescent-to-Parent Abuse of 'Domestic Violence': A Conceptual Review," *Trauma, Violence & Abuse*, 17, no. 5 (2016).

4. Jim Orford, Alex Copello, Richard Velleman, and Lorna Templeton, "Family Members Affected by a Close Relative's Addiction: The Stress-Strain-Coping-Support Model," *Drugs: Education, Prevention & Policy*, 17 (2010).

5. Jim Orford, Alex Copello, Richard Velleman, and Lorna Templeton, "Family Members Affected by a Close Relative's Addiction: The Stress-Strain-Coping-Support Model," *Drugs: Education, Prevention & Policy*, 17 (2010).

6. A. Copello and L. Templeton, *The Forgotten Carers: Support for Adult Family Members Affected by a Relative's Drug Problems* (UK Drug Policy Commission, 2012).

7. Jim Orford, Richard Velleman, Guillermina Natera, Lorna Templeton, and Alex Copello, "Addiction in the Family is a Major but Neglected Contributor to the Global Burden of Adult Ill-Health," *Social Science & Medicine*, 78 (2013).

8. Charlie Lloyd, "The Stigmatization of Problem Drug Users: A Narrative Literature Review," *Drugs: Education, Prevention and Policy*, 20, no. 2 (2013).

9. Natalie D. Crawford, Abby E Rudolph, Kandice Jones, and Crystal Fuller, "Differences in Self-Reported Discrimination by Primary Type of Drug Used among New York City Drug Users," *American Journal of Drug & Alcohol Abuse*, 38, no. 6 (2012); Michael Young, Jennifer Stuber, Jennifer Ahern, and Sandro Galea, "Interpersonal Discrimination and the Health of Illicit Drug Users," *The American Journal of Drug and Alcohol Abuse*, 31, no. 3 (2005).

10. M. Lachs and K. Pillemer, "Elder Abuse," *The New England Journal of Medicine*, 373, no. 20 (2015).

11. M. Williams, K. Tuffin, and P. Niland, "'It's Like He Just Goes Off, Boom!': Mothers and Grandmothers Make Sense of Child-to-Parent Violence," *Child and Family Social Work*, 22 (2017).

12. Carla Meurk, Doug Fraser, Megan Weier, Jayne Lucke, Adrian Carter, and Wayne Hall, "Assessing the Place of Neurobiological Explanations in Accounts of a Family Member's Addiction," *Drug and Alcohol Review*, 35, no. 4 (2016).

13. G. Heyman, *Addiction: A Disorder of Choice* (Cambridge, MA: Harvard University Press, 2009), 8.

14. Carla Meurk, Doug Fraser, Megan Weier, Jayne Lucke, Adrian Carter, and Wayne Hall, "Assessing the Place of Neurobiological Explanations in Accounts of a Family Member's Addiction," *Drug and Alcohol Review*, 35, no. 4 (2016).

15. B. Svensson, T. Richert, and B. Johnson, "Parents' Experiences of Abuse by Their Adult Children with Drug Problems," *NAD Nordic Studies on Alcohol and Drugs*, 37, no. 1 (2020).

16. Karen A. Roberto, Brandy Renee McCann, Pamela B. Teaster, and Emily Hoyt, "Elder Abuse and the Opioid Epidemic: Evidence from APS Cases in Central Appalachia," *Journal of Rural Mental Health* (2021).

17. Karen A. Roberto, Brandy Renee McCann, Pamela B. Teaster, and Emily Hoyt, "Elder Abuse and the Opioid Epidemic: Evidence from APS Cases in Central Appalachia," *Journal of Rural Mental Health* (2021).

18. Karen A. Roberto, Brandy Renee McCann, Pamela B. Teaster, and Emily Hoyt, "Elder Abuse and the Opioid Epidemic: Evidence from APS Cases in Central Appalachia," *Journal of Rural Mental Health* (2021).

19. Kathleen Sciacca and Agnes B. Hatfield, "The Family and the Dually Diagnosed Patient," in *Double Jeopardy: Chronic Mental Illness and Substance Use Disorder*, edited by A. F. Lehman and L. B. Dixon (Harwood Academic Publishers/Gordon, 1995), 193–209.

20. Jayati Das-Munshi, Maya Semrau, Corrado Barbui, Neerja Chowdhary, Petra C. Gronholm, Kavitha Kolappa, Dzmitry Krupchanka, Tarun Dua, and Graham Thornicroft, "'Gaps and Challenges: Who Treatment Recommendations for Tobacco Cessation and Management of Substance Use Disorders in People with Severe Mental Illness': Correction," *BMC Psychiatry*, 20 (2020).

21. A. Eden Evins, Corinne Cather, and Gail L. Daumit, "Smoking Cessation in People with Serious Mental Illness," *The Lancet Psychiatry*, 6, no. 7 (2019).

CHAPTER 9

1. Simon Olshansky, "Chronic Sorrow: A Response to Having a Mentally Defective Child," *Social Casework*, 43, no. 4 (1962).
2. A. Patrick-Ott and L. D. Ladd, "The Blending of Boss's Concept of Ambiguous Loss and Olshansky's Concept of Chronic Sorrow: A Case Study of a Family with a Child Who Has Significant Disabilities," *Journal of Creativity in Mental Health*, 5, no. 1 (2010).
3. Alicia Lucksted, William McFarlane, Donna Downing, and Lisa Dixon, "Recent Develpments in Family Psychoeducation as an Evidence-Based Practice," *Journal of Marriage & Family Therapy*, 38, no. 1 (2012); H. Thorning, *Grief: The Psychological Consequences of the Caregiving Dynamic on Family Caregivers of Persons with Severe Mental Illness* (New York University, 2004); H. Thorning and L. Dixon, *The Spectrum of Family Caregiving for Adults and Elders with Chronic Illness* (Oxford University Press, 2016).

CHAPTER 10

1. World Health Organization, *Missing Voices: Views of Older Persons on Elder Abuse* (World Health Organization, 2002).
2. M. Lachs and K. Pillemer, "Elder Abuse," *The New England Journal of Medicine*, 373, no. 20 (2015).
3. M. Lachs and K. Pillemer, "Elder Abuse," *The New England Journal of Medicine*, 373, no. 20 (2015); R. Wolf and K. Pillemer, "Elder Abuse and Case Outcome," *Journal of Applied Gerontology*, 19, no. 2 (2000).
4. Ron Acierno, Melba A. Hernandez, Ananda B. Amstadter, Heidi S. Resnick, Kenneth Steve, Wendy Muzzy, and Dean G. Kilpatrick, "Prevalence and Correlates of Emotional, Physical, Sexual, and Financial Abuse and Potential Neglect in the United States: The National Elder Mistreatment Study," *American Journal of Public Health*, 100, no. 2 (2010): 292–97.
5. Edward O. Laumann, Sara A. Leitsch, and Linda J. Waite, "Elder Mistreatment in the United States: Prevalence Estimates from a Nationally Representative Study," *The Journals of Gerontology: Series B* 63, no. 4 (2008): S248–S254.

6. Sherry Hamby, Alli Smith, Kimberly Mitchell, and Heather Turner, "Poly-victimization and Resilience Portfolios: Trends in Violence Research that can Enhance the Understanding and Prevention of Elder Abuse," *Journal of Elder Abuse & Neglect*, 28, no. 4-5 (2016): 217–34.

7. Henry T. Harbin and Denis J. Madden, "Battered Parents: A New Syndrome," *The American Journal of Psychiatry* (1979); Barbara Cottrell, *Parent Abuse: The Abuse of Parents by Their Teenage Children* (Ottawa, Canada: Family Violence Prevention Unit, Health Canada, 2001); Amanda Holt, "'The Terrorist in my Home': Teenagers' Violence Towards Parents—Constructions of Parent Experiences in Public Online Message Boards," *Child & Family Social Work*, 16, no. 4 (2011): 454–63.

8. Amanda Holt, "Adolescent-to-Parent Abuse as a Form of 'Domestic Violence': A Conceptual Review," *Trauma, Violence, & Abuse*, 17, no. 5 (2016): 490–99; Nicola Kennair and David Mellor, "Parent Abuse: A Review," *Child Psychiatry and Human Development*, 38, no. 3 (2007): 203–19.

9. B. Cottrell, *Parent Abuse: The Abuse of Parents by Their Teenage Children* (Ottawa: Family Violence Prevention, 2001); Amanda Holt, "Adolescent-to-Parent Abuse as a Form of 'Domestic Violence': A Conceptual Review," *Trauma, Violence, & Abuse*, 17, no. 5 (2016): 490–99.

10. Michel Edenborough, Debra Jackson, Judy Mannix, and Lesley M. Wilkes, "Living in the Red Zone: The Experience of Child–to–Mother Violence," *Child & Family Social Work*, 13, no. 4 (2008): 464–73.

11. M. Stewart, A. Burns, and R. Leonard, "Dark Side of the Mothering Role: Abuse of Mothers by Adolescent and Adut Children," *Sex Roles*, 56 (2007).

12. Amanda Holt, "Violence against Grandparents: Towards a Life Course Approach," in *Violence Against Older Women*, volume I (Palgrave Macmillan, Cham, 2019), 161–80; Karen Bullock and Rebecca L. Thomas, "The Vulnerability for Elder Abuse among a Sample of Custodial Grandfathers: An Exploratory Study," *Journal of Elder Abuse & Neglect*, 19, no. 3-4 (2007): 133–50; Megan Williams, Keith Tuffin, and Patricia Niland, "'It's Like He Just Goes Off, BOOM!': Mothers and Grandmothers Make Sense of Child–to–Parent Violence," *Child & Family Social Work*, 22, no. 2 (2017): 597–606.

13. N. Kennair and D. Mellor, "Parent Abuse: A Review," *Child Psychiatry Human Development*, 38 (2007).

14. Jennifer E. Storey, "Risk Factors for Elder Abuse and Neglect: A Review of the Literature," *Aggression and Violent Behavior*, 50 (2020).

15. Gunhild O. Hagestad, "On-Time, Off-Time, out of Time? Reflections on Continuity and Discontinuity from an Illness Process," in *Adulthood and Aging: Research on Continuities and Discontinuities*, edited by Vern L. Bengtson (New York: Springer Publishing Co, 1996).

242 *Notes*

16. Travis Labrum and Phyllis L. Solomon, "Elder Mistreatment Perpetrators with Substance Abuse and/or Mental Health Conditions: Results from the National Elder Mistreatment Study," *Psychiatric Quarterly*, 89, no. 1 (2018).
17. Karl Pillemer and David Finkelhor, "Causes of Elder Abuse: Caregiver Stress Versus Problem Relatives," *American Journal of Orthopsychiatry*, 59, no. 2 (1989).
18. K. A. Roberto, "The Complexities of Elder Abuse," *American Psychologist*, 71, no. 4 (2016).
19. Karl Pillemer, David Burnes, Catherine Riffin, and Mark S. Lachs, "Elder Abuse: Global Situation, Risk Factors, and Prevention Strategies," *The Gerontologist*, 56, no. Suppl. 2 (2016): S194–S205; K. A. Roberto, "The Complexities of Elder Abuse," *American Psychologist*, 71, no. 4 (2016).
20. Ron Acierno, Melba A. Hernandez, Ananda B. Amstadter, Heidi S. Resnick, Kenneth Steve, Wendy Muzzy, and Dean G. Kilpatrick, "Prevalence and Correlates of Emotional, Physical, Sexual, and Financial Abuse and Potential Neglect in the United States: The National Elder Mistreatment Study," *American Journal of Public Health*, 100, no. 2 (2010): 292–97.
21. Deborah Finfgeld-Connett, "Intimate Partner Abuse among Older Women: Qualitative Systematic Review," *Clinical Nursing Journal*, 23, no. 6 (2014); Deborah Courtney and Tina Maschi, "Trauma and Stress among Older Adults in Prison: Breaking the Cycle of Silence," *Traumatology*, 19, no. 1 (2013): 73–81.
22. D. Henderson, J. A. Buchanan, and J. E. Fisher, "Violence and the Elderly Population: Issues for Prevention," in *Preventing Violence in Relationships: Interventions across the Life Span*, edited by P. A. Schewe (Washington, DC: American Psychological Association, 2002).
23. K. A. Roberto, "The Complexities of Elder Abuse," *American Psychologist*, 71, no. 4 (2016).
24. K. Pillemer and J. Suitor, "Violence and Violent Feelings: What Causes Them among Family Caregivers?" *Journal of Gerontology*, 47, no. 4 (1992).
25. Ron Acierno, Melba A. Hernandez, Ananda B. Amstadter, Heidi S. Resnick, Kenneth Steve, Wendy Muzzy, and Dean G. Kilpatrick, "Prevalence and Correlates of Emotional, Physical, Sexual, and Financial Abuse and Potential Neglect in the United States: The National Elder Mistreatment Study," *American Journal of Public Health*, 100, no. 2 (2010): 292–97; K. A. Roberto, "The Complexities of Elder Abuse," *American Psychologist*, 71, no. 4 (2016); Karl Pillemer, J. J. Suitor, S. E. Mock, M. Sabir, T. B. Pardo, and J. Sechrist, "Capturing the Complexity of Intergenerational Relations: Exploring Ambivalence within Later-Life Families," *Journal of Social Issues*, 63, no. 4 (2007).
26. David Burnes, Karl Pillemer, Paul L. Caccamise, Art Mason, Charles R. Henderson Jr, Jacquelin Berman, Ann Marie Cook, et al., "Prevalence of and Risk Factors for Elder Abuse and Neglect in the Community: A Population–

based Study," *Journal of the American Geriatrics Society*, 63, no. 9 (2015): 1906–12; J. I. Kosberg and D. Nahmiash, "Characteristics of Victims and Perpetrators and Milieus of Abuse and Neglect," *Abuse, Neglect, and Exploitation of Older Persons: Strategies for Assessment and Intervention* (Health Professions Press, 1996).

27. Frederick L. Newman, Laura R. Seff, Richard L. Beaulaurier, and Richard C. Palmer, "Domestic Abuse against Elder Women and Perceived Barriers to Help-seeking," *Journal of Elder Abuse & Neglect*, 25, no. 3 (2013): 205–29; Briony Dow, Luke Gahan, Ellen Gaffy, Melanie Joosten, Freda Vrantsidis, and Meaghan Jarred, "Barriers to Disclosing Elder Abuse and Taking Action in Australia," *Journal of Family Violence* (2019): 1–9.

28. Marguerite DeLiema, Zachary D. Gassoumis, Diana C. Homeier, and Kathleen H. Wilber, "Determining Prevalence and Correlates of Elder Abuse Using Promotores: Low-Income Immigrant Latinos Report High Rates of Abuse and Neglect," *Journal of the American Geriatrics Society*, 60, no. 7 (2012).

29. Frederick L. Newman, Laura R. Seff, Richard L. Beaulaurier, and Richard C. Palmer, "Domestic Abuse against Elder Women and Perceived Barriers to Help-seeking," *Journal of Elder Abuse & Neglect*, 25, no. 3 (2013): 205–29.

30. Patient Protection and Affordable Care Act, Public Law 111-148, 111th Congress Sess. (2010).

CHAPTER 11

1. Ron Acierno, Melba A. Hernandez, Ananda B. Amstadter, Heidi S. Resnick, Kenneth Steve, Wendy Muzzy, and Dean G. Kilpatrick, "Prevalence and Correlates of Emotional, Physical, Sexual, and Financial Abuse and Potential Neglect in the United States: The National Elder Mistreatment Study," *American Journal of Public Health*, 100, no. 2 (2010): 292–97; M. Miszkurka, C. Steensma, and S. P. Phillips, "Correlates of Partner and Family Violence among Older Canadians: A Life-Course Approach," *Maladies Chroniques et Blessures au Canada*, 36, no. 3 (2016).

2. Vincent J. Felitti, Robert F. Anda, Dale Nordenberg, David F. Williamson, Alison M. Spitz, Valerie Edwards, Mary P. Koss, and James S. Marks, "Reprint Of: Relationship of Childhood Abuse and Household Dysfunction to Many of the Leading Causes of Death in Adults: The Adverse Childhood Experiences (Ace) Study," *American Journal of Preventive Medicine*, 56, no. 6 (2019).

PART II

1. J. O. Prochaska and J. M. Prochaska, *Changing to Thrive: Using the Stages of Change to Overcome the Top Threats to Your Health and Happiness* (Hazelden Publishing, 2016).

CHAPTER 12

1. J. O. Prochaska, J. C. Norcross, and C. C. DiClemente, *Changing for Good* (New York: Morrow, 1994).
2. J. O. Prochaska, J. C. Norcross, and C. C. DiClemente, *Changing for Good* (New York: Morrow, 1994).
3. J. O. Prochaska and J. M. Prochaska, *Changing to Thrive: Using the Stages of Change to Overcome the Top Threats to Your Health and Happiness* (Hazelden Publishing, 2016).
4. J. O. Prochaska, J. C. Norcross, and C. C. DiClemente, *Changing for Good* (New York: Morrow, 1994).

CHAPTER 13

1. Andreas Bartels and Semir Zeki, "The Neural Correlates of Maternal and Romantic Love," *Neuroimage*, 21, no. 3 (2004): 1155–66.

CHAPTER 14

1. W. R. Miller and G. S. Rose, "Motivational Interviewing and Decisional Balance: Contrasting Responses to Client Ambivalence," *Behavioral Cognitive Psychotherapy*, 43 (2015); W. R. Miller and S. Rollnick, *Motivational Interviewing: Helping People Change*, third edition (New York: Guilford Press, 2013); J. O. Prochaska, J. C. Norcross, and C. C. DiClemente, *Changing for Good* (New York: Morrow, 1994).

CHAPTER 15

1. G. R. VandenBos (Ed.), *APA Dictionary of Psychology* (Washington, DC: American Pyschological Association, 2007).

2. Oliver Huxhold, Katherine L. Fiori, Noah J. Webster, and Toni C. Antonucci, "The Strength of Weaker Ties: An Underexplored Resource for Maintaining Emotional Well-being in Later Life," *The Journals of Gerontology: Series B*, 75, no. 7 (2020): 1433–42.

3. National Academies of Sciences, Engineering, and Medicine, *Social Isolation and Loneliness in Older Adults: Opportunities for the Health Care System* (National Academies Press, 2020).

4. National Academies of Sciences, Engineering, and Medicine, *Social Isolation and Loneliness in Older Adults: Opportunities for the Health Care System* (National Academies Press, 2020).

5. Albert Bandura, "The Explanatory and Predictive Scope of Self-efficacy Theory," *Journal of Social and Clinical Psychology*, 4, no. 3 (1986): 359–73; Albert Bandura, "The Anatomy of Stages of Change," *American Journal of Health Promotion: AJHP*, 12, no. 1 (1997): 8–10.

6. M. L. Slepian and B. Bastian, "Truth or Punishment: Secrecy and Punishing the Self," *Personality and Social Psychology Bulletin*, 43 (2017): 1595–611.

7. Al-Anon Family Groups of South Carolina, "The Family Disease of Alcoholism," https://www.al-anon-sc.org/the-family-disease-of-alcoholism.html.

8. Lisa B. Dixon, Alicia Lucksted, Deborah R. Medoff, Joyce Burland, Bette Stewart, Anthony F. Lehman, Li Juan Fang, Vera Sturm, Clayton Brown, and Aaron Murray-Swank, "Outcomes of a Randomized Study of a Peer-Taught Family-to-Family Education Program for Mental Illness," *Psychiatric Services*, 62, no. 6 (2011); John F. Kelly, Lauren Hoffman, Corrie Vilsaint, Roger Weiss, Andrew Nierenberg, and Bettina Hoeppner, "Peer Support for Mood Disorder: Characteristics and Benefits from Attending the Depression and Bipolar Support Alliance Mutual-Help Organization," *Journal of Affective Disorders*, 255 (2019).

CHAPTER 16

1. J. Sirey, "Protect: A Pilot Program to Integrate Mental Health Treatment into Elder Abuse Services for Older Women," *Journal of Elder Abuse & Neglect*, 27 (2015).

CHAPTER 17

1. M. Lachs and J. Berman, *Under the Radar: New York State Elder Abuse Prevalence Study* (Lifespan of Greater Rochester, Inc., Weill Cornell Medical Center New York City Department of Aging, 2011).

CHAPTER 18

1. "Recovery from Mental Disorders, a Lecture by Patricia Deegan," *YouTube*, https://youtu.be/jhK-7DkWaKE.

CHAPTER 19

1. L. Funk and K. Kobayashi, "Choice: In Filial Care Work: Moving Beyond a Dischomy," *Canadian Sociological Review*, 46, no. 3 (2009).

2. N. Hooyman and J. Gonyea, *Feminist Perspectve on Family Care: Pleas for Gender Justice*, volume 6 (Thousand Oaks: Sage, 1995).

3. Jim Orford, Richard Velleman, Guillermina Natera, Lorna Templeton, and Alex Copello, "Addiction in the Family Is a Major but Neglected Contributor to the Global Burden of Adult Ill-Health," *Social Science and Medicine*, 78 (2013).

APPENDIX B

1. Judith R. Smith, "Expanding Constructions of Elder Abuse and Neglect: Older Mothers' Subjective Experiences," *J Elder Abuse Negl*, 27, no. 4-5 (2015): 328–55; J. R. Smith, "Elder Abuse, Impaired Adult Child, and Maternal Identity," in *Handbook of Interpersonal Violence*, edited by Robert Geffner, Jacquelyn W. White, L. Kevin Hamberger, Alan Rosenbaum, Viola Vaughan-Eden, and Victor I. Vieth (Springer, 2021); J. R. Smith, "Mothering in Later Life: Older Mothers and Their Challenging Adult Chiildren," *Ageing and Society*, no. 1 (2021).

2. Kathy Charmaz, *Constructing Grounded Theory*, second edition (Sage, 2014).

3. D. P. McAdams, *The Life Story Interview* (Evanston, IL: Northwestern University, 1995).

4. K. Charmaz, "Constructivist Grounded Theory," in *Handbook of Constructivist Research*, edited by J. H. Gubrium (New York: Guilford, 2008).

5. M. Hennick, B. Kaiser, and V. Mercino, "Code Saturation Versus Meaning Saturaction: How Many Interviews Are Enough?" *Qualitative Health Research*, 27, no. 4 (2017).

6. Kathy Charmaz, *Constructing Grounded Theory*, second edition (Sage, 2014).

References

Acierno, Ron, Melba A. Hernandez, Ananda B. Amstadter, Heidi S. Resnick, Kenneth Steve, Wendy Muzzy, and Dean G. Kilpatrick. "Prevalence and Correlates of Emotional, Physical, Sexual, and Financial Abuse and Potential Neglect in the United States: The National Elder Mistreatment Study." *American Journal of Public Health*, 100, no. 2 (2010): 292–97.

Appiah, Kwame Anthony. "My Adult Son Moved In. It's a Nightmare. Can I Kick Him Out?" *New York Times*, October 30, 2020.

Arnett, Jeffrey Jensen. *Emerging Adulthood: The Winding Road from the Late Teens through the Twenties*. Oxford University Press, 2014.

Aschbrenner, K. A., J. S. Greenberg, S. A. Allen, and M. M. Seltzer. "Subjective Burden and Personal Gains among Older Parents of Adults with Serious Mental Illness." *Psychiatric Services*, 61, no. 6 (2010): 605–11.

Avieli, H., Y. Smeloy, and T. Band-Winterstein. "Departure Scripts and Life Review of Parents Living with Abusive Adult Children with Mental Disorder." *Journal of Aging Studies*, 34 (2015): 48–56.

Band-Winterstein, T., and H. Avieli. "The Experience of Parenting a Child With Disability in Old Age," *Journal of Nursing Scholarship*, 49 (2017): 421–428.

Band-Winterstein, Tova, Hila Avieli, and Yael Smeloy. "Harmed? Harmful? Experiencing Abusive Adult Children With Mental Disorder Over the Life Course." *Journal of Interpersonal Violence* 31, no. 15 (September 2016): 2598–2621.

Band-Winterstein, Tova, Yael Smeloy, and Hila Avieli. "Shared Reality of the Abusive and the Vulnerable: The Experience of Aging for Parents Living with Abusive Adult Children Coping with Mental Disorder." *International Psychogeriatrics* 26, no. 11 (2014): 1917–1927.

Beck, C. T., and Indman, P. "The Many Faces of Postpartum Depression." *Journal of Obstet Gynecol Neonatal Nursing*, 34, no. 5.

Birditt, K. K., K. Fingerman, and S. Zarit. "Adult Children's Problems and Successes: Implications for Intergenerational Ambivalence." *Journals of Gerontology: Psychological Sciences and Social Sciences*, 65B (2010): 145–153.

Bleiszner, R., and J. Mancini. "Enduring Ties: Older Adults' Parental Role and Responsibilities." *Family Relations*, 36 (1997): 176–180.

Bouchard, G. "How Do Parents React When Their Children Leave Home? An Integrative Review." *Journal of Adult Development*, 21 (2014): 69–79.

Brent, Benjamin K., and Anthony J. Giuliano. "Psychotic-Spectrum Illness and Family-Based Treatments: A Case-Based Illustration of the Underuse of Family Interventions." *Harvard Review of Psychiatry*, 15, no. 4 (2007): 162–67.

Britton, Marcus L. "Race/Ethnicity, Attitudes, and Living with Parents During Young Adulthood." *Journal of Marriage and Family*, 75, no. 4 (2013): 995–1013.

Burnes, David, Karl Pillemer, Paul L. Caccamise, Art Mason, Charles R. Henderson Jr, Jacquelin Berman, Ann Marie Cook, Denise Shukoff, Patricia Brownell, Mebane Powell, Aurora Salamone, and Mark S. Lachs. "Prevalence of and Risk Factors for Elder Abuse and Neglect in the Community: A Population-Based Study." *Journal of the American Geriatrics Society*, 63, no. 9 (2015): 1906–12.

Caplan, Paula J., and Ian Hall-McCorquodale. "Mother-Blaming in Major Clinical Journals." *American Journal of Orthopsychiatry*, 55, no. 3 (1985): 345–53.

Carter, Elizabeth A., and Monica McGoldrick. *The Family Life Cycle: A Framework for Family Therapy*. Halsted Press, 1980.

Charmaz, K. *Constructing Grounded Theory*. Thousand Oaks, CA: Sage, 2014.

Choi, J., J. Zhu, and L. Goodman. *Young Adults Living in Parents' Basement: Causes and Consequences*. Washington, DC: Urban Institute, 2019.

Coleman, J. "Parents Are Sacrificing Their Social Lives on the Altar of Intensive Parenting." *The Atlantic*, 2021.

Collins, W. Andrew, Maccoby, Eleanor, Steinberg, Laurence, Hetherington, E. Mavis, and Bornstein, Marc H. "Contemporary Research on Parenting: The Case for Nature and Nurture." *The American Psychologist*, volume 55, no. 2 (2000).

Connidis, Ingrid Arnet, and Julie Ann McMullin. "Ambivalence, Family Ties, and Doing Sociology." *Journal of Marriage and Family*, 64, no. 3 (2002): 594–601.

Connidis, I. A. "Exploring Ambivalence in Family Ties: Progress and Prospects." *Family Relations*, 77 (2015): 77–95.

Copello, A., and L. Templeton. *The Forgotten Carers: Support for Adult Family Members Affected by a Relative's Drug Problems.* UK Drug Policy Commission (UKDPC), 2012.

Cottrell, Barbara, and Peter Monk. "Adolescent-to-Parent Abuse: A Qualitative Overview of Common Themes." *Journal of Family Issues,* 25, no. 8 (November 2004): 1072–95.

Counter, R. "Mom Shaming Is Running Rampant During the Pandemic." *New York Times,* September 10, 2020.

Courtin, E., and M. Avendano. "Under One Roof: The Effect of Co-Residing with Adult Children on Depression in Later Life." *Social Science & Medicine,* 168 (2016): 140–49.

Crawford, N. D., A. E. Rudolph, K. Jones, and C. Fuller. "Differences in Self-Reported Discrimination by Primary Type of Drug Used among New York City Drug Users." *American Journal of Drug & Alcohol Abuse,* 38, no. 6 (2012): 588–92.

Dain, N. "Critics and Dissenters: Reflections on Anti-Psychiatry in the United States." *Journal of the History of the Behavioral Sciences,* 25, no. 1 (1989): 3–25.

Das-Munshi, Jayati, Maya Semrau, Corrado Barbui, Neerja Chowdhary, Petra C. Gronholm, Kavitha Kolappa, Dzmitry Krupchanka, Tarun Dua, and Graham Thornicroft. "Gaps and Challenges: Who Treatment Recommendations for Tobacco Cessation and Management of Substance Use Disorders in People with Severe Mental Illness: Correction." *BMC Psychiatry,* 20 (2020).

Davis, E. M., K. Kim, and K. Fingerman. "Is an Empty Nest Best?: Co-residence with Adult Children and Parental Marital Quality before and after Recession." *J Gerontological B Psychol Soc Sci,* 73, no. 3 (2018): 372–81.

DeLiema, M., Z. D. Gassoumis, D. C. Homeier, and K. H. Wilber. "Determining Prevalence and Correlates of Elder Abuse Using Promotores: Low-Income Immigrant Latinos Report High Rates of Abuse and Neglect." *Journal of the American Geriatrics Society,* 60, no. 7 (2012): 1333–39.

Dixon, L., L. Postrado, J. Delahanty, P. J. Fischer, and A. Lehman. "The Association of Medical Comorbidity in Schizophrenia with Poor Physical and Mental Health." *The Journal of Nervous and Mental Diseases,* 187, no. 8 (1999): 496–502.

Dixon, Lisa B., Alicia Lucksted, Deborah R. Medoff, Joyce Burland, Bette Stewart, Anthony F. Lehman, Li Juan Fang, Vera Sturm, Clayton Brown, and Aaron Murray-Swank. "Outcomes of a Randomized Study of a Peer-Taught Family-to-Family Education Program for Mental Illness." *Psychiatric Services,* 62, no. 6 (2011): 591–97.

Dixon, Lisa B., Yael Holoshitz, and Ilana Nossel. "Treatment Engagement of Individuals Experiencing Mental Illness: Review and Update." *World Psychiatry,* 15 (2016): 13–26.

Dolbin-MacNab, Megan L. "Just Like Raising Your Own? Grandmothers' Perceptions of Parenting a Second Time Around." *Family Relations*, 55, no. 5 (2006): 564–75.

Dow, B., M Gahan, E. Gaffy, M. Joosten, and M. Jarred. "Barriers to Disclosing Elder Abuse and Taking Action in Australia." *Journal of Family Violence*, 35 (2020): 853–61.

Eassom, Erica, Domenico Giacco, Aysegul Dirik, and Stefan Priebe. "Implementing Family Involvement in the Treatment of Patients with Psychosis: A Systematic Review of Facilitating and Hindering Factors." *BMJ Open*, 4, no. 10 (2014).

Edenborough, M., J. Mannix, D. Jackson, and L. M. Wilkes. "Living in the Red Zone: The Experience of Child-to-Mother Violence." *Child and Family Social Work*, 13, no. 4 (2008): 464–73.

Elder, Glen H. Jr. "Time, Human Agency, and Social Change: Perspectives on the Life Course." *Social Psychology Quarterly*, 57, no. 1 (1994): 4.

Estroff, S. E., J. W. Swanson, W. S. Lachicotte, M. Swartz, and M. Bolduc. "Risk Reconsidered: Targets of Violence in the Social Networks of People with Serious Psychiatric Disorders." *Social Psychiatry and Psychiatric Epidemiology*, 33, Suppl 1 (1998): S95–S101.

Evans, Ellis D., and Luann Warren-Sohlberg. "A Pattern Analysis of Adolescent Abusive Behavior toward Parents." *Journal of Adolescent Research*, 3, no. 2 (1988): 201–16.

Felitti, Vincent J., Robert F. Anda, Dale Nordenberg, David F. Williamson, Alison M. Spitz, Valerie Edwards, Mary P. Koss, and James S. Marks. "Reprint Of: Relationship of Childhood Abuse and Household Dysfunction to Many of the Leading Causes of Death in Adults: The Adverse Childhood Experiences (Ace) Study." *American Journal of Preventive Medicine*, 56, no. 6 (2019): 774–86.

Finfgeld-Connett, Deborah. "Intimate Partner Abuse among Older Women: Qualitative Systematic Review." *Clinical Nursing Journal*, 23, no. 6 (2014): 664–83.

Fingerman, K. L., Y-P Cheng, K. Birditt, and S. Zarit. "Only as Happy as the Least Happy Child: Multiple Grown Children's Problems and Successes and Middle-Aged Parents' Well-being." *The Journals of Gerontology, Series B: Psychological Sciences and Social Sciences*, 67, no. 2 (2012): 184–193.

Fingerman, K., P-C Chen, E. Hay, K. E. Cichy, and E. S. Lefkowitz. "Ambivalent Reactions in the Parent and Offspring Relationship." *Journals of Gerontology: Psychological Sciences and Social Sciences*, 61B (2006).

Fingerman, K. L., Pitzer, E., Lefkowitz, K., Birditt, K., and D. Mroczek. "Ambivalent Relationship Qualities Between Adults and Their Parents: Implications for Both Parties' Well-Being." *Journals of Gerontology: Psychological Sciences and Social Sciences*, 63B (2008): 362–371.

Fuller Torrey, E., R. Bruce, H. R. Lamb, C., Jacobs, D. J. Jaffe, and J. Snook. *Raising Cain: The Role of Serious Mental Illness in Family Households.* Washington, DC: Treatment Advocacy Center, 2016.

Funk, Laura M., and Karen M. Kobayashi. "'Choice' in Filial Care Work: Moving Beyond a Dichotomy." *Canadian Sociological Review*, 46, no. 3 (2009): 235–52.

Galinsky, Ellen. *Six Stages of Parenthood.* Addison-Wesley Pub. Co., 1987.

García Coll, C., Lamberty, G., Jenkins, R. McAdoo, H. P., Crnic, K., Wasik, B. H., and Vázquez García, H. "An Integrative Model for the Study of Developmental Competencies in Minority Children." *Child Development*, volume 67, no. 5. (1986).

Gibson, P. "Intergenerational Parenting from the Perspective of African American Grandmothers." *Family Relations*, 54, no. 2 (2005): 280–97.

Goodman, Ellen. "Guilt Gap." *The Washington Post*, 1990, 21.

Grose, J. "Mothers Are the 'Shock Absorbers' of Our Society." *New York Times*, October 14, 2020.

Gueta, K. and Tam, S. "Intensive-Invisible Mothering: The Experiences of Mothers of Adult Children with Dual Diagnosis." *International Journal Mental Health Nurses*, 28 (2019): 997–1007.

Gueta, Keren, Peled, Einat, Sander-Almoznino, Nili. "'I Used to Be an Ordinary Mom': The Maternal Identity of Mothers of Women Abused by an Intimate Partner." *American Journal of Orthopsychiatry*, 86, no. 4 (2016): 456–466.

Hagestad, G., and V. Bengtson. "On-Time, Off-Time, Out of Time? Reflections on Continuity and Discontinuity from an Illness Process." In *Adulthood and Aging: Research on Continuities and Discontinuities*, edited by Vern L. Bengtson, 204–27. New York: Springer Publishing Co., 1996.

Harbin, H., and D. Maddfen. "Battered Parents: A New Syndrome." *American Journal of Psychiatry*, 136 (1979): 1288–91.

Hardie, J. H., and J. Seltzer. "Parent-Child Relationships at the Transition to Adulthood: A Comparison of Black, Hispanic, and White Immigrant and Native-Born Youth." *Social Forces*, 95, no. 1 (2016): 321–53.

Hays, S. *The Cultural Contradictions of Motherhood.* New Haven: Yale University Press, 1998.

Henderon, A., S. Harmon, and H. Newman. "The Price Mothers Pay, Even When They Are Not Buying It: Mental Health Consequences of Idealized Motherhood." *Sex Roles*, 74 (2016): 512–26.

Henderson, D., J. A. Buchanan, and J. E. Fisher. "Violence and the Elderly Population: Issues for Prevention." In *Preventing Violence in Relationships: Interventions across the Life Span*, edited by P. A. Schewe, 223–45. Washington, DC: American Psychological Association, 2002.

Heyman, G. *Addiction: A Disorder of Choice*. Cambridge, MA: Harvard University Press, 2009.

Holt, A. "Violence Against Grandmothers: A Lifespan Approach." In *Violence Against Older Women: Research, Policy and Practice*, edited by H. Bows. New York: Palgrave MacMillan, 2019.

Holt, A. "Adolescent-to-Parent Abuse of 'Domestic Violence': A Conceptual Review." *Trauma, Violence & Abuse*, 17, no. 5 (2016): 490–99.

Holt, A. *Adolescent-to-Parent Abuse: Current Understandings in Research, Policy and Practice*. Bristol, England: Policy Press, 2013.

Holt, A. "Room for Resistance?: Parenting Orders, Disciplinary Power and the Production of the Bad Parent." In *ASBO Nation: The Criminalization of Nuisance*, edited by P. Squires. Bristol, UK: Policy Press, 2008.

Hooyman, N., and J. Gonyea. *Feminist Perspective on Family Care: Pleas for Gender Justice*. Volume 6. Thousand Oaks: Sage, 1995.

Huang, Yangtao, Francisco Perales, and Mark Western. "The Long Arm of Parental Advantage: Socio-Economic Background and Parental Financial Transfers over Adult Children's Life Courses." *Research in Social Stratification and Mobility*, 71 (2021).

Hunt, G., R. Greene, and C. Whiting. *On Pins and Needles: Caregivers of Adults with Mental Illness*. Washington, DC: National Alliance for Caregivers, 2016.

Hunter, C., J. Nixon, and S. Parr, "Mother Abuse: A Matter of Youth Justice, Child Welfare or Domestic Violence?" *Journal of Law and Society*, 37, no. 2 (2010): 264–28.

Hyde, A. P. "Coping with Threatening, Intimidating, Violent Behaviors of People with Psychiatric Disabilities at Home: Guidelines for Family Caregivers." *Psychiatric Rehabilitation Journal*, 21 (1997): 144–49.

Ingersoll-Dayton, B., R. Dunkle, L. Chadiha, A. Lawrence-Jacobson, E. Weir, and J. Sarorius. "Intergenerational Ambivalence: Aging Mothers Whose Adult Daughters Are Mentally Ill." *Families in Society: The Journal of Contemporary Social Services*, 92 (2011): 114–119.

Jackson, D. "Broadening Constructions of family Violence: Mothers' Perspectives of Aggression from Their Children." *Child Family Social Work*, 8 (2003): 321–329.

Jackson, D., and J. Mannix. "Then Suddenly He Went Right Off the Rails: Mothers' Stories of Adolescent Cannabis Use." *Contemporary Nurse*, 14 (2002): 169–79.

Jackson, D., and J. Mannix. "Giving Voice to the Burden of Blame: A Feminist Study of Mothers' Experiences of Mother Blaming." *International Journal of Mental Health Nursing*, 10 (2004): 150–58.

Kahn, J., G. Goldscheider, and J. Garcia-Manglano. "Growing Parental Economic Power in Parent-Child Households: Co-Residence and Financial

Dependency in the United States, 1960-2010." *Demography*, 50 (2013): 1449–75.

Karp, D. *The Burden of Sympathy: How Families Cope with Mental Illness.* Oxford University Press, 2001.

Karp, D., and V. Tanarugsachock. "Mental Illness, Caregiving and Emotional Management." *Qualitative Health Research*, 10, no. 1 (2000).

Kelly, John F., Lauren Hoffman, Corrie Vilsaint, Roger Weiss, Andrew Nierenberg, and Bettina Hoeppner. "Peer Support for Mood Disorder: Characteristics and Benefits from Attending the Depression and Bipolar Support Alliance Mutual-Help Organization." *Journal of Affective Disorders*, 255 (2019): 127–35.

Kempe, C. Henry, Frederic N. Silverman, Brandt F. Steele, William Droegemueller, and Henry K. Silver. "The Battered-Child Syndrome." *JAMA*, 181, no. 1 (1962): 17–24.

Kennair, N., and D. Mellor. "Parent Abuse: A Review." *Child Psychiatry Human Development*, 38 (2007): 203–19.

Kennedy, Lauren Paige, and Patricia A. Farrell. "What to Do When Adult Children Want to Move Back In." *Grow by WebMD*, August 29, 2020.

Korabik, K., and A. K. McElwain. "Work-Family Guilt." In *Work and Family Encyclopedia*, edited by E. Kossek and M. Pitt-Catsouphes. Chestnut Hill, MA: Sloan Work and Family Research Network, 2005.

Kosberg, J. I., and D. Nahmiash. "Characteristics of Victims and Perpetrators and Milieus of Abuse and Neglect (From Abuse, Neglect, and Exploitation of Older Persons: Strategies for Assessment and Intervention, P 31–49, 1996, Lorin A Baumhover and S Colleen Beall, eds.—See 163840)." U.S. Department of Justice, Office of Justice Programs, 1996.

Labrum, T., and P. Solomon. "Safety Fears Held by Caregivers About Relatives with Psychiatric Disorders." *Health in Social Work*, 43 (2018): 3.

Labrum, Travis, and Phyllis L. Solomon. "Elder Mistreatment Perpetrators with Substance Abuse and/or Mental Health Conditions: Results from the National Elder Mistreatment Study." *Psychiatric Quarterly*, 89, no. 1 (2018): 117–28.

Lachs, M., and J. Berman. *Under the Radar: New York State Elder Abuse Prevalence Study.* Lifespan of Greater Rochester, Inc. Weill Cornell Medical Center, New York City Department of Aging, 2011.

Lachs, M., and K. Pillemer. "Elder Abuse." *The New England Journal of Medicine*, 373, no. 20 (2015): 1947–56.

Landeweer, E. "Sharing Care Responsibilities between Professionals and Personal Networks in Mental Healthcare: A Plea for Inclusion." *Ethics and Social Welfare*, 12, no. 2 (2018): 147–59.

Leach, P. *Your Baby and Child.* New York: Knopf, 2010.

Lefley, H. P. *Family Caregiving in Mental Illness*. Thousand Oaks, CA: Sage Publications, 1999.

Leventhal, Tama and Jeanne Brooks-Gunn. "The Neighborhoods They Live in: The Effects of Neighborhood Residence on Child and Adolescent Outcomes." *Psychological Bulletin*, volume 126, no. 2. (2000).

Liss, Miriam, H. Schiffrin, and K. Rizzo. "Maternal Guilt and Shame: The Role of Self-Discrepancy and Fear of Negative Evaluation." *Journal of Child and Family Studies*, 22, no. 8 (2013): 1112–19.

Lloyd, Charlie. "The Stigmatization of Problem Drug Users: A Narrative Literature Review." *Drugs: Education, Prevention and Policy* 20, no. 2 (2013): 85–95.

Lucksted, A., W. McFarlane, D. Downing, L. Dixon, and C. Adams. "Recent Developments in Family Psychoeducation as an Evidence-Based Practice." *Journal of Marriage & Family Therapy*, 38, no. 1 (2012): 101–21.

Lukens, E., and H. Thorning. "Psychoeducational Family Groups." In *Psychosocial Treatment of Schizophrenia*, edited by A. Rubin. D.W. Springer, 2011.

Luscher, K., and K. Pillemer. "Intergenerational Ambivalence: A New Approach to the Study of Parent–Child Relations in Later Life." *Journal of Marriage and the Family*, 60, no. 2 (1998): 413–25.

Meurk, Carla, Doug Fraser, Megan Weier, Jayne Lucke, Adrian Carter, and Wayne Hall. "Assessing the Place of Neurobiological Explanations in Accounts of a Family Member's Addiction." *Drug and Alcohol Review*, 35, no. 4 (2016): 461.

Mills, C. Wright. "The Promise." In *The Sociological Imagination*. Oxford University Press, 1959.

Miszkurka, M., C. Steensma, and S. P. Phillips. "Correlates of Partner and Family Violence among Older Canadians: A Life-Course Approach." *Maladies Chroniques et Blessures au Canada*, 36, no. 3 (2016): 45–53.

Mitchell, Barbara A., Andrew V. Wister, and Ellen M. Gee. "The Ethnic and Family Nexus of Homeleaving and Returning among Canadian Young Adults." *The Canadian Journal of Sociology / Cahiers canadiens de sociologie*, 29, no. 4 (2004): 543–75.

Myers, K. "Parents Skimp on Retirement to Support Adult Children." *Yahoo Finance*, 2019.

NBC10. "Walter Wallace Jr. Struggled With Mental Health Issues, Family Says." https://www.nbcphiladelphia.com/News/Local/Walter-Wallace-Jr-Struggled-with-Mental-Health-Issues-Family-Says/2575493/.

Nemzoff, R. *Don't Bite Your Tongue: How to Foster Rewarding Relationships with Your Adult Children*. New York: St. Martin's Press, 2008.

Newman, F., L. Seff, R. Beaulaurier, and R. Palmer. "Domestic Abuse against Elder Women and Perceived Barriers to Help-Seeking." *Journal of Elder Abuse & Neglect*, 25, no. 3 (2012): 205–29.

Newman, S. *Under One Roof Again: All Grown up and Re (Learning) to Live Happily Together*. Guilford, CT: Lyons Press, 2010.

National Institute for Mental Health. "Transforming the Understanding and Treatment of Mental Illness." National Institute for Mental Health Researchers. https://www.youtube.com/watch?v=Nin4V1MeFds.

Novella, E. J. "Mental Health Care in the Aftermath of Deinstitutionalization: A Retrospective and Prospective View." *Health Care Analysis*, 18 (2010): 222–38.

Olshansky, S. "Chronic Sorrow: A Response to Having a Mentally Defective Child." *Social Casework*, 43, no. 4 (1962): 190–98.

Orford, J, A. Copello, R. Velleman, and L. Templeton. "Family Members Affected by a Close Relative's Addiction: The Stress-Strain-Coping-Support Model." *Drugs: Education, Prevention & Policy*, 17 (2010): 36–43.

Orford, J., G. Natera, J. Mora, C. Atkinsobn, and A. Copello. *Coping with Alcohol and Drug Problems: The Experiences of Family Members in Three Contrasting Cultures*. Routledge, 2005.

Orford, J., R. Velleman, N. Guillermkna, L. Templeton, and A. Copello. "Addiction in the Family Is a Major but Neglected Contributor to the Global Burden of Adult Ill-Health." *Social Science and Medicine*, 78 (2013): 70–77.

Park, K., and M. Seo. "Care Burden of Parents of Adult Chldren with Mental Illness: The Role of Associative Stigma." *Comprehensive Psychiatry*, 70 (2016): 159–64.

Park, S. H., Yun Ju C. Song, E. A. Demetriou, K. L. Pepper, I. B. Hickie, N. Glozier, D. F. Hermens, E. M. Scott, and A. J. Guastella. "Distress, Quality of Life and Disability in Treatment–Seeking Young Adults with Social Anxiety Disorder." *Early Intervention in Psychiatry*, 15, no. 1 (2021): 57–67.

Parker, R. *Torn in Two: The Experience of Maternal Ambivalence*. London: Virago Press, 1995.

Patrick-Ott, A., and L. D. Ladd. "The Blending of Boss's Concept of Ambiguous Loss and Olshansky's Concept of Chronic Sorrow: A Case Study of a Family with a Child Who Has Significant Disabilities." *Journal of Creativity in Mental Health*, 5, no. 1 (2010): 74–86.

Peters, C., K. Hooker, and A. Zvonkovic. "Older Parents' Perceptions of Ambivalence in Relationships with Their Children." *Family Relations*, 55 (2006): 539–551.

Pillemer, K. "The Dangers of Dependency: New Findings on Domestic Violence against the Elderly." *Social Problems*, 33 (1985): 146–158

Pillemer, K., and D. Finkelhor. "Causes of Elder Abuse: Caregiver Stress Versus Problem Relatives." *American Journal of Orthopsychiatry*, 59, no. 2 (1989): 179–87.

Pillemer, K., and K. Luscher. *New Perspectives on Parent-Child Relations in Later Life*. Amsterdam: Elsevier Science, 2004.

Pillemer, K., and J. Suitor. "'Will I Ever Escape My Child's Problems?' Effects of Adult Chldren's Problems on Elderly Parents." *Journal of Marriage & Family*, 53 (1991): 585–94.

Pillemer, K., and J. Suitor. "Violence and Violent Feelings: What Causes Them among Family Caregivers?" *Journal of Gerontology*, 47, no. 4 (1992): S165–S172.

Pillemer, K., and J. Suitor. "Exploring Mothers' Ambivalence toward Their Adult Children." *Journal of Marriage & Family*, 64 (2002): 602–13.

Pillemer, Karl, J. Jill Suitor, Steven E. Mock, Myra Sabir, Tamara B. Pardo, and Jori Sechrist. "Capturing the Complexity of Intergenerational Relations: Exploring Ambivalence within Later-Life Families." *Journal of Social Issues*, 63, no. 4 (2007): 775–91.

Pope, M. A., A. K. Malla, S. N. Iyer, S. Venkataraman, and G. Jordan. "'Everyone Has a Role': Perspectives of Service Users with First-Episode Psychosis, Family Caregivers, Treatment Providers, and Policymakers on Responsibility for Supporting Individuals with Mental Health Problems." *Qualitative Health Research*, 29, no. 9 (2019): 1299–312.

Prochaska, J. O., J. C. Norcross, and C. C. DiClemente. *Changing for Good*. New York: Morrow, 1994.

Prochaska, J. O., and J.M. Prochaska. *Changing to Thrive: Using the Stages of Change to Overcome the Top Threats to Your Health and Happiness*. Hazelden Publishing, 2016.

Roberto, K. A. "The Complexities of Elder Abuse." *American Psychologist*, 71, no. 4 (2016): 302–11.

Roberto, Karen A., Brandy Renee McCann, Pamela B. Teaster, and Emily Hoyt. "Elder Abuse and the Opioid Epidemic: Evidence from Aps Cases in Central Appalachia." *Journal of Rural Mental Health* (2021).

Rodgers-Farmer, A. Y. "Parenting Stress, Depression, and Parenting in Grandmothers Raising Their Grandchildren." *Children and Youth Services Review*, 21, no. 5 (1999): 377–88.

Rossi, A., and P. Rossi. *Of Human Bonding: Parent-Child Relations across the Life Course. Social Institutions and Social Change*. A. de Gruyter, 1990.

Rotkirch, A., and K. Janhunen. "Maternal Guilt." *Evolutionary Psychology*, 8, no. 1 (2010): 90–106.

Rowe, J. "Great Expectations: A Systematic Review of the Literature on the Role of Family Carers in Severe Mental Illness, and Their Relationships and

Engagements with Professionals." *Journal of Psychiatric and Mental Health Nursing*, 19 (2012): 70–82.

Ruddick, S. *Maternal Thinking: Toward a Politics of Peace*. Beacon Press, 1989.

Ryff, C., P. Schmutte, and Y. Lee. "How Children Turn Out: Implications for Parental Self-Evaluation." In *The Parental Experience in Midlife*, edited by Carol D. Ryff and Marsha Mailick Seltzer, 383–422. Chicago, IL: University of Chicago Press, 1996.

Seccombe, Karen, Delores James, and Kimberly Battle Walters. "'They Think You Ain't Much of Nothing': The Social Construction of the Welfare Mother." *Journal of Marriage & Family*, 60, no. 4 (1998): 849–65.

Seltzer, J. A., C. Q. Lau, and S. M. Bianchi. "Doubling up When Times Are Tough: A Study of Obligations to Share a Home in Response to Economic Hardship." *Social Science Research*, 41, no. 5 (2012): 1307–19.

Silfver, M., and K. Helkama. "Empathy, Guilt, and Gender: A Comparison of Two Measures of Guilt." *Scandinavian Journal of Psychology*, 48 (2007): 239–46.

Silverstein, M., and V. Bengtson. "Intergenerational Solidarity and the Structure of Adult Child–Parent Relationships in American Families 1." *American Journal of Sociology*, 103, no. 2 (1997): 429–35.

Sirey, J. "Protect: A Pilot Program to Integrate Mental Health Treatment into Elder Abuse Services for Older Women." *Journal of Elder Abuse & Neglect*, no. 27 (2015): 438–53.

Smith, Judith R. "Listening to Older Adult Parents of Adult Children with Mental Illness." *Journal of Family Social Work*, no. 15 (2012): 126–40.

Smith, Judith R. "Expanding Constructions of Elder Abuse and Neglect: Older Mothers' Subjective Experiences." *Journal of Elder Abuse & Neglect*, 27, no. 4–5 (2015): 1–28.

Smith, Judith R. "Elder Abuse, Impaired Adult Child, and Maternal Identity." In *Handbook of Interpersonal Violence*, edited by Robert Geffner, Jacquelyn W. White, L. Kevin Hamberger, Alan Rosenbaum, Viola Vaughan-Eden, and Victor I. Vieth. Springer Publishing, 2021.

Smith, Judith R. "Mothering in Later Life: Older Mothers and Their Challenging Adult Children." *Ageing and Society* (2021): 1–21.

Smith, Judith R., Brooks-Gunn, Jeanne. & Klebanov, Pamela. "Consequences of Living in Poverty for Young Children's Cognitive and Verbal Ability and School Readiness." In G. Duncan & J. Brooks-Gunn (Eds.). *Growing Up Poor* (pp. 132–189). NY: Russell Sage. (1997).

Smith, Judith R., and Manoj Pardasani. "Parenting in Later Life: A Cross-Cultural Study." *Journal of Family Social Work*, no. 3 (2014): 209–28.

Stewart, M., A. Burns, and R. Leonard. "Dark Side of the Mothering Role: Abuse of Mothers by Adolescent and Adut Children." *Sex Roles*, 56 (2007): 183–91.

Suitor, J., M. Gilligan, and K. Pillemer. "Conceptualizing and Measuring Intergenerational Ambivalence in Later Life." *The Journals of Gerontology: Series B: Psychological Sciences and Social Sciences*, 66, no. 6 (2011): 769–81.

Svensson, B., T. Richert, and B. Johnson. "Parents' Experiences of Abuse by Their Adult Children with Drug Problems." *NAD Nordic Studies on Alcohol and Drugs*, 37, no. 1 (2020): 69–85.

Thorning, H. *Grief: The Psychological Consequences of the Caregiving Dynamic on Family Caregivers of Persons with Severe Mental Illness*. New York University, 2004.

Thorning, H., and L. Dixon. "Caregiving for Individuals with Serious Mental Illness: A Life Cycle Perspective." In *The Spectrum of Family Caregiving for Adults and Elders with Chronic Illness*. Oxford, 2016.

Turrini, P. "Mothers' Center: Research, Service and Advocacy." *Social Work*, 22 (1977): 478–83.

van Gaalen, R., P Dykstra, and A. Komter. "Where Is the Exit? Intergenerational Ambivalence and Relationship Quality in High Contact Ties." *Journal of Aging Studies*, 24, no. 2 (2010): 105–14.

Van Zeijl, J, J. Mesman, M. H. Van Ijzendoorn, M. J. Bakermans-Kranenburg, F. Juffer, M. N. Stolk, H. M. Koot, and R. A. Alink. "Attachment-Based Intervention for Enhancing Sensitive Discipline in Mothers of 1- to 3-Year-Old Children at Risk for Externalizing Behavior Problems: A Randomized Controlled Trial." *Journal of Consulting and Clinical Psychology*, 74, no. 6 (2006): 994–1005.

Waldman, A. *Bad Mother: A Chronicle of Maternal Crimes, Minor Calamities, and Occasional Moments of Grace*. New York: Doubleday, 2009.

Williams, M, K. Tuffin, and P. Niland. "'It's Like He Just Goes Off, Boom!': Mothers and Grandmothers Make Sense of Child-to-Parent Violence." *Child and Family Social Work*, 22 (2017): 597–606.

Wolf, R., and K. Pillemer. "Elder Abuse and Case Outcome." *Journal of Applied Gerontology*, 19, no. 2 (2000): 203–20.

Young, M., J. Stuber, J. Ahern, and S. Galea. "Interpersonal Discrimination and the Health of Illicit Drug Users." *The American Journal of Drug and Alcohol Abuse*, 31, no. 3 (2005): 371–91.

Index

259

Department of Aging, 51
Department of Child Welfare, 51
dependence: of adult children, 69,
121; ethics of, 37–38; financial
support by parents and, 20;
on help, 25–26; for infants,
19; long-term planning for,
200–201; psychology of, 191–92;
responsibility related to, 24; of
young adults, 12–13
depression: of adult children, 79,
143–44; awareness of, 51, 166–
67; elder abuse and 122; self-
assessment of, 151, *152*
development: of children, 46, 50, 58;
developmental stake, 56–57
diagnoses, for SMI, 85
Di Clemente, Carlo, 13, 136, 138–40
difficult adult children: definition,
10–12; delays in self-sufficiency,
12–13; structural problem, 191–
93. *See also specific topics*
difficult mothering, 23–24, 57, 68
disappointment, 4, 13–14, 57, 61,
109–12, 159–60
discharge plans, 39
disorganized thinking, 72
disrespect, 14, 34, 48, 145, 218
distress: from adult children, 63;
for parents, 98–99, 128–29;
from SMI, 79; from unrealistic
expectations, 9
divorce, 190–91;
Domenici, Pete, 101
domestic violence, 5; blame for, 53;
public issue 11; shelters, 116
drug addiction, 96–98; finances for,
147–48; for parents, 7–8, 187–88;
theft for, 143–44. *See also*
substance abuse
Durene (mother), 34, 62–64, 76, 157,
161, 216

Earley, Pete, 92
elder abuse. *See* elder mistreatment
elder abuse shelter, 116, 198–99
elder mistreatment: awareness of, 4,
100, 122–23, 125; calling "311,"
113–14; definition, 117–20;
domestic violence and, 11, 116,
117–19; JASA/LEAP for, 162,
169–70, 173–74, 187; National
Center on Elder Abuse, 125;
neglect, 47–48; not reporting,
reasons for, 53, 120, 123–25;
perpetrator, 117–18; protecting
oneself, 114, 118–19, 195–96,
198–200; protection of mother,
114; research on, 118, 121–22;
risks for elder abuse, 117–18;
statistics, 113–14; staying safe,
116–19, 173–82; types of, 117;
victims of, 113–14, 121–22
Ellen (mother), 60–61, 111, 216–17
emerging adulthood, 12–13, 25–26
employment: during COVID-19,
30–31, 113; unemployment, 5; in
United States, 32
empty nest, 70–71
erratic behavior, 148–49
Esther (mother), 34, 37, 41, 60, 217
estrangement, 102, 110, 111,147,
225
ethics: of dependence, 37–38;
moral commitment, 41–42; of
motherhood, 45
evolutionary psychology, 43
exclusionary orders of protection,
178–79
exercise, 167, 200
expectations, unrealistic, 9

Facebook, 56, 86, 117
facing the problem: seeing *vs.*
avoidance, 143–49

About the Author

Judith R. Smith, PhD, LCSW, is a leader in gerontological research focusing on women's experiences as they age. She is a psychotherapist, professor, and researcher. Her years of experience as a mental health practitioner and researcher on child and adult development inform her work. She currently offers support groups to mothers with difficult adult children.

Dr. Smith coined the phrase "difficult adult children" to describe the dilemmas older mothers experience as they cope with the needs of their adult children who have problems related to mental health issues, substance misuse disorder, or chronic unemployment. These mothers, although conflicted, attempt to provide financial, emotional, and/or housing support. Dr. Smith hopes that by giving a name to a growing national and international problem, the needs of older mothers who are now the default caregivers for their vulnerable adult children will be included in policy discussions about family caregiving, mental health, and substance use policies. She hopes to help create a network of mothers of difficult adult children to share resources, find social support, influence policy, and lessen the stigma that many carry of being a "bad mother."

Dr. Smith is an associate professor emerita at the Graduate School of Social Services at Fordham University. She lives in New York City with her husband. She welcomes feedback, questions, and conversation with parents. Contact her by email judithrsmith@difficultmothering.com, on her website https://difficultmothering.com, or on Facebook @difficultmothering.

Milton Keynes UK
Ingram Content Group UK Ltd.
UKHW051011240324
440027UK00006B/20